# Managing Innovation Adoption

*This book is dedicated to my parents, Md. Nazrul Islam Talukder and Anwara Begum, and to my wife, Sultana Parvin, and to my daughters, Rumaysa Talukder and Umayma Talukder*

# Managing Innovation Adoption

## From Innovation to Implementation

MAJHARUL TALUKDER
*University of Canberra, Australia*

Routledge
Taylor & Francis Group

LONDON AND NEW YORK

First published 2014 by Gower Publishing

2 Park Square, Milton Park, Abingdon, Oxfordshire OX14 4RN
52 Vanderbilt Avenue, New York, NY 10017

*Routledge is an imprint of the Taylor & Francis Group, an informa business*

First issued in paperback 2020

**Gower Applied Business Research**
Our programme provides leaders, practitioners, scholars and researchers with thought provoking, cutting edge books that combine conceptual insights, interdisciplinary rigour and practical relevance in key areas of business and management.

**British Library Cataloguing in Publication Data.**
**A catalogue record for this book is available from the British Library.**

**The Library of Congress has cataloged the printed edition as follows:**
Talukder, Majharul.
   Managing innovation adoption: from innovation to implementation / by Majharul Talukder.
      pages cm
   Includes bibliographical references and index.
ISBN 978-1-4724-1335-2 (hardback: alk. paper) – ISBN 978-1-4724-1336-9 (ebook) –
ISBN 978-1-4724-1337-6 (epub)
   1. Technological innovations – Management. 2. Diffusion of innovations – Management.
3. Organizational change. I. Title.

   HD45.T355 2014
   658.4'063—dc23

                                                                              2013037637

ISBN 13: 978-1-4724-1335-2 (hbk)
ISBN 13: 978-0-367-60079-2 (pbk)

# Contents

| | | |
|---|---|---:|
| *List of Figures* | | *ix* |
| *List of Tables* | | *xi* |
| *Acknowledgements* | | *xv* |
| *Preface* | | *xvii* |

| **Chapter 1** | **Introduction to Innovation Adoption** | **1** |
|---|---|---:|
| | 1.1 Background of the Problem | 1 |
| | 1.2 Research Questions | 4 |
| | 1.3 Study's Rationale | 4 |
| | 1.4 Study's Contribution to Knowledge | 5 |
| | 1.5 Study's Contribution to Practice | 5 |
| | 1.6 Conclusion | 6 |

| **Chapter 2** | **Innovation Adoption by Individual Employees** | **7** |
|---|---|---:|
| | 2.1 Introduction | 7 |
| | 2.2 Definitions of Innovation | 8 |
| | 2.3 Types of Innovation | 9 |
| | 2.4 The Innovation Adoption Process | 12 |
| | 2.5 Organizational Innovation Adoption | 13 |
| | 2.6 Factors That Affect Individual Adoption | 16 |
| | 2.7 Organizational Factors | 16 |
| | 2.8 Individual Factors | 19 |
| | 2.9 Social Factors | 22 |
| | 2.10 Demographics | 24 |
| | 2.11 Attitude Toward Innovation | 26 |
| | 2.12 Conclusion | 26 |

| **Chapter 3** | **Theories of Innovation Adoption** | **29** |
|---|---|---:|
| | 3.1 Introduction | 29 |
| | 3.2 Theory of Reasoned Action (TRA) | 30 |
| | 3.3 Technology Acceptance Model (TAM) | 33 |
| | 3.4 Conceptual Framework Provided by Frambach and Schillewaert | 35 |

3.5 Unified Theory of Acceptance and Use of
Technology (UTAUT)                                       36
3.6 DeLone and McLean IS Success Model                   37
3.7 Conclusion                                           38

Chapter 4    **Advanced Research Model of Innovation Adoption    39**
4.1 Introduction                                         39
4.2 Outline of the Research Model                        39
4.3 Proposed Advanced Research Model                     41
4.4 Individual Factors                                   42
4.5 Social Influence                                     44
4.6 Organizational Factors                               46
4.7 Demographics                                         47
4.8 Conclusion                                           48

Chapter 5    **Research Methods and Analytical Framework          51**
5.1 Introduction                                         51
5.2 Research Design                                      51
5.3 Quantitative Study                                   54
5.4 Definitions of the Constructs and Measures
of the Variables                                         57
5.5 Validity and Reliability of the Study                64
5.6 Data Collection Process                              68
5.7 Data Analysis                                        69
5.8 Qualitative Study                                    72
5.9 Conclusion                                           74

Chapter 6    **Impact of Organizational, Individual and Social Factors    77**
6.1 Introduction                                         77
6.2 Analysis of Demographic Data                         78
6.3 Employees' Level of Using Calendar                   79
6.4 Cross-tabulations for Level of Usage According
to Respondents' Demographic Characteristics              84
6.5 Inter-correlations Among Study Variables             98
6.6 Reliability and Validity of the Instruments          99
6.7 Multiple Regressions with Usage as Dependent
Variable                                                 104
6.8 The Impact of Respondents' Demographic
Characteristics on Usage                                 115

6.9 Hierarchical Regression Model for Impact
of Demographic Variables 126
6.10 Regression Analysis for Attitude with
Organizational, Individual and Social Factors 133
6.11 Discussion of Quantitative Results 136
6.12 Implications of Quantitative Results 139
6.13 Conclusion 142

Chapter 7   **Perception of Professionals and Management
Personnel**   **145**
7.1 Introduction 145
7.2 Analysis of Interview Findings 145
7.3 Summary of Interviews 166
7.4 Conclusion 169

Chapter 8   **Conclusion and Implications**   **173**
8.1 Introduction 173
8.2 Summary of Research 173
8.3 Conclusions and Implications for
Innovation Adoption 175
8.4 Contribution to Knowledge 181
8.5 Study Limitations 183
8.6 Future Research 183

*References* 185
*Index* 193

# List of Figures

| | | |
|---|---|---|
| 4.1 | The outline of the research model | 40 |
| 4.2 | Advanced research model of innovation adoption | 42 |
| 6.1 | Extent of use by gender | 85 |
| 6.2 | Number of calendar features used by gender | 87 |
| 6.3 | Extent of use by academic and professional staff | 93 |
| 6.4 | Number of features used by academic and administrative staff | 94 |
| 6.5 | Relationship between usage with other variables | 100–101 |
| 6.6 | Plot of standardized residuals against standardized predicted values | 113 |
| 6.7 | Histogram of normally distributed residuals | 114 |
| 6.8 | Normal P-P plot of regression standardized residuals | 114 |
| 6.9 | Mean usage level by gender | 116 |
| 6.10 | Mean usage level by age | 117 |
| 6.11 | Mean usage level by divisions | 119 |
| 6.12 | Mean usage by classification of employees | 121 |
| 6.13 | Mean usage level by employed as full-time and part-time employees | 123 |
| 6.14 | Mean usage level by academic qualifications | 124 |
| 6.15 | Plot of standardized residuals against standardized predicted values | 131 |
| 6.16 | Histogram of normally distributed residuals | 131 |
| 6.17 | Normal P-P plot of regression standardized residuals | 132 |

# List of Tables

| | | |
|---|---|---|
| 5.1 | Variables of the study | 56 |
| 5.2 | Participants in various studies | 64 |
| 6.1 | Demographic information about the respondents | 78 |
| 6.2 | Frequency of use of calendar in job-related activities | 80 |
| 6.3 | Average time spent on calendar per week | 81 |
| 6.4 | Level of usage of creating appointment | 81 |
| 6.5 | Level of usage of meeting request | 82 |
| 6.6 | Level of usage of sharing calendar | 83 |
| 6.7 | Number of different calendar applications have worked with or used | 83 |
| 6.8 | Use of sophisticated elements of calendar (recurring appointment, sharing and permissions, import and export to other applications, etc.) | 84 |
| 6.9 | Frequency of use of calendar by gender | 85 |
| 6.10 | Average time spent per week on using calendar for job-related activities by gender | 86 |
| 6.11 | Usage of number of different calendar applications by gender | 87 |
| 6.12 | Use of sophisticated elements of calendar by gender | 88 |
| 6.13 | Frequency of use of calendar by faculty (division) | 88 |
| 6.14 | Average time spent per week on using calendar for job-related activities by division | 89 |
| 6.15 | Usage of number of different calendar applications by division | 90 |
| 6.16 | Use of sophisticated elements of calendar by division | 91 |
| 6.17 | Frequency of use of calendar by academic and administrative staff | 92 |
| 6.18 | Average time spent per week on using calendar for job-related activities by academic and administrative staff | 93 |

6.19   Usage of number of different calendar applications
       by academic and administrative staff                              94
6.20   Use of sophisticated elements of calendar by
       academic and administrative staff                                 95
6.21   Frequency of use of calendar by full-time and
       part-time employees                                               96
6.22   Average time spent per week on using calendar for
       job-related activities by full-time and part-time employees       96
6.23   Usage of number of different calendar applications
       by full-time and part-time employees                              97
6.24   Use of sophisticated elements of calendar by
       full-time and part-time employees                                 98
6.25   Inter-correlations among study variables                         102
6.26   Variable means, standard deviations and scale reliability        103
6.27   Test for multicollinearity                                       104
6.28   Descriptive statistics                                           106
6.29   Regression model summary                                         107
6.30   ANOVA                                                            107
6.31   Coefficients                                                     108
6.32   Collinearity statistics                                          112
6.33   Summary statistics of gender distribution                        116
6.34   Test of homogeneity of variances between
       types of gender                                                  116
6.35   Oneway ANOVA test for usage level by gender                      116
6.36   Summary statistics of age distributions                          118
6.37   Test of homogeneity of variances among age group                 118
6.38   Oneway ANOVA test for usage level by age group                   118
6.39   Summary statistics of divisions distribution                     119
6.40   Test of homogeneity of variances among divisions                 120
6.41   Oneway ANOVA test for usage level by division
6.42   Oneway ANOVA post hoc (Tamhane) test for usage
       level by division                                                120
6.43   Summary statistics of classification of employees                122
6.44   Test of homogeneity of variances between
       classifications of employees                                     122
6.45   Oneway ANOVA test for usage level by
       classification of employees                                      122
6.46   Summary statistics of employment status
       (full-time and part-time employees)                              123

| 6.47 | Test of homogeneity of variances between employment status (full-time and part-time employees) | 123 |
| 6.48 | Oneway ANOVA test for usage level by employment status | 124 |
| 6.49 | Summary statistics of academic qualifications | 125 |
| 6.50 | Test of homogeneity of variances among academic qualifications | 125 |
| 6.51 | Oneway ANOVA test for usage level by academic qualifications | 125 |
| 6.52 | Model summary | 127 |
| 6.53 | Analysis of variance (ANOVA) | 128 |
| 6.54 | Coefficients | 128 |
| 6.55 | Regression model for organizational factors | 134 |
| 6.56 | Regression model for individual factors | 134 |
| 6.57 | Regression model for social factors | 135 |
| 6.58 | Regression model for organizational, individual and social factors | 136 |

# Acknowledgements

In doing this study, I was the recipient of gracious help from many people. Without their support and advice, this study would have been difficult to accomplish. For their help, I am grateful to all of them. I wish to express my deepest appreciation and gratitude to Associate Professor Howard Harris and Dr. Gido Mapunda. They provided me with sincere help, valuable suggestions, encouragement and scholarly advice throughout this study. I am very grateful and indebted to them for responding promptly, sharing their ideas, motivating and guiding me toward the accomplishment of the study.

I take this opportunity to express my gratitude to the following individuals: Professor Monir Mir, Professor Phyllis Tharenou, Associate Professor Chris Provis, Associate Professor Gary Howat, Professor John Benson, Professor Atique Islam, Dr. Lindsay Ryan, Dr. Anna Ciccarelli, Professor Ali Quazi and Dr. Sheila Strawn for their sincere guidance, valued assistance, advice and encouragement in advancing this research.

I would like to acknowledge Martin West and Chris Muddiman at Ashgate/ Gower Publishing for their assistance and cooperation. I also sincerely thank all respondents who used their valuable time to complete the survey questionnaire and give interviews.

I would like to express my appreciation to my colleagues and friends Carmen Joham, Mahfuz Ashraf, ABM Abdullah and Chris Obi, who have made contributions to this book often with a short notice. Their scholarly writings and collective endeavors have added to the variety and quality of this book.

A special appreciation goes to my beloved parents whose exceptional love, prayers and moral support always reinforced me to complete this work. I acknowledge my brothers and sisters for their support, advice, love and encouragement that provided me with so much strength and energy to complete my research. I would like to thank my beloved wife, Sultana Parvin, and my daughters, Rumaysa Talukder and Umayma Talukder, whose understanding, love, inspiration and encouragement were very important in the completion of this study. I would also like to thank my friends, colleagues and relatives who have seen me through this process, offering intellectual support, love, wishes and encouragement along the way.

Majharul Talukder
Canberra, Australia

# Preface

Innovation is generally considered to be one of the key drivers of corporate success. One of the important issues organizations face is how to implement innovation successfully. Research has identified that many innovations fail due to the lack of acceptance by employees. Thus, in order for an organization to be successful in bringing innovation to the workplace, an understanding of potential adopters and the factors influencing their adoption decision is important. Despite much research on organizational adoption of innovation, little is currently known about the adoption of innovation by individual employees within the organization. The purpose of this study is to investigate empirically the determinants and provide a new theoretical framework that addresses the adoption decision by individual employees in the organization.

This study develops and tests an advanced model of innovation adoption considering the strength and limitations of existing models. The theoretical framework for this study is based on the theory of reasoned action (TRA), the technology acceptance model (TAM), the conceptual framework provided by Frambach and Schillewaert (2002), the unified theory of acceptance and use of technology (UTAUT) and DeLone and McLean IS Success Model. The advanced model includes several modifications that were not in these models.

The advanced model combines multiple sets of factors found in previous models and incorporates factors that have been suggested in previous models. Furthermore, it incorporates additional variables found in other innovation acceptance-related studies to create a coherent model of innovation adoption. The combination of factors in this study goes beyond previous research in an attempt to bring together relevant factors, which can influence adoption into a single model to examine the relationships between individual adoption and the factors that affect the adoption. Multiple avenues of data collection are employed to test the relevance of the proposed enhanced model including a questionnaire survey to test the advanced model and interviews to provide additional information.

The empirical results show that the proposed enhanced model is supported and can be used to identify factors that would be effective for broader understanding of the adoption and usage behavior by employees. The findings indicate that perceived usefulness and managerial support are the two dominant variables in explaining adoption. The results show that individual adoption of innovation can be influenced by three organizational factors – training, managerial support and incentives; and by five individual factors – perceived usefulness, personal innovativeness, prior experience, image and enjoyment with innovation. Contrary to previous research, the results show that individual adoption of innovation is also influenced by two social factors – peers and social network. The results also indicate that individual adoption of innovation is influenced by demographic factors such as gender, academic discipline, occupation category and tenure.

The theoretical model developed in this study provides a valuable alternative and comprehensive theoretical basis for improving our understanding of individual users' acceptance of innovation. The study contributes to knowledge and has practical implications for organizations, managers, administrators and employees concerned with adoption of innovation.

Chapter 1 introduces the study by stating the background of the research problem upon which the research questions were established. It focuses on the problems with adoption of innovation by employees within an organization. The chapter also discusses why the proposed research model is important to researchers and practitioners. In addition, it explores three broad categories of factors: organizational, individual and social, which affect employees' adoption of innovation. The significance of this study, explained at the end of the chapter, articulates how this study can contribute towards discovering new knowledge and establishing an enhanced model of innovation adoption.

Chapter 2 starts by providing various definitions of innovation and types of innovation adoption. It explains Rogers's model of the innovation adoption process in the organization. The chapter also discusses the organizational innovation adoption. Although this study is about individuals' adoption of innovation, this section focuses on such adoption by organizations and identifies the reasons that influence organizational decisions to do so.

Chapter 3 focuses on the theories of innovation adoption by reviewing existing innovation adoption models: the theory of reasoned action (TRA); the technology acceptance model (TAM); the conceptual framework provided by Frambach and Schillewaert (2002); the unified theory of acceptance and use of technology (UTAUT); the DeLone and McLean IS Success Model and shows inadequacies or limitations of those models.

Chapter 4 describes an advanced research model proposed by the researcher. It starts with an outline of the proposed model. The new model is based on the theory of reasoned action, incorporates elements of the technology acceptance model, the model provided by Frambach and Schillewaert (2002), the unified theory of acceptance and use of technology (UTAUT) and DeLone and McLean IS Success Model while introducing several modifications that were not in these models. The chapter then develops an enhanced research model of innovation adoption. In the development of this model four categories of factors are included – individual, social, organizational and demographics. The chapter also discusses demographic factors that influence individuals' adoption of innovation.

Chapter 5 describes the research design and methodology used in the empirical study. Initially, it explains the rationale behind the selection of the multi-methods strategy approach. The next section discusses the location of the study, sample size, research instruments, definition of constructs, validity and reliability, experts' opinions, pilot study, data collection procedures and data analysis techniques.

Chapter 6 provides a systematic analysis of data collected from individual employees. In this chapter, the proposed enhanced model of innovation adoption is tested statistically using data from the questionnaire survey. The statistical testing assists and supports the development of a theoretical construct that brings individual innovation adoption issues into a coherent model.

Chapter 7 contains analysis of the perception of professionals and management personnel on adoption of innovation. The chapter focuses on interviews with academic and administrative staff to gain additional information and support for the enhanced model developed in this study. It presents an analysis and discussion of interview findings, summary of interviews and conclusion, highlighting the factors affecting individual adoption of innovation in an organizational context and supporting the development of the enhanced model of innovation adoption.

Chapter 8 concludes the book. It begins with summary of the research and then moves on to the conclusion and implications. The conclusion shows how this research has extended previous research and contributes to knowledge and the broader theoretical understanding of individual adoption of innovation. The chapter discusses the practical implications for managers and practitioners. Finally, it states limitations and an agenda for future research.

# 1

# Introduction to Innovation Adoption

## 1.1 Background of the Problem

Innovation offers the potential for substantially improving the performance of organizations, such as businesses in the global economy. However, performance gains are often obstructed by users' unwillingness to accept and use the available innovation. Due to the persistence and importance of this problem, explaining users' acceptance of innovation has been a long-term study issue in organizations and information systems research (Davis, 1989). According to Frambach, Barkema, Nooteboom and Wedel (1998, p.161) "environmental conditions increasingly force organizations to innovate and bring new products to the market. As only a fraction of new products are successful, a thorough understanding of factors underlying the innovation adoption decisions by potential adopters is necessary." Similarly, Bhattacherjee and Sanford (2006, p.805) state that "understanding IT acceptance is important because the expected benefits of IT usage, such as gain in efficiency, effectiveness or productivity, cannot be realized if individual users do not accept these systems for task performance." Venkatesh, Morris and Ackerman (2000) note that organizational investments in information technologies have increased significantly in the past decade and these investments specifically aim to increase individual productivity, which consequently contributes to organizational productivity. While advances in innovation continue at an astronomical pace, the use of these innovations have fallen well below expectations and has been identified as one of the reasonable explanations for productivity gains from innovation investments being less than expected (Venkatesh, Morris & Ackerman, 2000). Consequently, understanding the factors influencing user acceptance of innovation in the workplace has long been a concern of scholars and practitioners (Sherif, Zmud & Browne, 2006, p.339; Venkatesh, Morris & Ackerman, 2000, p.34).

According to Bhattacherjee (1998) investment in innovation represents substantial capital budget expenditure for any organization. Management expects that innovation will be appropriately utilized by employees within the organization in order to achieve increased worker productivity, better decision making, efficiency in performing jobs or other expected benefits. However, the availability of innovation does not automatically guarantee that employees will use it. According to Bhattacherjee (1998), the 'shelf-ware syndrome' has been coined to describe software productivity packages sitting idle on book-shelves without being utilized by the individuals for whom they are intended. Motivating users to use innovation remains a major problem for organizations. Nelson (1990, p.79) concluded that "the adoption of new technology in the workplace has become a transition experience common to many organizations. The success of these endeavors depends on the nature of the individuals within the organization and the technology itself." Innovation represents a social change affecting the behaviors of individuals within the organization as well as a structural change that alters the work design of the organization. The introduction of innovation in an organization requires its employees to change their attitude and behavior. Without employees' behavior changes the organization's plans may fail to reach its desired outcomes as they may either refuse to adopt it, or not use it to its potential (Nelson, 1990). As Youngblood (2005) put it, a "solution without the involvement of those who use the system is not a solution at all. A successful technology solution needs early and ongoing involvement of the people who use the system" (Youngblood, 2005, p.12).

Organizational innovations that need to be incorporated in the work processes of an organization are of little value if they are not adopted by employees (Frambach & Schillewaert, 2002). Employees must actually use an innovation to realize the intended benefits. According to Rogers's (2003) model of innovation adoption, innovation passes through a set of stages before it is implemented by people. Individuals develop the ability to formulate attitudes, make decisions, implement and confirm whether or not innovations should be practiced. Despite an organizational decision to adopt an innovation, its actual usage depends on how employees implement an innovation. Therefore, it is important to examine the adoption of innovations by employees within organizations because if there is no acceptance among employees, the desired benefits cannot be realized and the organization may eventually abandon the innovation. People, by nature will resist change unless they can be convinced that they can directly benefit from the change (Ajzen, 1991). New technologies are rapidly replacing old ones by providing more powerful tools, efficiency and speed for users. "Their adoption can be successful, however, only when the employees accept and effectively use them, which means an organization should understand the acceptance process and factors that are essential in making this process effective" (Lee, Kim, Rhee & Trimi, 2006, p.470).

Although innovation adoption has been studied extensively, drivers of adoption and research on individual innovation acceptance remains limited (Frambach & Schillewaert, 2002). Designing an effective approach for increasing end-user acceptance and subsequent use of innovation continues to be a fundamental challenge that has not always provided straight-forward solutions. "While advances in hardware and software capabilities continue at an extraordinary pace, the problem of underutilized systems remains" (Kukafka, Johnson, Linfante & Allegrante, 2003, p.218). The current literature indicates that we know relatively little about the ways in which individuals adopt and the factors that influence individual adoption of innovation (Bhattacherjee, 1998; Frambach & Schillewaert, 2002; van Everdingen & Wierenga, 2002; Venkatesh & Davis, 2000). Hence, further research is required regarding the role of organizational, individual and social processes affecting individual adoption of innovation (Frambach & Schillewaert, 2002; Schepers & Wetzels, 2007; Yi, Jackson, Park & Probst, 2006). This study is designed to fill that gap. The identification of these factors is important to organizations that want to create a work environment that is conducive to individual adoption of innovation and thereby gain the expected benefits from the innovation.

From an empirical study conducted in South Australia, this study proposes a new theoretical framework and develops an advanced research model of innovation adoption taking into account the strength and limitations of previous innovation acceptance models such as the theory of reasoned action (Ajzen & Fishbein, 1980), the technology acceptance model (Davis, 1989) and the conceptual framework provided by Frambach and Schillewaert (2002) while introducing several modifications, which were not in these earlier models. The new theoretical framework and improved model will help greater learning in innovation adoption and facilitate an understanding of the factors affecting individuals' adoption of innovation. Theoretically, such research will enrich the innovation acceptance literature by addressing a construct that combines innovation adoption issues into a coherent model. The combination of variables and the testing of a wide range of factors in this study represent a novel approach to the understanding of an individual's adoption of innovation. In addition, this research examines moderating factors that influence the process of innovation adoption, a previously unexplored area of research. In the case of practitioners, this research can help managers to identify and benchmark strategies to motivate innovation adoption in their organizations and customize these strategies to best fit the unique characteristics of their organizational users.

## 1.2 Research Questions

The implementation of an innovation in an organization when it has committed to it often happens slowly. This being the case, this study seeks to analyze the following:

1.  What is the impact of organizational factors – training, managerial support and incentives – on individual adoption of innovation?

2.  Do individual factors – perceived usefulness, personal innovativeness, prior experience, image and enjoyment of innovation – affect individuals' adoption of innovation?

3.  What is the impact of social factors – peers and social network – on individual adoption of innovation?

## 1.3 Study's Rationale

1.  The study will develop a new model and extend previous research by investigating multiple factors in individual adoption of innovation.

2.  Findings of the study will contribute to the existing knowledge in the context of factors affecting the use and continued use of innovation.

3.  The study will help organizations understand the determinants and the process of innovation adoption by individuals within an organization.

4.  The results of the study will help organizations understand what changes are needed in organizational policies and strategies in order to develop and promote the adoption of innovation and

consequently improve the wellbeing of employees as well as productivity of the organization.

5.  The study will provide better understanding of employees' adoption of innovation and thereby increase the level of innovation usage in the organization.

The research contributes to knowledge and promotes the adoption of innovations by individual employees within organizations.

## 1.4 Study's Contribution to Knowledge

**Development of a theoretical construct that correlates individual innovation adoption issues into a coherent model.**

The combination of variables in this study goes beyond previous research in an attempt to bring together all the relevant factors that may influence adoption into a coherent model. It examines the relationship between individual adoption and the factors that affect and determine the adoption and continued use of an innovation by individual employees within an organization. This research involves the combination of multiple variables, found in different innovation adoption-related studies, into a single-study context. Organizational, individual and social factors influence individual attitudes that consequently lead to individual adoption. In short, this study addresses numerous factors, tests whether they are significant and assesses differences between the factors; thereby contributing to knowledge and the broader theoretical understanding of the phenomenon.

## 1.5 Study's Contribution to Practice

**Promotion of management awareness, understanding and support of innovation adoption by individual employees.**

In addition to being of academic interest, the results of this research will be useful for various groups of practitioners engaged in introducing innovation in an organization. With the trend towards end-user applications, these findings will be crucial for guiding management toward more effective adoption and usage of innovation in an organization. The study will help to identify the extent to which the innovation can be used to support organizational needs and improve the work environment within the organization. Furthermore, it will determine the factors that affect individuals to adopt innovation. For management, this research may help to reduce innovation implementation-related cost and enable faster and more efficient individual uptake of innovation in the organization.

## 1.6 Conclusion

This chapter has provided background information on the research effort, research questions and the study's contribution to knowledge and practice. Chapter 2, which presents a literature review, will examine various studies dealing with different aspects of adoption of innovation within an organization, theoretical foundations and relevant factors that affect individuals' adoption of innovation.

# 2

# Innovation Adoption by Individual Employees

## 2.1 Introduction

The purpose of this chapter is to present a review of related literature on the issue of individual employees' adoption of innovation in an organization. The chapter provides an analysis of the definitions of innovation, innovation adoption and implementation, the theoretical framework, the relevant factors that influence adoption of innovation and conclusion.

This chapter explains the various definitions of innovation and the problems with information innovation adoption and implementation. It includes three theoretical and conceptual models – the theory of reasoned action, the technology acceptance model and the conceptual framework provided by Frambach and Schillewaert (2002) to develop an advanced research model of individual innovation adoption. The chapter then discusses relevant factors that influence adoption of innovation. The chapter particularly focuses on three organizational factors – training, managerial support and incentives; five individual factors – perceived usefulness, personal innovativeness, prior experience, image and enjoyment with innovation and two social factors – peers and social network which affect individuals' adoption of innovation. The chapter also discusses demographic factors that influence individuals' attitude toward innovation adoption.

## 2.2 Definitions of Innovation

There are various definitions of innovation that appear in the literature. The purpose of this section is to explain and compare the major definitions.

Rogers (2003, p.12) defines "innovation as an idea, practice or object that is perceived as new by an individual or other unit of adoption. If an idea or object seems new to the individual, it is considered as an innovation." Furthermore, according to Rogers (2003, p.12), "the concept of newness in an innovation need not just involve new knowledge. An individual may have known of an innovation for some time but not yet developed a favorable or unfavorable attitude toward it." He argues that "the newness aspect of an innovation can be expressed in terms of knowledge, persuasion or a decision to adopt" (Rogers, 2003, p.12).

Afuah (2003) states that innovation is the use of a new technological system that offers a better and improved service. The outcome of the new system is more efficiency and that it is new to the employees. According to Higgins (1995, p.9), "innovation is the development of something new that has significant value to an individual, a group, an organization, an industry or a society." This definition explains that an innovation is something – an object or a system – that has significant value to individuals or to organizations. Organizations intend that individual employees will adopt an innovation that consequently will enhance work efficiency, gain competitive advantage and maintain superior management systems. Holt (1983) makes similar claims that innovation is a process, which uses knowledge and information to create or introduce something that is new and useful to individuals or to organizations.

According to Zaltman, Duncan and Holbek (1973, p.8), "innovation can be defined as an idea, practice, or material artifact perceived to be new by the relevant unit of adoption." They argued that innovation is any new system or program, which is new to individuals or organizations who are adopting it no matter how old the system may be or how many other organizations may have adopted it. The length of time the system has been in existence and the number of other organizations that have adopted it does not directly affect its newness to the organization or to the individuals considering its adoption (Zaltman, Duncan & Holbek, 1973). They state that "this does not imply that each new idea or system or technology adopted by an organization is necessarily new to society. A particular new technology may be new only to an organization or to individuals who are adopting it" (1973, p.11). The idea is also supported by

Rogers (2003). The key point in this definition is that any technology or system is considered an innovation if it is new to the individual who plans to adopt it even though the technology has been in existence for a long time.

Although the Zaltman, Duncan and Holbek (1973) definition and arguments are plausible, logical and relevant to this study, from the above definitions a more comprehensive definition of innovation can be derived. Accordingly, innovation can be defined as something – an idea or a system or a technology which is new or significantly improved, which can be implemented or adopted by an organization or individual to create added value, improve performance or efficiencies of activities in an organization. From this definition, it can be said that innovation is something that adds value to an organization and it will only be regarded as innovation when it can be implemented. A new abstract idea or a new technology cannot be considered an innovation if it cannot be incorporated into daily activities of an organization. Note that to assimilate or incorporate innovation into organizational activities, it requires substantial efforts from all elements of the organization, especially the involvement of employees who will be using the targeted innovation.

## 2.3 Types of Innovation

Today's world is characterized by profound social, economic and technological changes. "Change is ubiquitous and pervasive, and innovation facilitates the process of adaptation to many of these changes" (Gopalakrishnan & Damanpour, 1997, p.15). Innovation plays a role in nurturing the economy, in enhancing and sustaining high performance of organizations, in building competitiveness, in creating better quality, and in improving standards and efficiency (Gopalakrishnan & Damanpour, 1997). Innovations have usually been categorized by researchers into a set of contrasting types each providing insight to our understanding of the innovation process. Three of the most popular typologies are based on distinctions between administrative and technical innovation, product and process innovation and radical and incremental innovation (Gopalakrishnan & Bierly, 2001; Gopalakrishnan & Damanpour, 1997).

Administrative and technical innovations reflect a more general distinction between social and technical system of an organization (Damanpour, 1996). "Technical innovations include products, process and technologies used to produce or render services related to the basic work activity of an organization" (Gopalakrishnan & Bierly, 2001, p.109). Technical innovations would be adopted in an organization, as they are perceived to be relatively more advantageous than administrative innovations (Damanpour, 1996). On the other hand, "administrative innovations pertain to organizational structures, administrative processes and human resources; these innovations are indirectly related to basic work activity of the organization and are more directly related to its management" (Gopalakrishnan & Damanpour, 1997, p.19). Administrative innovations are primarily adopted in larger and structurally more complex organizations to control and coordinate differentiated units. Technical innovations usually occur in the technical core where as administrative innovations are more often initiated in the administrative core of an organization (Gopalakrishnan & Bierly, 2001).

Product and process innovations are distinct, based on different areas and activities that each of them affect within the organization (Gopalakrishnan & Bierly, 2001). According to Gopalakrishnan and Damanpour (1997, p.18), "process innovations are tools, devices and knowledge in throughput technology that mediate between inputs and outputs and are new to an industry, organizations or sub-units." While product innovations are outputs or services that are introduced for the benefits of customers, employees or clients (Gopalakrishnan & Damanpour, 1997), studies found that organizations adopt more products than process innovations because process innovations are less observable and perceived to be relatively less advantageous as they relate to the delivery of outcomes rather than being outcomes themselves and they are more difficult to implement. This is because their successful implementation depends on widespread changes in organizational structure and administrative systems (Damanpour, 1996). When an organization is small and its structure is simple, it primarily introduces product innovations, but as the organization grows and becomes more complex, it also introduces process innovations because conditions of high complexity and large size are more advantageous for process than product innovations (Damanpour, 1996). A more recent study conducted by Damanpour and Schneider (2006) confirmed that organizational complexity and size influence every phase of innovation (p.226).

The difference between radical and incremental innovations is based on the degree of change an innovation causes to the structure and processes of an organization (Gopalakrishnan & Bierly, 2001; Gopalakrishnan & Damanpour, 1997). According to Gopalakrishnan and Bierly (2001, p.109), "radical innovations produce fundamental changes in the activities of an organization and produce clear departure from the existing practice." On the other hand, "incremental innovations call for marginal a departure from existing products or processes and reinforce the existing capabilities of organizations" (Gopalakrishnan & Bierly, 2001, p.109).

According to Damanpour (1996), radical innovations on average are less frequently adopted than incremental innovations because they present a more severe challenge to existing structures of organizations causing more internal resistance during their adoption and implementation process. Radical innovations appear more complex to organizational members and generate greater uncertainty in the organization (Gopalakrishnan & Damanpour, 1997). Research findings suggest that organizations with large numbers of employees are more successful than smaller ones in introducing radical innovation because technological knowledge and resources are required to overcome obstacles against it (Damanpour, 1996).

Dewar and Dutton (1986) state that incremental innovation is improvement or adjustment to current technology, whereas radical innovation is dramatic change to an existing system or technology. Complexity and knowledge depth is less important for incremental innovations because adoption of this type of innovation requires less knowledge resources in the organization for development, support and implementation. Instead, "adoption of these kinds of changes should be facilitated by mere exposure to the innovation through contact with the external environment" (Dewar & Dutton, 1986, p.1424). Individual exposure may occur through membership in trade or professional association or contact with other members within the organization or members in other organizations (Dewar & Dutton, 1986). These represent the means for individuals to keep abreast of developments for improving current operations and introducing efficiency into daily activities.

This research is about technical innovation because it intends to produce or render services related to work activities of an organization. The research is seen as process innovation because it is a tool, new to employees and intended for creating efficiency and productivity of employees in an organization. It is about incremental innovation and its purpose is to find out how an organization's internal and external environment affects employees adoption of innovation. The usage of advanced features of innovation that has been implemented for years is considered to be incremental innovation. Adoption of this kind of innovation can be influenced by organizational support, external influence and employees' personal characteristics or circumstances.

## 2.4 The Innovation Adoption Process

Intra-organizational adoption refers to the adoption that occurs at the individual level within the organization (Frambach & Schillewaert, 2002). Inter-organizational adoption is the process whereby the organization benefits from the fact that its business partners in the same industry have previously taken up an innovation. Organizations are inclined to adopt an innovation when its suppliers, customers, competitors and other organizations use it as well (Frambach & Schillewaert, 2002). Organizational adoption is therefore the process whereby an organization adopts a new idea to achieve organizational advantages such as productivity, increased profits, strategic domination, efficiency and effectiveness.

The adoption process consists of a sequence the potential adopter passes through before acceptance of innovation. An innovation can only be considered a success when the innovation is adopted by employees and integrated into the organization and the adopters demonstrate commitment by continuing to use the innovation over a period of time (Bhattacherjee, 1998). Rogers (2003) defines adoption as the decision to make full use of an innovation by the adopter as the best course of action. Adoption of innovation in an organization implies that adoption also occurs at the individual level within the organization, which is also referred to as intra-organizational adoption (Frambach & Schillewaert, 2002).

According to Rogers's (2003) innovation adoption model, every innovation passes through a set of stages before it is adopted. Decision processes play an important role in innovation adoption because employees in an organization are faced with choices to innovate or not, to select different innovations or to use different methods of implementation. Rogers (2003) states that the innovation decision process is the process through which an individual passes from first knowledge of an innovation to forming an attitude toward innovation, to a decision to adopt or reject, to implementation and use of the new idea and to confirmation of this decision. The process consists of a series of actions and choices over time through which an individual evaluates a new idea and decides whether or not to incorporate the innovation into ongoing practice.

This research is concerned with the last two stages of Rogers's innovation adoption model, i.e., implementation and confirmation. An organization may have made a decision to adopt an innovation but confirmation will then depend on how employees implement innovation in their daily functions and continued use of innovation in the activities of an organization. If employees are neither influenced nor interested in adopting innovation, then the expected benefits may not be achieved. Therefore, it is essential to look at what influences individual employees and what makes them interested in adopting and continued use of innovation.

## 2.5 Organizational Innovation Adoption

Although this study is about individuals' adoption of innovation, this section of the literature review focuses on such adoption by organizations and identifies the reasons that influence organizational decisions to do so. Organizations innovate in order to achieve benefits such as productivity gains and increased profits. Strategic importance and organizational effectiveness also stimulate a business's decisions for upgrading systems. In contrast, individual employees adopt innovative ideas or processes to realize personal benefits such as career advancement. Individuals also adopt innovations when they feel that they will help them do their jobs better. Individual adoption of innovation also depends on organizational attitudes toward innovation because organizations, within which employees work, make innovation available to employees. If an organization does not adopt an innovation then there is no chance for its employees to adopt and use it. An organization needs to create an environment for employees to be innovative and creative. Organizations need to encourage lifelong learning, assisting and encouraging employees' skills and knowledge enhancement and continuous improvement.

Two types of organizational adoption decisions can be identified: firstly, the decision made by an organization and secondly, the decision made by an individual within an organization (Frambach & Schillewaert, 2002). In regard to organizational adoption, two main stages may be identified: initiation and implementation (Zaltman, Duncan & Holbek, 1973). The adoption decision occurs at the organizational level between the initiation and the implementation stage. "In the initiation stage, the organization becomes aware of the innovation, forms an attitude toward it and evaluates the new product; and in the implementation stage, the organization decides to purchase and make use of the innovation" (Frambach & Schillewaert, 2002, p.164). Frambach and Schillewaert (2002) have contended that this organizational adoption decision is only the beginning of implementation of innovation because the acceptance of innovation within the organization now becomes important.

There are various factors that affect adoption at the organizational level. According to Frambach and Schillewaert (2002) the perceptions of an innovation by relevant decision makers in the organization affect their evaluation of and propensity to adopt an innovation. The perceived net benefits, including economic incentives the innovation offers has an important effect on organizational adaptation (Mansfield, 1993). Other innovation characteristics that influence organizational adoption decision include compatibility, complexity, observability, trialability and perceived uncertainty (Frambach & Schillewaert, 2002; Nooteboom, 1988; Rogers, 2003).

Adoption decisions in organizations are also influenced by organizational characteristics. There are several types of characteristics at the organizational level such as organizational size, organizational structure, organizational innovativeness and organizational strategic posture (Kennedy, 1983; Zaltman, Duncan & Holbek, 1973). According to Frambach and Schillewaert (2002, p.165), "size has repeatedly been found to influence the propensity to adopt and size is usually found to be positively related to innovation adoption." This is because larger organizations have a greater need to adopt an innovation in order to support and improve their performance. In contrast, it is argued that small organizations are more flexible and innovative, which lead to receptiveness toward innovation. In addition, Frambach and Schillewaert (2002, p.165) state that "these apparently contrasting relations may be largely attributable to the correlation of organization size with other variables such as structure, strategy and culture." For instance, Zaltman, Duncan and Holbek (1973) assert that more formalized and centralized organizations are less likely to initiate innovation adoption decisions but they are better equipped to implement an innovation (Frambach & Schillewaert, 2002). Frambach and Schillewaert (2002) argue that the degree to which an organization is receptive to innovation will influence its propensity to adopt new products or ideas. Organizations that pursue aggressive strategies are more likely to conduct their activities with an orientation that is open to innovation (Han, Kim & Srivastava, 1998).

An organization that manufactures or supplies innovations can significantly influence the probability that an innovation will be adopted by an organization (Frambach, Barkema, Nooteboom & Wedel, 1998). According to Easingwood and Beard (1989), although different factors may stimulate or facilitate adoption, three factors are important: targeting, communication and risk reduction. Careful and specific targeting of an innovation toward selected potential adopters can facilitate adoption for the organization. Potential adopters such as innovative organizations may be more receptive to innovation than other organizations (Frambach & Schillewaert, 2002). Gauvin and Rajib (1993) argue that to target an organization, it is necessary to consider what benefits and opportunities an organization can have to adopt an innovation.

Manufacturers or suppliers need to communicate with the potential trading partners about innovation because innovation adoption is largely an information processing activity. Communication indirectly affects potential adopters' propensity to adopt (Frambach & Schillewaert, 2002). According to Frambach and Schillewaert (2002), this communication will not only create awareness but also influence potential adopters' perceptions of innovation. Manufacturers or suppliers of innovation can ensure risk reduction in terms of implementation risk, financial risk and operational risk, which may stimulate organizations to adopt (Frambach & Schillewaert, 2002). They may offer innovation to potential adopters on a trial basis for a certain period of time or offer innovation at a low introduction price (Ram & Jung, 1994). According to Frambach and Schillewaert (2002), in the high tech market, initiating a risk reduction strategy may even be necessary to gain market acceptance.

Organizations in their business environment can influence each other to adopt an innovation. Organizations in formal or informal networks facilitate the spread of information about an innovation, which may positively influence the probability of adoption (Frambach & Schillewaert, 2002). Lefebvre, Lefebvre, Elia and Boeck (2005) make this point specifically for the adoption of e-commerce processes in small and medium sized enterprises. Furthermore, the business environment can affect adoption behavior in various ways. Potential adopters may perceive benefits from the fact that their business partners within their environment have previously adopted innovation (Frambach & Schillewaert, 2002). Organizations are more inclined to adopt when its suppliers, customers, competitors and other organizations also use innovation (Frambach & Schillewaert, 2002).

In a competitive market environment, organizations may be forced to adopt an innovation to maintain market position (Robertson & Gatignon, 1986). According to Frambach and Schillewaert (2002), non-adoption of an innovation that is adopted by other organizations in the market environment may result in competitive disadvantage. The strategic importance of innovation and its potential implications for effectiveness and efficiency of an organization stimulates the intention to adopt innovation (Frambach & Schillewaert, 2002).

## 2.6 Factors That Affect Individual Adoption

The following section defines variables and explains factors that affect individuals' adoption of innovation. In order to explore an individual's attitude toward innovation and subsequently adoption, it is necessary to understand the factors that influence his or her attitude and adoption of innovation. Based on the literature review, there are three broad categories of variables – organizational, individual and social. These are further sub categorized into ten factors – training, managerial support, incentives, perceived usefulness, personal innovativeness, prior experience, image, enjoyment with innovation, peers and social network. They affect and determine an individual's acceptance and continued use of innovation. In addition, demographic characteristics are included in the model as moderating factors in adoption. These factors are crucial for the use and continuous use of innovation. It is necessary to describe each variable to determine why they are important and required in investigating employees' adoption of innovation.

## 2.7 Organizational Factors

Several studies have indicated that an individual's adoption of innovation not only depends on individual attitudes but also on organizational policies, approaches and actions (Peansupap & Walker, 2005). Organizational factors are external to an individual who is considering adopting the innovation. These are organizational factors where individuals work. Organizations need to provide facilitating conditions, which include the extent and type of support provided to individuals that would influence their use of innovation. Facilitating conditions are believed to include the availability of training and provision of support. Facilitating conditions have been identified as having an effect on infusion or adoption of a number of new information system innovations (Lu, Yu & Liu, 2005). These factors include training (Al-Gahtani & King, 1999; Clegg, Carey, Dean, Hornby & Bolden, 1997), managerial support (Ahuja & Thatcher, 2005; Igbaria, Parasuraman & Baroudi, 1996) and incentives (Bhattacherjee, 1998). These influences affect an individual's awareness of the functioning and application of an innovation, its usefulness and fit with the job, which leads to its adoption (Frambach & Schillewaert, 2002). Organizational influences can motivate employees to adopt an innovation.

## TRAINING

This refers to the extent of training that is provided to individual employees in an organization. This will indicate the extent to which training is provided to employees that would contribute to the increase of their knowledge and expertise using a new system (Al-Gahtani & King, 1999). Training plays an important role in increasing user confidence in the ability to learn and use the innovation. It increases individual skills and abilities to do related work (Lee, Kim, Rhee & Trimi, 2006). According to Igbaria, Zinatelli, Cragg and Cavaye (1997), training promotes greater understanding, favourable attitude, more frequent use, and more diverse use of applications. Several studies have reported that training encourages an individual to adopt innovation (Igbaria, Parasuraman & Baroudi, 1996; Jasperson, Carter & Zmud, 2005). Such training decreases anxiety and increases favourable perceptions about the innovation and consequently influences its adoption (Igbaria, 1993). A review of the relevant literature suggests that adoption of innovation is directly affected by specialized instructions, guidance, coaching and consulting with the potential adopters (Igbaria, 1993; Yuan et al., 2005). With training, educating and assisting employees when they encounter difficulties, some of the potential barriers to adoption can be reduced or eliminated (Burgess, Jackson & Edwards, 2005; Thompson, Higgins & Howell, 1991). Individual adoption of innovation is positively influenced by the amount of relevant formal training. Such training enhances an individual's belief, possession of skills and knowledge that permit successful task performance (Ligon, Abdullah & Talukder, 2007). Instructional procedures that are more individualized and focus on the relative amount of learning and progress are likely to enhance the adoption process (Farr & Ford, 1990; Yuan et al., 2005).

## MANAGERIAL SUPPORT

Davis, Bagozzi and Warshaw (1989) propose that managerial support is an important variable that is likely to affect the adoption of innovation by employees. Managerial support includes senior management encouragement and allocation of adequate resources (Igbaria, Parasuraman & Baroudi, 1996; Igbaria, Zinatelli, Cragg & Cavaye, 1997). Managerial support was found to be associated with adoption and use of innovation. Other studies also indicate that managerial support is positively related to the individual's adoption of innovation (Trevino & Webster, 1992). In this context, managerial support facilitates employees' adoption and utilization of innovation. Managerial support is associated with greater adoption; usage while lack of organizational support is seen as a critical barrier to adopting innovation (Lee, Lee & Kwon, 2005). Employees tend to innovate more if they believe adoption will be valued by management.

Management can enhance an individual's adoption of innovation by reinforcing the individual's role in successful task performance. Management can help employees adopt innovation by structuring work arrangements to permit a greater chance of short-term success while building employees' long-term abilities. Supportive and consultative feedback from management that is specific to the introduction of innovation will not only build confidence of employees but is also likely to encourage adoption intention via direct reinforcement effort (Farr & Ford, 1990). According to Attewel (1992), regarding complex innovation adoption involving higher knowledge barriers, the decision of employees is constrained by an individual's ability to obtain support from an organization's senior management. Top or senior management support is an important factor in individual adoption decisions in an organization. Previous studies found that managerial support significantly influences the use of innovation (Lee, Kim, Rhee & Trimi, 2006).

## INCENTIVES

Incentive refers to the individual's beliefs about the benefits or consequences of adopting an innovation (Chang & Cheung, 2001; Cheung, Chang & Lai, 2000). Incentive is often considered a powerful motivator of employee behavior in adopting an innovation (Nilakant & Rao, 1994). Sappington (1991) found that incentives can motivate individual employees to adopt and use new innovations to achieve goals that management has developed. Managers typically acquire innovation to achieve organizational benefits such as productivity gains and increased profits and want employees to adopt the innovation and use it appropriately so that the intended benefits are realized. Employees value individual benefits such as career advancement, and personal or organizational achievements. In order to encourage adoption, managers must provide individual employees with incentives, such as commissions, recognition and praise for the adoption (Bhattacherjee, 1998).

According to Currid (1995), incentives need not only be financial. Innovative, non-monetary incentives such as yielding control over employees' working agenda, providing public recognition and changing of titles can be equally effective over the long run as salary raises or bonuses (Bhattacherjee, 1998). Individuals must foresee a reasonable set of positive outcomes from a possible adoption of innovation before they attempt to take it on. Outcomes that may be positively valued by individuals can be broadly conceived to include financial rewards, organizational advancement, formal and informal recognition, increased autonomy, beliefs about self-worth and achievement and greater job security (Bhattacherjee, 1998; Farr & Ford, 1990). If the innovation is believed to result in favourable outcomes for the individual, then the individual will be more likely to adopt it. Factors such as the provision of discretionary time to individuals working with the innovation or recommendation of bonuses for working with innovation have an impact on individual adoption of innovation (Bhattacherjee, 1998; Chen & Ching, 2002; Farr & Ford, 1990).

## 2.8 Individual Factors

According to Lewis, Agarwal and Sambamurthy (2003), individual factors are one of the most important determinants of adopting innovation. It refers to individuals' cognitive interpretations of innovation and themselves. Several studies found that individual factors such as perceived usefulness, personal innovativeness, prior experience, image and enjoyment with innovation have stronger influence on an individual's adoption of innovation (Al-Gahtani & King, 1999; Davis, 1989; Igbaria, Parasuraman & Baroudi, 1996; Lewis, Agarwal & Sambamurthy, 2003; Venkatesh & Davis, 2000). It has been noted that "individual characteristics have been reported to play a key role in management information systems success" (Lee, Kim, Rhee & Trimi, 2006, p.472).

### PERCEIVED USEFULNESS

There are many reasons why employees accept or reject innovation. For example, previous research suggests that individuals tend to use or not use an application to the extent that they think it will help them perform their job better. This variable is referred to as perceived usefulness, which is defined as "the degree to which an individual feels that using a particular system would enhance his or her job performance" (Davis, 1989, p.320). Usefulness is also defined as the total value a user perceives from using an innovation (Kim, Chan & Gupta, 2007). According to Davis (1989, p.320), "a system high in perceived usefulness is the one for which an individual user believes in the existence of a positive use-performance relationship." Davis (1989) also found that perceived usefulness has a stronger and consistent relationship with system use. Other studies have reported that perceived usefulness is positively associated with system usage (Al-Gahtani & King, 1999; Igbaria, 1993). Studies have shown perceived usefulness is one of the strongest predictors and remains significant at all points of measurement (Agarwal & Prasad, 1998; Venkatesh & Davis, 2000; Venkatesh, Morris, Davis & Davis, 2003). When an individual perceives that an innovation offers a relative advantage over the firm's current practice, it is more likely to be adopted and implemented. "Individuals evaluate the consequences of their behavior in terms of perceived usefulness and base their choice of behavior on the desirability of the usefulness" (Kim, Chan & Gupta, 2007, p.116). If an individual thinks that the new system usage will enhance efficiency and effectiveness or offer greater control over the job, the innovation is more likely to be adopted (Lee, 2004).

## PERSONAL INNOVATIVENESS

Personal innovativeness refers to the willingness of an individual to try out any innovation (Agarwal & Prasad, 1998; Lewis, Agarwal & Sambamurthy, 2003; Thatcher, Stepina, Srite & Liu, 2003). According to Yi, Jackson, Park and Probst (2006) "some individuals are more willing to take a risk by trying out an innovation, whereas others are hesitant to change their practice" (p.356). All organizations try to influence their employees' attitudes concerning the adoption of innovation. However, some individuals more readily adopt certain innovations while others do not. According to Agarwal and Prasad (1998), the adoption of innovation by employees is influenced by each individual's personal innovativeness. Frambach and Schillewaert (2002) mentioned that personal innovativeness is the innate tendency of a person to adopt an innovation. Innovativeness may influence perception regarding innovation (Yi, Wu & Tung, 2006). Rogers (2003) defined it as the time at which an individual adopts an innovation during the diffusion process. Innovative individuals are characterized as those who adopt an innovation at an early stage in the diffusion process. According to Agarwal and Prasad (1998), personal innovativeness in the domain of innovation is an individual propensity that is associated with a more positive attitude toward innovation adoption and usage. According to Rogers's (2003) diffusion of innovation theory, individuals develop beliefs about new technology by synthesizing information from a variety of sources including the mass media and interpersonal channels. Individuals with higher personal innovativeness are expected to develop a more positive attitude toward innovation adoption (Agarwal & Prasad, 1998; Lewis, Agarwal & Sambamurthy, 2003). Innovativeness or receptivity to change by an organization's employee is an important determinant of innovation success (Lee, Kim, Rhee & Trimi, 2006).

## PRIOR EXPERIENCE

Prior experience refers to a user's prior experience with innovation and the overall skills of using innovation. This indicates an individual's prior experience in using innovations or systems (Igbaria, Guimaraes & Davis, 1995; Igbaria, Parasuraman & Baroudi, 1996). Prior experience with successful innovation leads employees to an early adoption of innovation. According to Farr and Ford (1990), members of an organization who are innovative in a specific technical area will exhibit more positive attitudes toward adopting similar and different innovations. Previous experience with innovation is likely to increase the individual's faith in adopting innovation (Igbaria, Parasuraman & Baroudi, 1996). Favourable or successful experiences are likely to result in a more positive impression. However, even experiences that were not successful may enhance an individual's beliefs that he or she has learned from failure, or how to be successful in future (Farr & Ford, 1990). Prior experience and familiarity with innovation reduce anxiety and build confidence (Fuller, Vician & Brown, 2006). Hill, Smith and Mann (1987) mentioned that previous experience positively influences behavioral intentions. Research found that previous experience with a computer was positively related to more general belief about the use of other innovative technologies. Thus, generalization from experience with one form of innovation may lead to the decision to adopt another kind of innovation. According to Bandura (1986), individuals may intend to adopt innovation on the basis of vicarious experience. Observing others being successful in the performance of a task with innovation can enhance an individual's behavioral intentions about using that innovation in order to perform that task. Prior experience was found to have a positive effect on system use (Lee, Kim, Rhee & Trimi, 2006).

## IMAGE

Image refers to the degree to which the use of innovation enhances one's image or status within the organization (Moore & Benbasat, 1996). Individuals often respond to the factors that establish or maintain a favourable image within a reference group (Venkatesh & Davis, 2000). In the typical work environment, with a high degree of interdependence with other employees in carrying out one's duties, increased image and status within the group is important to many individuals (Venkatesh & Davis, 2000). According to them "the increased power and influence resulting from elevated status provides a general basis for greater productivity" (2000, p.189). An individual may thus perceive that using a system will lead to improvement in his or her image regarding job performance (Venkatesh & Davis, 2000). Similarly, Jackson, Park and Probst (2006, p.355) state that "an individual may believe that a system is useful because the system enhances their image and social status."

## ENJOYMENT WITH INNOVATION

Enjoyment with innovation refers to the extent to which the activity of using the system is perceived to be enjoyable and satisfies the individual (Al-Gahtani & King, 1999). According to Venkatesh & Brown (2001), an individual adoption decision is influenced by hedonic outcomes. Research described hedonic outcomes as the pleasure driven from the consumption or use of innovation (Babin, Darden & Griffin, 1994). Entertainment potential is expected to have a strong influence on adoption decision and it provides an opportunity to escape reality and become absorbed in a new world (Van der Heijden, 2004). Motivation literature suggests that there are two main types of motivations: extrinsic and intrinsic. Extrinsic motivation refers to achievement of a specific goal whereas intrinsic motivation is the pleasure and satisfaction derived from a specific behavior (Vallerand, 1997; Venkatesh & Brown, 2001). According to Venkatesh and Brown (2001) extrinsic and intrinsic motivation are primary drivers of adoption and usage of innovation. Research suggests that individual employees with higher perceived productivity and hedonic outcomes are more likely to adopt whereas the desire for social outcomes is more important for earlier adopters (Venkatesh & Brown, 2001; Venkatesh & Davis, 2000).

## 2.9 Social Factors

Arguably, employees' adoption of innovation is driven by their social environment. Innovation used by others in employees' social environment is likely to play an important role in adoption of innovation. Social influence is the extent to which members of a social group influence one another's behavior in adoption (Konana & Balasubramanian, 2005; Venkatesh & Brown, 2001). It is perceived pressure and influence that peers feel when adopting an innovation and this influence is exerted through messages and signals that help to form perceptions of the value of innovation or activity (Fulk & Boyd, 1991). Ajzen and Fishbein (1980) refer to such influence as normative beliefs about the appropriateness of adoption of innovation. According to this perspective, employees may adopt an innovation not because of its usefulness but because of perceived social pressure. Such pressure may be perceived as coming from individuals whose beliefs and opinions are important, including peers and people who are in social networks (Igbaria, Parasuraman & Baroudi, 1996). According to Abrahamson and Rosenkopf (1997), it is a largely internal influence that potential adopters exert on each other that persuades them to adopt. Several studies found that social factors were more significant than economic factors in driving adoption of innovation by individuals within an organization (Peansupap & Walker, 2005; Westphal, Gulati & Shortell, 1997).

## PEERS

Employees are influenced by peers in the adoption of an innovation. Moral support, motivation and encouragement from peers can greatly influence employees in this way (Farr & Ford, 1990; Lewis, Agarwal & Sambamurthy, 2003; Yuan et al., 2005). The adoption of an innovation by peers may signal its importance and certain advantages and thus eventually motivate an individual to adopt. Individuals normally imitate by looking at their peers (Frambach & Schillewaert, 2002). Social persuasion and communication from peers have been suggested as factors influencing acceptance of an innovation (Davis, Bagozzi & Warshaw, 1989; Mirvis, Sales & Hackett, 1991). According to Brancheau and Wetherbe (1990), in the case of intra-firm adoption decisions of employees, interpersonal contacts were more important in all phases of the adoption decision process. They found that the adoption decision of employees within an organization has a significant impact on both management and peers. The greater the amount of communication among adopters within an organization, the greater the probability that other will adopt an innovation (van Everdingen & Wierenga, 2002).

## SOCIAL NETWORK

According to Lewis, Agarwal and Sambamurthy (2003) the term social network refers to the extent to which individual employees are influenced by members of other organizations. Communication between members of a social network can enhance the speed of innovation adoption. The participation of employees in an organization in informal networks facilitates the spread of information about the innovation, which consequently positively influences the probability of adoption. These informal networks connect members within the organization or organization in different industries (Frambach & Schillewaert, 2002). The opinions and positive attitude of important referents could be the basis for a person's feelings about the utility and functioning of the innovation (Yi, Jackson, Park & Probst, 2006, p.355). The extent to which organizational members share information with other organizations is referred to as their degree of interconnectedness. The greater the level of informal information sharing, the more likely organizational members are exposed to new ideas and objects (Frambach & Schillewaert, 2002; Rogers, 2003). Members of an organization may adopt an innovation based on the information that other employees in the interrelated organization in their market environment have developed (Brown & Venkatesh, 2005; Katz & Shapiro, 1994; Kraut, Rice, Cool & Fish, 1998). Empirical evidence confirms that external influences are important factors for adoption of innovation (Khoumbati, Themistocleous & Irani, 2006; Standen & Sinclair-Jones, 2004).

## 2.10 Demographics

The following section discusses demographic variables in the model. These moderating variables affect individual beliefs and attitudes about the adoption of innovation. This research is interested to find out whether male or female has a higher rate of adoption of innovation.

Gender has been of interest as a variable to account for some differences in innovation research outcomes that concern individual adoption and sustained usage of innovation in the workplace. There have been conflicting opinions in regard to whether men use innovation more than women. For example, Lerouge, Newton and Blanton (2005) found that males use innovation significantly higher than females. One explanation proposed in some studies is that males are more attracted to and skilled in the use of computers than are females. However, another study found that females are higher innovation users than males (Bhatnagar & Ghose, 2004, p.759).

There is a common perception that innovation users are quite young. Significant age differences were found regarding preferences in using innovation, finding that older groups, aged 50 and above, preferred to use innovation skills significantly less than those aged between 20–29 and 40–49 (Lerouge, Newton & Blanton, 2005). Since many older people have limited experience using computers and the internet in comparison to younger people, it is likely that learning to use innovation creates an anxiety-provoking situation that many would choose to avoid due to perceived difficulty associated with the task (Porter & Donthu, 2006). Younger people – 20–29 years old – are likely to be newer to their professions and recently graduated from formal schooling, hence having stronger preferences to use their newly acquired skills. Professionals aged 40–49 may welcome innovation to spark the second half of their career life. Those in the 30–39 age group also have the potential to learn much from using the innovation. However, the study conducted by Lerouge, Newton and Blanton (2005) did not find that innovation usage was significantly influenced by people in the 30–39 age group (Lerouge, Newton & Blanton, 2005, p.20).

Academic disciplines are also important demographic factors that influence the adoption and use of innovation. Employees in science and technology disciplines have adequate knowledge about innovation compared to their counterparts in social science disciplines.

There have not been many studies on whether academic staff use innovation more than administrative staff. Academic staff mainly deal with teaching and research. On the other hand, administrative or clerical staff perform many administrative duties and they are sometimes required to use innovation in order to produce certain files, maintain databases and conduct internal and external communication with various parties. Consequently, administrative staff may be greater users of certain innovation than academic staff.

Although there have not been studies regarding whether full-time employees use innovation more than part-time employees, it is obvious that full-time employees have more duties to perform in their workplace compared to employees who are part-time. Part-time employees work only certain hours and they have fewer responsibilities than full-time employees. Part-time employees might use innovation but on a limited scale because they have limited obligations and tasks to execute.

Education is another important demographic variable determining the use of innovation. Education enables users to operate and appreciate innovation use. According to Porter and Donthu (2006, p.1001), "the decision to adopt a new technology is related to the amount of knowledge one has regarding how to use the technology appropriately." Early adopters of new technologies tend to have higher educational levels and better knowledge, perhaps reflecting their ability to understand more quickly than those with less education (Porter & Donthu, 2006; Rogers, 2003). Less educated individuals may feel they have insufficient knowledge and more computer anxiety and have less sophisticated cognitive structures that impede their ability to learn (Porter & Donthu, 2006).

## 2.11 Attitude Toward Innovation

There are various definitions of attitude. For example, Ajzen and Fishbein (1980) define attitude as a pre-disposition to respond favorably or unfavorably to an object, person, event or institution. According to Lam, Cho and Qu (2007, p.54) "attitude is an individual's feelings of the favorableness or un-favorableness of his or her performance of the behavior." Ajzen and Fishbein (1980) state that attitude is the function of behavioral beliefs and evaluation of outcomes. They explained that "behavioral belief is one's belief in performing a specific behavior that will lead to a specific consequence, and evaluation of outcome is one's assessment of that specific consequence" (Lam, Cho & Qu, 2007, p.54). Attitudes toward information systems have been extensively studied in the past. For instance, Liao and Landry (2000) assert that employees' attitudes toward the acceptance of innovation would affect the intention of the innovation adoption (Lam, Cho & Qu, 2007). According to Pavlou and Fygenson (2005) attitude has been shown to influence behavioral intentions and this relationship has received substantial empirical support. Based on the work of Ajzen and Fishbein (1980), Davis (1989) developed an attitude construct scale. The instruments ask individuals to rate five items according to how they felt about using the innovation on a five-point scale (Lam, Cho & Qu, 2007; Taylor & Todd, 1995). Employees may behave differently when their attitude toward a certain type of behavior has changed. Specifically, employees are more likely to perform a behavior if they possess a positive attitude and are more likely not to perform a behavior when they possess a negative attitude (Kwok & Gao, 2006). Attitude toward innovation adoption is an aggregate belief of organizational, individual and social factors in the proposed advanced research model. A favourable attitude is likely to encourage individual employees to adopt and use the innovation.

## 2.12 Conclusion

This chapter has reviewed relevant literature on the issue of innovation adoption by organizations' personnel. The review of literature has shown that the term innovation means an idea or a system or an innovation perceived to be new or significantly improved by the relevant unit of adoption to create added value, or improve performance of activities in organizations. It is any new system or technology that is new to individuals or an organization that is adopting such technology or system, no matter how old it may be or how many others individuals or organizations have adopted it.

The review then discusses Rogers's innovation adoption process model, which states that every innovation adoption process passes through a set of stages before it is adopted. It is a process that occurs over time, consisting of five stages – knowledge, persuasion, decision, implementation and confirmation. This study is concerned with the last two stages, implementation and confirmation, because an organization may have made a decision to adopt an innovation but confirmation will then depend on how employees implement it in their daily activities as well as continued use of the innovation in organizational activities.

The chapter then discusses relevant factors that affect employees' adoption of innovation. The factors that influence employees' adoption of innovation can be grouped into three main areas: organizational factors, individual factors and social factors. More specifically, there is a total of ten variables under the three main categories of factors: training, managerial support, incentives, perceived usefulness, personal innovativeness, prior experience, image, enjoyment with innovation, peers and social network. In addition, demographic factors were also discussed. The next chapter will discuss the theories of innovation adoption for the development of the proposed advanced model of innovation adoption.

# 3

# Theories of Innovation Adoption

## 3.1 Introduction

The theoretical framework for this study is based on the theory of reasoned action (TRA), the technology acceptance model (TAM), the conceptual framework provided by Frambach and Schillewaert (2002), the unified theory of acceptance and use of technology (UTAUT) and DeLone and McLean IS success model. This chapter shows how the models used to examine innovation adoption have developed over time, and concludes by proposing a further development. The foundation of the models is Fishbein and Ajzen's 1967 theory of reasoned action, which postulates that the intention to any particular behavior is determined by the agent's attitude toward that behavior and the relevant subjective norms. However, the model did not make any reference to external factors and personality characteristics (demographic factors). There is evidence that external and demographic factors influence behavior (Ajzen & Fishbein, 1980).

Davis (1989) used this as the basis for TAM, discarding the subjective norms element as insignificant, and defining two key beliefs – the perceived usefulness and ease of use of the new technology – as the determinants of attitude. The model also did not include external and demographic factors as affecting attitude toward usage. Whilst Fishbein and Ajzen had noted the importance of external factors, it was not included in TRA, but the 2002 model developed by Frambach and Schillewaert (2002) does include external factors. They include nine factors affecting attitude grouped in three categories – social, organizational and personal – and return social norms to the model. A number of other studies have shown that certain other factors also influence adoption, as do demographic factors. The unified theory of acceptance and use of technology (UTAUT) and DeLone and McLean IS success model are discussed briefly. Each of the main models is now discussed in turn, showing how the core of the TRA, that beliefs determine attitude, which in turn determines action, persists throughout and how the array of factors influencing use have been developed and ordered.

## 3.2 Theory of Reasoned Action (TRA)

Theory of reasoned action (TRA) is a widely studied model that had its origins in social psychology, which is concerned with the determinants of conscious intended behavior. The foundation of the TRA conceptual framework is based on a distinction between beliefs, attitudes, intentions and behaviors (Al-Gahtani & King, 1999). The theory of reasoned action is an especially well-researched model that has proved successful in predicting and explaining behavior across a wide variety of domains (Davis, Bagozzi & Warshaw, 1989; Kukafka, Johnson, Linfante & Allegrante, 2003).

The theory of reasoned action was introduced in 1967 and it has, over the years, been refined, developed and tested. The theory is based on the assumption that human beings are usually quite rational and they can make systematic use of information available to them (Ajzen & Fishbein, 1980). Generally, human beings consider the implications of their actions before they decide to engage or not to engage in a given behavior. For this reason the approach was referred to as the theory of reasoned action (Ajzen & Fishbein, 1980). The ultimate goal of the theory is to predict and understand an individual's behavior. "The theory views a person's intention to perform a behavior as the immediate determinants of the action and since the purpose of the theory is to understand human behavior, therefore, it is essential to identify what determines intentions" (Ajzen & Fishbein, 1980, p.6).

According to TRA, a person's performance of a specific behavior is determined by his or her behavioral intention to perform the behavior, and behavioral intention is jointly determined by two basic determinants: a person's attitude toward a particular behavior and subjective norms concerning the behavior in question (Ajzen & Fishbein, 1980, p.6; Kukafka, Johnson, Linfante & Allegrante, 2003, p.220). Consequently, "behavioral intention is a measure of strength of one's intention to perform a specified behavior" (Ajzen & Fishbein, 1980, p.6). In addition, "attitude is defined as an individual's positive or negative evaluation of performing the behavior. Attitude refers to the person's judgment that performing the behavior is good or bad, that he is in favor of or against performing the behavior" (Ajzen & Fishbein, 1980, p.6).

According to the theory, attitudes are a function of beliefs. A person who believes that performing a given behavior will lead to mostly positive outcomes will hold a favourable attitude toward performing the behavior, while a person who believes that performing the behavior will lead to mostly negative outcomes will hold an unfavourable attitude toward the behavior (Ajzen & Fishbein, 1980; Bhattacherjee & Sanford, 2006). TRA theorizes that a person's attitude toward a behavior is determined by his or her salient beliefs about consequences of performing the behavior and an evaluation of the outcome of that behavior (Davis, Bagozzi & Warshaw, 1989). Beliefs are defined as an individual's subjective probability that performing the target behavior will result in consequences and the evaluation term refers to an implicit evaluative response to the consequence (Ajzen & Fishbein, 1980). According to Ajzen and Fishbein (1980), the beliefs that underline a person's attitude toward behavior are termed behavioral beliefs.

Subjective norms are also a function of beliefs, but beliefs of a different kind, namely the person's beliefs that specific individuals or groups think he or she should or should not perform the behavior (Ajzen & Fishbein, 1980; Yi, Jackson, Park & Probst, 2006). These beliefs underlying a person's subjective norm are termed normative beliefs. According to Ajzen and Fishbein, "a person who believes that most referents with whom he is motivated to comply think he should perform the behavior will perceive social pressure to do so" (1980, p.7). On the other hand, "a person who believes that most referents with whom he is motivated to comply think he should not perform the behavior will have a subjective norm that puts pressure on him to avoid performing the behavior" (Ajzen & Fishbein, 1980, p.7). Therefore, individuals are more likely to perform an act if they perceive the existence of greater social pressure from salient referents to perform that act (Lam, Cho & Qu, 2007).

Ajzen and Fishbein (1980, p.8) assert that their analysis of behavior did not make reference to various factors other than attitudes toward targets that social and behavioral scientists have invoked to explain behavior. The factors that have not been included in their analysis were personality characteristics such as demographic variables and external variables. There is plenty of evidence that those factors influence behavior (Ajzen & Fishbein, 1980). TRA postulates that external stimuli influence attitude through changes in a person's belief structure (Ajzen & Fishbein, 1980). Yet again, Ajzen and Fishbein (1980, p.8) state that "from our point of view, external variables may influence the beliefs a person holds or the relative importance he attaches to attitudinal and normative considerations." Their arguments show that external factors may indeed influence behavior.

The theory of reasoned action is a unique and well-researched model that seeks to predict and understand human behavior. The model has been used and proved successful in predicting and explaining behavior across a wide variety of domains. According to Davis, Bagozzi and Warshaw (1989, p.985), "a substantial body of empirical data in support of TRA has accumulated and has been widely used in applied research settings spanning a variety of subject areas." The theory of reasoned action has also stimulated a great deal of theoretical research aimed at understanding theoretical frameworks, testing assumptions and analyzing various refinements and extensions. For instance, Davis (1989) extended the TRA by providing two variables: perceived usefulness and perceived ease of use to trace the impact of external factors on beliefs, attitude and intentions. These variables were relevant in the acceptance behavior regarding computers.

External factors were not included in the TRA but it is suggested that they are just as important since Ajzen and Fishbein (1980, p.9) argued that "investigation of the effects of external variables can enhance the understanding of a given behavioral phenomenon." Although Ajzen and Fishbein (1980) state that external factors can help understand behavioral phenomena, they did not include external variables explicitly and this is the form most frequently referred to by Ajzen and Fishbein and other writers. Specifically, Ajzen and Fishbein (1980, p.84) stated that there are three categories of external variables: demographic variables (age, sex, occupation, socioeconomic status, religion and education), attitude toward organizational targets (including attitude regarding other people and institutions) and personality traits (introversion-extraversion, neuroticism, authoritarianism and dominance). Ajzen and Fishbein (1980, p.91) state that "on the basis of different experiences, people may form different beliefs about the consequences of performing a behavior and different normative beliefs. These beliefs in turn determine attitudes and subjective norms which then determine intention and the corresponding behavior." External variables are assumed to influence an individual's interpretation of the environment and thus the beliefs that a person holds. This study acknowledges Ajzen and Fishbein's reference to the possible influence of external variables and expands on their model by including explicitly external and demographic variables. These affect employees' behavior by influencing their attitude on an innovation being considered for implementation.

## 3.3 Technology Acceptance Model (TAM)

The technology acceptance model (TAM), first introduced in 1986, is an adaptation of the theory of reasoned action (Ajzen & Fishbein, 1980) that is specifically tailored for explaining user acceptance of information technology (Davis, Bagozzi & Warshaw, 1989). "The model has been shown to have good predictive validity for both initial adoption as well as continued use of a variety of information technologies" (Karahanna, Agarwal & Angst, 2006, p.782). The theory serves to provide an explanation of the determinants of technology acceptance. The theory is capable of explaining user behavior across a broad range of technologies, while at the same time being both parsimonious and theoretically justified (Davis, Bagozzi & Warshaw, 1989). This applies to decision to adopt an innovation. A key aim of TAM is to provide a basis for tracing the impact of two fundamental variables dealing with cognitive and affective determinants of technology acceptance (Al-Gahtani & King, 1999).

TAM postulates that two particular beliefs, perceived usefulness and perceived ease of use, are of primary relevance for computer acceptance behaviors (Bruner & Kumar, 2005; Davis, 1989; King & He, 2006). "Perceived usefulness is defined as the prospective user's subjective probability that using a specific application system will increase his or her job performance. In addition, perceived ease of use refers to the degree to which the prospective user expects the target system to be free of effort" (Davis, Bagozzi & Warshaw, 1989, p.985). Davis (1989, p.320), asks: "what causes people to accept or reject information technology? Among the many variables that may influence system use, previous research suggested two determinants that are especially important." The first determinant is that individuals tend to use an application to the extent they believe it will help them perform their job better. This variable is referred to as perceived usefulness (Davis, 1989). Second, "even if potential users believe that a given application is useful, but they may feel that the system is too hard to use and that the performance benefits of usage are outweighed by the effort of using the application" (Davis, 1989, p.320). Therefore, in addition to usefulness, usage is theorized as being influenced by ease of use.

According to Davis, Bagozzi and Warshaw (1989, p.985), "ideally one would like a model that is helpful not only for prediction but also for explanation, so that researchers and practitioners can identify why a particular system may be acceptable or unacceptable, and pursue appropriate corrective steps." They further note that "the technology acceptance model was formulated in an attempt to achieve these goals by identifying a small number of fundamental variables suggested by previous research dealing with the cognitive and affective determinants of computer acceptance" (Davis, Bagozzi & Warshaw, 1989, p.985). The foundation of the TRA conceptual framework is provided by the distinction between beliefs, attitude, intentions and behavior (Al-Gahtani & King, 1999, p.278). According to TRA "a person's performance of a specific behavior is determined by his or her behavioral intentions to perform the behavior, and a behavioral intention is jointly determined by the person's attitude and subjective norms concerning the behavior in question" (Al-Gahtani & King, 1999, p.278). Similar to TRA, TAM proposes that computer usage is determined by behavioral intentions. But it differs with TRA in that behavioral intention is viewed as being jointly determined by the person's attitude toward using technology and its perceived usefulness (Davis, Bagozzi & Warshaw, 1989). In TAM, attitude toward using technology is jointly determined by perceived usefulness and ease of use. TAM does not include TRA's subjective norms as determinants of behavioral intention since this is one of the least understood aspects of TRA (Davis, Bagozzi & Warshaw, 1989; Schepers & Wetzels, 2007).

From the arguments provided by Thompson, Higgins and Howell (1991) it seems that the model should not include behavioral intention and link attitude to actual behavior directly. Thompson, Higgins and Howell (1991) contend that behavioral intention should be excluded from the model because studies are interested in actual behavior directly. "Such behavior has already taken place in the past, while behavioral intention is the person's subjective probability that he or she will perform the behavior in question and is thus dealing with future behavior" (Al-Gahtani & King, 1999, p.278). This study intends to assess the model, which is developed based on TRA, TAM and Frambach and Schillewaert's models using actual measures of usage with multiple sets of variables in order to fully examine the extent to which the new model can help to understand usage behavior. The study also intends to include a subjective norms construct, which was not included in TAM.

A number of studies have been done on technology adoption (Ahuja & Thatcher, 2005; Al-Gahtani & King, 1999; Chang & Cheung, 2001; Cheung, Chang & Lai, 2000; Igbaria, Guimaraes & Davis, 1995; Igbaria, Zinatelli, Cragg & Cavaye, 1997; Jasperson, Carter & Zmud, 2005; Lewis, Agarwal & Sambamurthy, 2003; Schepers & Wetzels, 2007; Van der Heijden, 2004; Venkatesh & Davis, 2000), many using TAM. Although several of these studies provided insight into the acceptance of technology using TAM, their research focused on attitudinal and behavioral intentions as determining factors of technology usage. King and He (2006, p.740) argue that "TAM has come to be one of the most widely used models in information systems because of its understandability and simplicity." However, they assert that "it is imperfect, and all TAM relationships are not borne out in all studies; there is a wide variation in the predicted effects in various studies with different types of users and systems" (p.740). In addition, Yi, Jackson, Park and Probst (2006) state that "TAM should be integrated into a more inclusive model incorporating variables related to both human and social change processes as well as the adoption of innovation" (p.352). Furthermore, "recent studies on IT adoption are generally based on TAM or extensions to it by including one variable, for instance, enjoyment with technology, as one of the predictors" (Chang & Cheung, 2001, p.2; Huang, 2005). Note that TAM does not test as many variables compared to the model provided by Frambach and Schillewaert (2002).

Consequently, an advanced innovation adoption model, which will include a combination of variables found in different elements of innovation adoption, is required. Most of the previous innovation adoption studies are industry and firm specific, and studies have not proceeded to investigate its subsequent adoption at the individual level and there has been no such study conducted to examine determinants of individual adoption of innovation (Bhattacherjee, 1998; Frambach & Schillewaert, 2002; Venkatesh & Davis, 2000). This study seeks to develop an advanced innovation adoption model combining multiple sets of factors found in previous models and various innovation and management literature in order to examine a broader perspective which will help in understanding individuals' adoption of innovation and usage levels.

## 3.4 Conceptual Framework Provided by Frambach and Schillewaert

The advanced model proposed in this study is also based on the theoretical framework provided by Frambach and Schillewaert (2002). According to Frambach and Schillewaert (2002), individual acceptance of an innovation is based on perceived beliefs and affects regarding the focal innovation. These beliefs and effects are reflected in an individual's attitude towards a particular innovation. Frambach and Schillewaert (2002, p.171) state that "attitudes can change and there is evidence that a person's attitudes mediate the influence of external variables and stimuli."

Based on Frambach and Schillewaert's model, individual usage of innovation also depends on management strategies, policies and actions; and, these factors include training, social persuasion and organizational support. These factors influence an individual's awareness of the functioning and application of innovations and their advantages and fit with the job (Frambach & Schillewaert, 2002). These variables are categorized under organizational facilitators in their model. According to this model, an organization tries to influence its employees' attitudes toward adoption of innovation but some individuals may readily accept certain innovations while others may not. This concept is referred to as personal innovativeness – "the tendency of a person to accept an innovation within a product class, independent of the communicated experience of others" (Frambach & Schillewaert, 2002, p.171). Personal innovativeness influences individual acceptance both directly and indirectly through attitudes. The model further proposes that personal innovativeness is determined by various personal characteristics such as demographics, tenure, product experience and personal values (Frambach & Schillewaert, 2002). Individual acceptance of innovation is also influenced by social factors. In addition, individual acceptance of innovations is also driven by the usage of an innovation within their social environment. Such social influences may stem from two sources – network externalities and peers (Frambach & Schillewaert, 2002). These two variables are categorized under social usage.

Frambach and Schillewaert's conceptual model has not been tested yet and they have recommended a study testing their model. Although Frambach and Schillewaert included a long list of factors in their model compared to previous technology acceptance models, they did not include several important factors such as perceived usefulness, image and enjoyment with innovation, which were included in other innovation acceptance studies. Therefore, a more comprehensive model is needed that will include and test the wide range of factors affecting individual adoption of innovation. Chapter 3 of this study develops such a model – an advanced model of innovation adoption (AMIA).

## 3.5 Unified Theory of Acceptance and Use of Technology (UTAUT)

The unified theory of acceptance and use of technology (UTAUT) was developed by Venkatesh, Morris, Davis and Davis (2003) and it integrates eight previously developed models and theories concerning the acceptance and use of technology. Based on in-depth review of eight prominent theories of technology adoption, Venkatesh, Morris, Davis and Davis (2003) constructed the UTAUT model, which became more popular to predict innovation usage behavior of individual employees. Venkatesh, Morris, Davis and Davis (2003) integrated theory of reasoned action (TRA) (Fishbein & Ajzen, 1975), technology acceptance model (TAM) (Davis, 1989), motivational model (MM) (Davis, Bagozzi & Warshaw, 1992), theory of planned behavior (TPB) (Ajzen, 1991), combined TAM-TPB (C-TAM-TPB) (Taylor & Todd, 1995a), model of PC utilization (MPCU) (Thompson, Higgins & Howell, 1991), innovation diffusion theory (IDT) (Rogers, 1995) and social cognitive theory (SCT) (Compeau & Higgins, 1995). The theory postulates that the behavioral intention to use technology is determined by performance expectancy, effort expectancy and social influence. Facilitating conditions directly impact on usage behavior. The moderating factors such as gender, age, experience and voluntariness of use are also used in the model to examine the relationship among the independent variables and behavioral intention to use. The UTAUT is used to construct the advanced research model of innovation adoption.

## 3.6 DeLone and McLean IS Success Model

Information system (IS) success model was developed by DeLone and McLean (1992) that describe the impact of system quality and information quality on user satisfaction and usage behavior. DeLone and McLean describe system quality as the characteristics of the information system itself and it measures technical success and information quality indicates the characteristics of the information product and the measurement of semantic success. The model also indicates that the use, user satisfaction, individual and organizational impact measure success in terms of effectiveness of an information system and this refers to the impact that information has on the user (DeLone & McLean, 1992; Lin, 2008). DeLone and McLean propose that there are six interrelated dimensions in the model and there is a causal relationship among these dimensions. The model suggests that when an information system is created which contains important features and characteristics exhibiting various degrees of the system quality and information quality. According to DeLone and McLean, individual users and managers experience those features by utilizing the system and they are either satisfied or dissatisfied with the system quality or the information products. The usage of the system and the information impact the individual users conducting their work and these individual impacts collectively results on the organization (DeLone & McLean, 1992). The model has been used to develop the advanced model of innovation adoption since the study has proven very applicable for studies on information systems.

## 3.7 Conclusion

This chapter discusses the theories of innovation adoption and looked into the limitations of previous innovation acceptance models in order to develop a more comprehensive model that will investigate a wider range of factors that affect individuals' adoption of innovation. This study proposes an advanced model of innovation adoption based on the theory of reasoned action (TRA), technology acceptance model (TAM) and the conceptual framework provided by Frambach and Schillewaert (2002), unified theory of acceptance and use of technology (UTAUT), and DeLone and McLean IS success model. Several modifications that had not been part of these models were introduced. The next chapter will discuss the advanced research model of innovation adoption.

# 4

# Advanced Research Model of Innovation Adoption

## 4.1 Introduction

The purpose of this chapter is to present the conceptual development of the research model and consequently, the proposed advanced research model of innovation adoption. This chapter has four sections – introduction, outline of the research model, proposed advanced research model of innovation adoption (AMIA) and the conclusion.

## 4.2 Outline of the Research Model

The conceptual model of this research is based on the theory of reasoned action (TRA) and it incorporates elements of the technology acceptance model (TAM) and the model provided by Frambach and Schillewaert (2000). Several modifications, which were not in these models, are discussed. From the analysis of relevant literature the researcher found four categories of factors that affect individuals' adoption of innovation. These four distinctive categories of factors are individual factors, social influence, organizational factors and demographics. Based on these categories of factors the researcher first provided an outline of the research model. The outline of the research model is depicted in Figure 4.1.

The first two elements of the model are behavioral and normative beliefs, similar to the two elements of TRA as discussed in Chapter 3, section 3.2. The researcher has chosen to call the two categories individual factors and social influence.

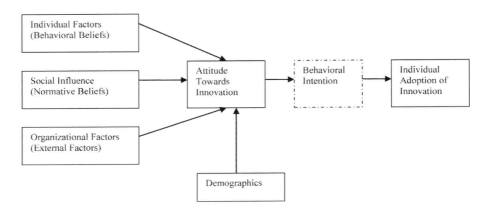

**Figure 4.1     The outline of the research model**

The first element of the model is called "individual factors," which is similar to behavioral beliefs factors described in TRA and TAM. TRA used a single belief construct called behavioral beliefs. TAM used two particular behavioral beliefs – perceived usefulness and ease of use, as discussed in Chapter 3, section 3.3. These behavioral beliefs factors are users' perceptions about the innovation and themselves.

The second element of the model is called "social influence," which is similar to the normative beliefs factor of TRA. TAM did not include normative beliefs factor as it was considered to be non-significant and the least understood factor of TRA. Despite this, it has been included in the research model because the researcher believes that normative beliefs are important in influencing an individual's attitude toward adoption. Frambach and Schillewaert (2000) also used this social factor in their conceptual model and recommended a future study. They described these factors as individual perceptions that most people who are important to him or her think he or she should or should not perform a particular behavior, and are therefore, normative beliefs.

The third element of the model is called "organizational factors." These are external to the individual who is considering adopting an innovation. Ajzen and Fishbein (1980, p.8) did not include external factors in TRA but state that investigation of external factors can enhance the understanding of a given behavioral phenomenon. Frambach and Schillewaert (2000) included organizational facilitators as external factors in their model. The researcher has included external factors in the model because Ajzen and Fishbein (1980) highlighted their importance. Furthermore, Frambach and Schillewaert included external factors. In the proposed model the external factors category is limited to factors within the organization where individuals work. These factors come from management policies, strategies and actions.

The fourth element of the model is "demographics." Ajzen and Fishbein (1980, p.8) did not include demographic factors in TRA but state that demographic characteristics also influence behavior. Frambach and Schillewaert (2000) included demographics but not as a separate major category. The researcher has included demographics into the model as a separate and major category because this is different from other categories and it is directly related to individuals' characteristics and defines the individuals, which influence behavior.

These behavioral beliefs, normative beliefs, external factors and demographic factors affect individual attitude toward innovation, which consequently influence individuals' adoption of innovation. The link between attitude and adoption is strongly supported in the literature and well recognized (Kwok & Gao, 2006; Lam, Cho & Qu, 2007). The proposed model retains behavioral intention as a stage between attitude toward innovation and its adoption because this will allow researchers to use the model to predict future intention to use an innovation. However, this empirical study will investigate actual behavior and does not make any use of future intention.

## 4.3 Proposed Advanced Research Model

This section describes the model in more detail and discusses the development of the new theoretical framework.

The model for this study maintains the basic structure of the theory of reasoned action and incorporates certain elements of the technology acceptance model. However, Frambach and Schillewaert (2002) proposed a longer list of variables, which determine attitude and they recommended a study to test these variables. This study incorporates that list. Figure 4.2 presents the proposed advanced model of innovation adoption (AMIA).

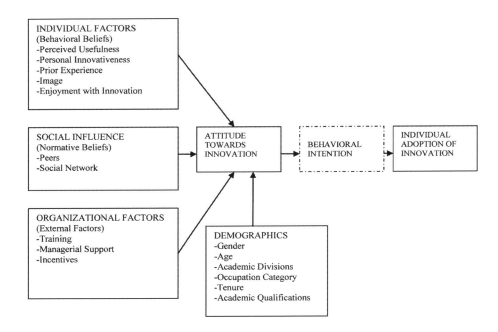

**Figure 4.2    Advanced research model of innovation adoption**


## 4.4 Individual Factors

In the development of the advanced model the researcher included a behavioral beliefs factor in the model and called it "individual factors." Lewis, Agarwal and Sambamurthy (2003, p.663) used the term individual factors to describe individuals' cognitive interpretations of innovation and themselves. This study used the term individual factors as used by Lewis, Agarwal and Sambamurthy (2003). Under the individual factors or behavioral beliefs factors category TRA had one, TAM had two and the AMIA model included five variables – perceived usefulness, personal innovativeness, prior experience, image and enjoyment with innovation.

### PERCEIVED USEFULNESS

The first variable under individual factors is perceived usefulness. This variable is used by TAM – it is a well-recognized factor. Perceived usefulness is defined as the degree to which an individual believes that using a particular innovation would enhance his or her job performance (Davis, 1989, p.320). Ease of use, the second of the belief variables in TAM and other variables which are related to specific innovation have not been included separately because they form part of perceived usefulness.

## PERSONAL INNOVATIVENESS

The second variable under individual factors is personal innovativeness. This variable was not used in TRA or TAM but Lewis, Agarwal and Sambamurthy (2003), whose model is based on TAM, included this variable under individual factors. Personal innovativeness refers to an individual's willingness of to use any innovation (Agarwal & Prasad, 1998). Personal innovativeness does influence employees to adopt innovation. Studies such as Lee (2004), Lee, Kim, Rhee and Trimi (2006) used the term "innovativeness." However, Agarwal and Prasad (1998), Yi, Jackson, Park and Probst (2006), and Yi, Wu and Tung (2006) used the term "personal innovativeness." Frambach and Schillewaert (2002) used the term in their model as "personal dispositional innovativeness" to explain the same concept of personal innovativeness. In fact, in the diagrammatic representation of the model they used personal dispositional innovativeness but in the written explanation they referred to it as personal innovativeness. They define "personal innovativeness as the tendency of a person to accept an innovation within a product class, independent of the communicated experience of other" (p.171). Therefore this study used the term personal innovativeness because it is more appropriate and has been recognized.

## PRIOR EXPERIENCE

The third variable under individual factors is prior experience. Prior experience refers to individuals' previous use of the same or similar innovation and general innovation skills. It indicates the extent of experience individuals have received from previous work, self training, training courses and in any other ways with similar innovation. Frambach and Schillewaert (2002) included a variable called product experience, which they defined as experience with the product being implemented and which influenced adoption. Igbaria, Parasuraman and Baroudi (1996) used the term "skills"; Igbaria, Guimaraes and Davis (1995) used the term "user computer experience"; Farr and Ford (1990) used the term "previous relevant job experience" and Lee, Kim, Rhee and Trimi (2006) used the term "experience." This study uses the term "prior experience" because it is the most appropriate. The researcher did not want to specify any particular innovation or product class but keep it open so that it could be linked to prior experience with any innovation concerned with adoption.

## IMAGE

The fourth variable under individual factors is image. This refers to the degree to which the use of innovation enhances one's image within an organization. It is the perception that an individual has of oneself and is thus included among behavioral beliefs, which this study has called individual factors. TRA, TAM and Frambach and Schillewaert (2002) did not include this variable in their models. Studies such as those of Yi, Jackson, Park and Probst (2006), Al-Gahtani and King (1999) and Venkatesh and Davis (2000) – whose models are based on TAM – used image as a variable under belief factors that affect attitude to adoption. Other studies such as those of Moore and Benbasat (1996), and Lee (2004) also used image variable as belief factors in their studies. This study has introduced image variable in the advanced model, which affect attitude toward adoption.

## ENJOYMENT WITH INNOVATION

The fifth variable under individual factors is enjoyment with innovation. This refers to the extent to which the activity of using innovation is perceived to be enjoyable and satisfy the individual. TRA, TAM and Frambach and Schillewaert (2000) also did not include this variable in their models. However, Al-Gahtani and King (1999), Igbaria, Parasuraman and Baroudi (1996), and Van der Heijden (2004) whose models are based on TAM, used this variable. Al-Gahtani and King (1999) used the term "enjoyment," Igbaria, Parasuraman and Baroudi (1996) used the term "perceived fun/enjoyment" and Van der Heijden (2004) used the similar term "perceived enjoyment." This study has used the term enjoyment with innovation as joy driven from the use of innovation and that it affects individuals' attitude toward adoption.

## 4.5 Social Influence

In the development of AMIA the researcher has incorporated social norms factors in the model and called them "social influence." This is because the influence is derived from the social environment. Lewis, Agarwal and Sambamurthy (2003) used a social norms construct in their model and called them "social factors." Van Everdingen and Wierenga (2002) used the term "social influence." There are two variables under social influence – peers and social network.

Social influence is a normative factor. TRA used a normative factor but TAM did not include TRA's subjective norms construct as it was not significant and it was one of the least understood aspects of TRA (Davis, Bagozzi & Warshaw, 1989, p.986). "Davis, Bagozzi and Warshaw (1989) dropped social norms from TAM on grounds that it is empirically non-significant and probably less relevant in the IT acceptance context" (Bhattacherjee & Sanford, 2006, p.806). While TAM does not include subjective norms, TRA identifies subjective norms as one of the sole determinants of behavioral intention (Yi, Jackson, Park & Probst, 2006). According to Lam, Cho and Qu (2007), TRA theorizes that an individual's subjective norm is determined by the functions of his or her normative beliefs and his or her motivation to comply with these expectations. Consequently, individuals are more likely to perform an act if they perceive the existence of greater social pressure from salient referents to perform that act. Studies such as Lam, Cho and Qu (2007) and Westbay (2005), whose models were built on the theory of reasoned action, held that social factors influence an individual's intention toward adopting innovation. Frambach and Schillewaert (2002) point out that "organizational members will exhibit more positive attitudes if people in their social environment also use focal innovation" (p.172). The researcher also believes that normative beliefs are important in affecting individuals' behavior toward adoption. Therefore, two variables – peers and social network are included in the advanced model as directly affecting individual attitude toward adoption.

## PEERS

The first variable under social influence is peers. Peers influence represents the extent to which co-workers influence behavior. It is the influence, motivation and encouragement to an employee by colleagues in adopting innovation. Frambach and Schillewaert (2000) also used this variable in their diagrammatic representation of the model called "peers usage." However, in the written explanation of the variable they used the phrase "peers." Brown and Venkatesh (2005) used the term "work place referent's influence." This study has used the term peers, which is simple and easy to understand.

## SOCIAL NETWORK

The second variable under social influence is social network. It is the extent to which members of a social network influence each other's behavior. This refers to the extent to which employees are influenced by members in a similar discipline or other organizations outside of their own working environment.

Frambach and Schillewaert (2002) called it "network externalities." Frambach and Schillewaert (2002) state that "when there is a critical mass users within a person's reference or work group and innovation usage by others in an individual's social environment is likely to play an important role in all types of innovations" (p.171). Venkatesh and Brown (2001) used the term "social network." Lewis, Agarwal and Sambamurthy (2003) used a similar concept – "professional peers" and Brown and Venkatesh (2005) used a concept called "friends and family influence." This study has used the term "social network," borrowed from Venkatesh and Brown (2001). It is a term that is easy to understand and easy to differentiate between peers and social network.

## 4.6 Organizational Factors

In the development of the advanced model of innovation adoption organizational factors are incorporated as external factors. Organizational factors are the external factors and these include where individuals work. These external factors were not included in TRA and TAM. However, Ajzen and Fishbein (1980) said that external factors are important in understanding behavioral phenomenon. Frambach and Schillewaert (2000) also argued that external factors affect attitude and usage. They included organizational factors as external factors in their model and recommended they be tested in future research. For example, Frambach and Schillewaert (2002) point out that these external influences affect an individual's awareness of the functioning and application of innovations and their fit with the job. Organizational factors are the equivalent to "organizational facilitators," as mentioned by Frambach and Schillewaert (2000). Igbaria, Zinatelli, Cragg and Cavaye (1997) used the term "intra-organizational factors" and Lewis, Agarwal and Sambamurthy (2003) termed it "institutional factors." This study used the term "organizational factors." Under organizational factors there are three variables – training, managerial support and incentives.

### TRAINING

The first variable under organizational factors is training. It refers to the extent of training provided to individual employees. It indicates the extent to which training is provided to individuals and contributes to increasing their knowledge and expertise in using innovation. Frambach and Schillewaert's model shows training as an organizational factor. Igbaria, Zinatelli, Cragg and Cavaye (1997), Al-Gahtani and King (1999) and Lee, Kim, Rhee and Trimi (2006) also used the variable training. This study has also used the training variable as influencing attitude toward adoption.

## MANAGERIAL SUPPORT

The second variable under organizational factors is managerial support. It refers to the extent to which managerial support is provided to employees to take up innovation. Managerial support includes senior management encouragement and allocation of adequate resources. Frambach and Schillewaert's model shows it as a form of organizational support. However, Igbaria, Zinatelli, Cragg and Cavaye (1997) and Igbaria (1993) called the variable "managerial support." This study has used the term managerial support because it is more specific and it refers to the manager who provides support to employees.

## INCENTIVES

The third variable under organizational factors is incentives. Incentives are material or other benefits that an organization may provide to employees who adopt innovation. Frambach and Schillewaert (2000) used the term social persuasion in their model. Although Frambach and Schillewaert (2002) used the term social persuasion in their diagrammatic representation of the model, in their written explanation they used the term "incentives." This study has adopted the term "incentives" because it is easy to understand.

## 4.7 Demographics

In developing an advanced model, demographic factors have been included. These factors are the characteristics of employees. Demographics play an important part in influencing individuals' attitudes toward adoption. TRA and TAM did not include demographics in their models but suggested that these factors do influence behavior. Frambach and Schillewaert (2002) also state that demographic factors influence behavior. A study conducted by Igbaria (1993) found that demographic factors – gender, age and education – have a significant impact on adoption. Lee, Lee and Kwon (2005) also investigated gender, age and education in addition to three other factors, which constituted a significant part of their study. This study included gender, age and education as used by Igbaria (1993) and Lee, Lee and Kwon (2005). The study also included tenure, since Frambach and Schillewaert's model had this variable. In addition, the present study used two other variables – academic divisions and occupation category (academic and administrative staff). These two variables were not found in any other related studies but the researcher feels that they are important for identifying whether academic disciplines and occupation category exert any influence on individual adoption. Therefore five demographic variables are included in the advanced model of innovation adoption: gender, age, academic disciplines, occupation category, tenure and academic qualifications.

Previous studies have used behavioral intention in their models to explain adoption (Agarwal & Prasad, 1998; Davis, 1989) and the findings imply that an effective use of innovation relies on positive intention toward adoption (Lam, Cho & Qu, 2007). In contrast, Thompson, Higgins and Howell (1991) dropped behavioral intention and linked attitude to actual behavior directly. Thompson, Higgins and Howell (1991) argue that behavioral intention should be excluded where behavior itself can be measured because we are interested in actual behavior adoption. Although the advanced model keeps behavioral intention as surrogate because this allows the model to be used for predicting future use of an innovation, the empirical study investigates actual behavior. Results of this integrated study will identify actual adoption of innovation.

The terms "individual acceptance," "individual adoption," "individual adoption decision" and "system use" are used synonymously in the literature but the advanced model uses the term "individual adoption" of innovation, since the study is interested in investigating the adoption of innovation.

## 4.8 Conclusion

This chapter has discussed the outline of the research model and then proposed an advanced research model of innovation adoption. This model is built on the theory of reasoned action and incorporates elements from the technology acceptance model and that provided by Frambach and Schillewaert (2002) while at the same time introducing several modifications, which were not in these models. The advanced model developed here combines factors found in the previous models; incorporates factors which have been suggested in the previous models and includes additional variables found in other innovation acceptance related studies to create a coherent model of innovation adoption. The model contains four categories of factors – individual factors, social influence, organizational factors and demographics – which have the most significant influence on attitude and adoption. Within the four categories of factors there are ten independent variables (perceived usefulness, personal innovativeness, prior experience, image, enjoyment with innovation, peers, social network, training, managerial support and incentives) and five moderating variables (gender, age, academic disciplines, occupation category, tenure and academic qualifications). These variables affect attitude, which in turn influences adoption. The model retains behavioral intention as a surrogate, which will allow the model to be used in predicting future intention but empirical study will investigate actual usage behavior.

The proposed advanced model is easy to understand. The model has a direct link in attitude and adoption because these factors affect attitude, which influences adoption. This model is more comprehensive than TRA, TAM or Frambach and Schillewaert's model in explaining individual's adoption of innovation because it has ten independent variables and five moderating variables compared to two variables in both TRA and TAM. In addition, the researcher has removed some unnecessary complexities compared to previous models, which will provide greater explanatory power in practical settings. The advanced model can be used for a long period of time in testing innovation adoption in an organization because as individual, social, organizational or demographic factors change over time and new factors emerge in the future, they can be added to the four categories of factors identified as individual, social and organizational factors or demographics.

If AMIA can be proven, then it can be applied to a large number of innovation adoption and management problems in innovation adoption areas. Future research in innovation and adoption can benefit from the use of this advanced model. The model will be tested through an empirical study. The next chapter will discuss the methodology used in this study.

# 5

# Research Methods and Analytical Framework

## 5.1 Introduction

This chapter discusses the research procedures used in this study. The chapter consists of five sections: introduction; research design, location of the study and reasons for using calendar; quantitative research method and a discussion of the sample size for the study, research instruments, variables of the study, reliability and validity of the study, experts' opinions, pilot study, data collection procedures and data analysis; a qualitative study that addresses in-depth interviews and interview data analysis technique and the conclusion.

## 5.2 Research Design

According to Neuman (2000, p.124), "observing something from different angles or viewpoints, they get a fix on its true location." He added that "applied to social research, it means it is better to look at something from several angles than to look at it only one way" (p.124). Campbell and Fiske probably originated the concept of mixing different methods in 1959 when they used multiple methods to study the validity of psychological traits (Scandura & Williams, 2000). This study has adopted the multi-method approach for collecting and analyzing both quantitative and qualitative data in a single study. This study has used a multi-method research strategy that combines quantitative and qualitative approaches to collect, analyze and present both types of data.

After reviewing relevant literature, a two-step methodology was developed. In the first step the study used a quantitative method – survey – as the primary data collection method. The procedure for obtaining data for the study was through an online survey questionnaire. The study used the University of South Australia's TellUs software to collect online data. The survey method was used because the study wanted to precisely measure variables and test the advanced model that are linked to general casual explanation (Neuman, 2000). The quantitative study aims to test an extensive list of factors that affect individual adoption of innovation and examine the advanced model of innovation adoption developed in this study. The study also used the qualitative method in the form of interviews to provide additional information. The rationale for interviews was to provide further evidence in the form of people's experiences for the proposed advanced model.

Scandura and Williams (2000) argue that using different methods for the same subject of research lead to greater validity and reliability than a single method. Neuman (2000, p.125) supports this by arguing that "by measuring something in more than one way, researchers are more likely to see all aspects of it." In support of the multi-method approach, Scandura and Williams (2000, p.1250), state that the ability of researchers to draw conclusions from their studies will be improved as the use of a variety of methods to examine a topic might result in more robust and generalizable findings and the recommendations for managers can be made with greater clarity and confidence. The purpose of using a multi-method approach in this study was to increase validity and reliability and provide better conclusions as well as provide recommendations with greater clarity and confidence.

## LOCATION OF THE STUDY

The study was conducted at the University of South Australia (UniSA), Adelaide, South Australia. The university has long recognized that innovation is a key driver for growth in improving its competitive advantage. The university puts much emphasis on continuously developing its innovation capabilities. Innovation is a significant contributor to success and the role of innovation is to develop a competitive advantage and take advantage of new opportunities worldwide. The university is in the process of emphasizing continuous improvement of its academic and professional staff in innovation management through the provision of access and availability of innovation to everyone on all campuses. The research questions were tested in the context of calendar application of Microsoft Outlook software used by the university's academic and administrative (professional) staff. The study examined the extent to which individuals in a single organization have adopted a specific innovation or selected advanced features of Microsoft Outlook, such as calendar applications.

The approach of this study is to focus on a single organization using multi-methods of data collection. The study focuses on one organization having multiple units or divisions. It also means that the study involves only one innovation, one organizational culture and the same starting date for its adoption and usage. The different units allow the researcher to collect data from individuals with different innovation backgrounds and experiences in using computer software. It also increases the breadth of the sample and allows a good spread of the data. The university setting is ideal for analysis because it provides an autonomous and decentralized environment where opinions are valued. Furthermore, multiple influences on an individual's interpretation about the adoption, usage and feature use of the calendar application of Microsoft Outlook for job activities will be apparent to staff. The influences range from strategic direction of the university as espoused and communicated by senior administration officials, influence exercised by one's immediate social circle and messages emanating from external colleagues. The study was conducted using a particular innovation, calendar, to test an advanced model of innovation adoption (AMIA).

## REASONS FOR USING CALENDAR

The study examines the use of selected advanced features of Microsoft Outlook (such as calendar applications). Microsoft Outlook is good for this reason because it has been widely used by university employees for many years. However, it has many advanced features beyond the core (email) function, in that there is a large variation in the usage of these advanced features, and the university is keen to increase their use. Microsoft Outlook is a personal information manager incorporated into the Microsoft Office suite. Although often used mainly as an email application, it also provides a calendar and has the capacity for contact management, task tracking, note taking, journal writing and web browsing. It can be used as a stand-alone application, but can also operate in conjunction with other Microsoft Servers to provide enhanced functions for multiple users, such as sharing mailboxes, calendars, public folders and meeting time allocation (Poremsky, 2003).

The features of any software that have not been used by many are considered new and innovative. This refers to the definition of innovation used by Zaltman, Duncan and Holbek (1973, p.8) who stated that "innovation can be defined as an idea, practice, or material artifact perceived to be new by the relevant unit of adoption." It is any new system or program, which is new to individuals who are adopting it, no matter how old the system may be or how many other organizations may have adopted it. The length of time the innovation has been in existence and the number of other organizations that have adopted it do not directly affect its newness to organizations or to the individuals considering its adoption (Zaltman, Duncan & Holbek, 1973). They state that "this does not imply that each new idea or system or technology adopted by an organization is necessarily new to society. A particular new system may be new only to organizations or to individuals who are adopting it" (1973, p.11). For example, one of the advanced features of Microsoft Outlook is "calendar." It is an advanced feature because it is only used by a few employees who are especially trained due to their particular needs and interests.

Calendar works as a personal information manager (Poremsky, 2003). As such, it supports three types of activities: creating appointments, using "meeting invitation" and "sharing calendar." Calendar helps in scheduling and tracking daily activities. It reminds the user of the time for various activities and appointments. Calendar can help schedule meetings by showing others' free and busy times, transmitting meeting invitations and tracking responses. Recipients can accept, reject or suggest another time. If accepted, a meeting is automatically added to all participants' calendars. There is also the option of making it compulsory or optional for the attendee and adding the meeting to a resource calendar (Poremsky, 2003). Calendar helps in sharing one's calendar with others. It enables an authorized person to only read another employee's a calendar. There are other advanced or sophisticated elements of calendar such as recurring appointments, sharing and permissions, importing and exporting to other applications, etc. The aim of this study is to therefore to test the proposed advanced model of innovation adoption using the calendar application.

## 5.3 Quantitative Study

While the qualitative research approach helps to organize and describe subjective data in a systematic way, quantitative research precisely measures variables, quantifies data and generalizes the results from a sample to the population of interest (Neuman, 2000). According to Creswell (1994, p.2), quantitative research is an inquiry "based on testing a theory composed of variables, measured with numbers, and analyzed with statistical procedures, in order to determine whether the predictive generalization of the theory hold true." In the quantitative approach the researcher uses a literature review to identify questions and variables linked to a general causal explanation or interrelationship before collecting actual data. In the quantitative approach the researcher should remain distant and attempt to control for bias and be "objective" in assessing a situation or a phenomenon. It is characterized as traditional, experimental and empirical (Creswell, 1994, p.4). In this research an online survey questionnaire was used as the primary quantitative data collection method. Statistical analysis was carried out using SPSS (Statistical Package for the Social Sciences). The study investigated variables in the advanced model of innovation adoption, which has been discussed in Chapter 3.

## SAMPLE SIZE FOR THIS STUDY

The study was conducted using staff from four faculties (divisions). These divisions are: Division of Business; Education, Arts and Social Sciences; Health Science and Information Technology, Engineering and Environment. One of the main statistical tools that were applied for data analysis was multiple regressions. Hair, Anderson, Tatham and Black (1998) suggest that for the analysis of variances test a minimum of 20 observations is recommended in a cell, although a larger size may be required for acceptable and more emphatic statistical power.

For the regression analysis, Hair, Anderson, Tatham and Black (1998, p.166) suggest that for each independent variable, there should be five observations. Reduction in this ratio below five to one exposes the researcher to the risk of over-fitting the variate to the sample, making the results too specific to the sample and rendering a lack of generalizability. Although the minimum ratio is five to one, the desired level is between 15 to 20 observations for each dependent and independent variable. When this level is reached, the results should be generalizable if the sample meets the criteria. Similarly, Stevens (2001) suggested that 15 subjects are needed for every predictor (independent variable) for a thorough cross-validation as required in the social sciences. Based on the suggestion of Hair, Anderson, Tatham and Black (1998) that 15 to 20 observations for each dependent and independent variable were to be used to determine the sample size, a sample of 165 to 220 respondents would be needed because this study uses 11 variables – 1 dependent and 10 independent.

## RESEARCH INSTRUMENT FOR THE STUDY

The quantitative data for this study was collected by using a questionnaire that was administered online to the respondents. The questionnaire items had their origins in related studies and empirically tested and validated in the context of innovation adoption. The instruments collected respondents' responses about various issues concerning the adoption and use of calendar application in an organizational context. The selection of factors was based on the research questions and from the developed model. The questionnaire was constructed based on a five-point Likert type scale (Likert, 1932): 1 = Strongly Disagree (SD), 2 = Disagree (D), 3 = Neutral (N), 4 = Agree (A), 5 = Strongly Agree (SA).

## VARIABLES OF THE STUDY

The following are the factors (independent variables) identified and discussed in the literature review as influencing the uptake of innovation by employees in organizations. There are 10 independent variables: training, managerial support, incentives, perceived usefulness, personal innovativeness, prior experience, image, enjoyment with innovation, peers and social network. Research questions with corresponding independent variables and dependent variable are shown in Table 5.1.

**Table 5.1    Variables of the study**

| Research questions | Independent variables | Dependent variable |
|---|---|---|
| **Research Question no 1**<br>What is the impact of organizational factors such as training, managerial support and incentives on individual adoption of innovation? | 1. Training<br>2. Managerial support<br>3. Incentives | Individual adoption of innovation |
| **Research Question no 2**<br>Do the individual factors such as perceived usefulness, personal innovativeness, prior experience, image and enjoyment with innovation affect individuals' adoption of innovation? | 4. Perceived usefulness<br>5. Personal innovativeness<br>6. Prior experience<br>7. Image<br>8. Enjoyment with innovation | |
| **Research Question no 3**<br>What is the impact of social factors such as peers and social network on the individual adoption of innovation? | 9. Peers<br>10. Social network | |

## 5.4 Definitions of the Constructs and Measures of the Variables

The items used to construct the questionnaire were adopted from previously developed and validated measures with appropriate modifications to make them specifically relevant to this study. Definitions of constructs and measures of the independent and dependent variables are given below.

## 1. INDIVIDUAL ADOPTION OF INNOVATION

Based on several studies (Al-Gahtani & King, 1999; Igbaria, Guimaraes & Davis, 1995; Igbaria, Zinatelli, Cragg & Cavaye, 1997), system usage was selected as the primary indicator of individual adoption. System usage is often operationalized using self-reported measures of actual adoption. Based on previous studies (Al-Gahtani & King, 1999; Igbaria, Guimaraes & Davis, 1995; Igbaria, Zinatelli, Cragg & Cavaye, 1997), five indicators were implemented for this study to measure individual adoption. They are:

(1) **Actual amount of time spent**. Individuals were asked to indicate the amount of time spent on using calendar application per week on average using a five-point scale ranging from (1) less than half an hour to (5) more than three hours per week.

On average, how frequently do you use the calendar feature in Microsoft Outlook for job-related work?

(2) **Frequency of use**. Individuals were asked to indicate on average how frequently they use the calendar feature in Microsoft Outlook. Frequency was measured on a five-point scale ranging from (1) once a month or less to (5) several times a day.

On average, how much time do you spend per week using calendar for job related work?

(3) **Usage level.** Usage level of different features can provide a good indication of overall adoption and variety of task performed. Thus, respondents were asked to indicate their level of usage on a five-point scale ranging from (1) not used at all to (5) used extensively.

Please indicate your level of usage of Creating Appointment (scheduling and tracking daily activities).

Please indicate your level of usage of Sharing Calendar (giving permission to others to see your calendar).

(4) **Number of features used.** Calendar has three applications. Respondents were asked to indicate how many features they use ranging from (1) nil to (4) three features.

How many different calendar applications (creating appointment, meeting request, sharing calendar) have you worked with or used?

(5) **Sophistication level of features used.** Calendar has a wide range of advanced features. A good indication of overall adoption of innovation can be provided by measuring the sophistication level of the features used (recurring appointment, sharing and permissions, import and export to other applications, etc.). Sophistication level was measured by asking respondents to indicate how much they use sophisticated elements of calendar on a five point scale ranging from (1) not used at all to (5) used extensively.

Do you use sophisticated elements of calendar (recurring appointment, sharing and permissions, import and export to other applications etc.)?

## 2. TRAINING

The measurement of training was assessed by the extent of training provided to employees. Respondents were asked to indicate the extent to which training is provided to them, and the extent to which it contributes to increasing their knowledge and expertise in using innovation. Training was assessed using five criteria. These criteria were used by Al-Gahtani and King (1999) and Igbaria, Zinatelli, Cragg and Cavaye (1997).

1.    UniSA provides me with internal training to explain the features of calendar.

2.    Internal training courses are readily available for me to improve calendar usage abilities.

3.    A specific person is available for individualized support when I face difficulties with using calendar.

4.      Specialized instructions and education concerning calendar usage are available for me.

5.      Guidance is available for me on how to use calendar.

## 3. MANAGERIAL SUPPORT

The measurement of managerial support includes the assessment of top or senior management encouragement and allocation of adequate resources. Individuals were asked to indicate the extent of agreement or disagreement with the five statements concerning managerial support. These items were used by Igbaria, Zinatelli, Cragg and Cavaye (1997) and Igbaria, Parasurman and Baroudi (1996).

1.      Management is aware of the benefits that can be achieved with the use of calendar.

2.      Management always supports and encourages me to use MS Outlook for job related work.

3.      Management provides most of the necessary help and resources to enable me to use calendar.

4.      Management is really keen to see that employees are happy with using calendar.

5.      Management provides good access to various types of computer resources when I need to use the system.

## 4. INCENTIVES

Incentives were measured as an individual's belief about benefits or consequences of adopting innovation. Individuals were asked to rate their perceived benefits. These items were created after looking at the items in "long-term consequences" used by Chang and Cheung (2001) and Cheung, Chang and Lai (2000).

1.      Use of calendar is a means of effective self organizing.

2.      Use of calendar saves time in organizing my work.

3.    Use of calendar keeps my personal data more secure than conventional methods (i.e., diary).

4.    Use of calendar motivates me as it is being recognized by the university.

## 5. PERCEIVED USEFULNESS

Perceived usefulness is defined as the degree to which an individual believes that using a particular system would enhance his or her job performance. Perceived usefulness was measured by an eight-item scale used by Davis (1989), Moore and Benbaset (1996) and Al-Gahtani and King (1999).

1.    Using calendar enables me to accomplish tasks more quickly.

2.    Using calendar improves the quality of the work I do.

3.    Using calendar makes it easier to do my job.

4.    Using calendar improves my job performance.

5.    Using calendar enhances my effectiveness on the job.

6.    Using calendar gives me greater control over my work.

7.    Using calendar increases my productivity.

8.    Overall, I find using calendar to be advantageous in my job.

## 6. PERSONAL INNOVATIVENESS

This refers to the willingness of an individual to try any innovation. Personal innovativeness was measured by a five-item scale. Two items were created and three items were adopted from Lewis, Agarwal and Sambamurthy (2003).

1.    If I heard about a new information technology, I would look for ways to experiment with it.

2.    Among my peers, I am usually the first to try out a new system.

3.    I like to experiment with new information technologies/software.

4.    I am always enthusiastic to learn about new technology/system.

5.    I learned more about calendar by my own initiatives.

## 7. PRIOR EXPERIENCE

Prior experience was assessed by the users' prior experience with innovation and overall skills in using innovation. Prior experience was measured by individuals' responses to four questions asking them to report the extent of experience they had received from four sources: prior work, self training and training courses and previous experience with similar systems. These items were adopted from Igbaria, Parasurman and Baroudi (1996) and Igbaria, Guimaraes and Davis (1995).

1.    I learned from my previous work experience to use calendar.

2.    I learned from my earlier self-training to use calendar.

3.    I learned from prior training courses to use calendar.

4.    I learned from previous experience with similar system/technology to use calendar.

## 8. IMAGE

This refers to the degree to which the use of innovation enhances one's image within the organization. Image was measured by a five-item scale. These items were adopted from Moore and Benbasat (1996); Venkatesh and Davis (2000); Al-Gahtani and King (1999).

1.    Using calendar improves my image within the organization.

2.    Because of my use of calendar, others in the organization see me as more organized.

3.    People in this organization who use calendar are more efficient than those who do not.

4.    High profile people in this organization are using calendar.

5.    Using calendar is a standardized operational symbol in this organization.

## 9. ENJOYMENT WITH INNOVATION

This refers to the extent to which using the system is perceived to be enjoyable and satisfying to the individual. Enjoyment was measured by a five items scale. Two items were created and three items were adopted from Al-Gahtani and King (1999).

1.    I believe using calendar is enjoyable.

2.    I believe the actual process of using calendar is pleasant.

3.    I believe while I use calendar, I enjoy using the system.

4.    I believe using calendar is convenient.

5.    I believe using calendar is interesting.

## 10. PEERS (AT THE FACULTY OR DIVISION)

The measurement of peers was assessed by the influence, motivation and encouragement given to an individual employee by peers in adopting innovation. Individuals were asked to indicate the extent of agreement or disagreement with the five statements concerning peers' influence, motivation and encouragement on a five-item scale. Three items were created and two items were adopted from Lewis, Agarwal and Sambamurthy (2003).

1.    People in informal groups to which I belong think using calendar is valuable.

2.    The opinions of the people in informal groups to which I belong are important to me.

3.    I learned from my friends how to use calendar successfully.

4.    Communicating with my friends helped me to learn more about calendar.

5.    Observing my friends performing a task enhanced my intention to use calendar to perform a similar task.

## 11. SOCIAL NETWORK (AT UNISA OR OTHER ORGANIZATIONS)

This refers to the extent to which employees are influenced by people in a similar discipline or other organizations. Social network was measured by the five-item scale below. Three items were created and two items were adopted from Lewis, Agarwal and Sambamurthy (2003).

1.    People in my discipline think that using calendar is valuable.

2.    The opinion of people in my discipline is important to me.

3.    I use calendar because our interrelated organizations also use calendar.

4.    I use calendar because many of my friends in other divisions are using calendar.

5.    I use calendar because UniSA students and employees use the similar system.

## 12. ATTITUDE

Attitude is a pre-disposition to respond favourably or unfavourably to an object, person, event or institution. It is an individual's feelings of favourableness or unfavourableness of his or her performance of the behavior. It is also the function of behavioral beliefs and evaluation of outcomes. Behavioral belief is one's belief in performing a specific behavior that will lead to a specific consequence, while evaluation of outcome is one's assessment of that specific consequence. The instrument asked individuals to rate five items according to how they feel about using innovation on a five-point scale. The items for this study were adopted from Taylor and Todd (1995), Al-Gahtani and King (1999) and Lam, Cho and Qu (2007).

1.    Using calendar is important to my job.

2.    Using calendar is relevant to my job.

3.    Using calendar is helpful.

4.    Using calendar is practical.

5.    I like the idea of using calendar.

## 5.5 Validity and Reliability of the Study

Two major criteria of a good research instrument are validity and reliability (Hair, Anderson, Tatham & Black, 1998). The validity and reliability of the research instruments were established by taking a number of measurements. Validity is the degree to which a measurement accurately represents what it is supposed to measure (Hair, Anderson, Tatham & Black, 1998). It is concerned with the accuracy of scientific findings. The items of the research instruments were drawn from the literature review and previous studies in similar areas. The participants who took part in this study were academic and administrative (professional) staff at the University of South Australia (UniSA). The specific questions in the questionnaire were derived from studies conducted among similar groups of people. This is shown in Table 5.2 below.

**Table 5.2      Participants in various studies**

| Studies | Participants |
|---|---|
| Lewis, Agarwal and Sambamurthy (2003) | Academic staff |
| Moore and Benbaset (1996) | Academic staff |
| Igbaria, Parasurman and Baroudi (1996) | Managers and professionals |
| Igbaria, Zinatelli, Cragg and Cavaye (1997) | General employees |
| Igbaria, Guimaraes and Davis (1995) | Professional and managerial staff |
| Chang and Cheung (2001) | Management and general staff |
| Cheung, Chang and Lai (2000) | Managers, professional and technical support staff |

In designing the instruments, the language was kept simple and straightforward so as to make items easily understood by respondents. Minor modifications were made to the survey questions to acknowledge the local context and the specific innovation involved. Apart from this, the questions follow well-established patterns as shown in the previous section, and this underpins the validity of the questionnaire.

On the other hand, reliability applies to a measure when similar results are obtained over time and across situations. Reliability is expressed numerically, usually as a coefficient – a higher coefficient indicates high reliability. Cronbach's alpha is the most widely used to measure reliability (Hair, Anderson, Tatham & Black, 1998). Steps were taken to ensure that any measurement represents what it was intended to measure and it is free from any systematic error or bias. To ensure the study's reliability, several measurements were taken such as experts' opinions, data examination, pilot study and reporting the reliability coefficient. Furthermore, three types of triangulation were used – methodological triangulation, data triangulation and theoretical triangulation – in an attempt to enhance the validity and reliability of the study. For methodological triangulation, different methods were employed including the quantitative survey and qualitative interviews after analyzing data in the quantitative study. For data triangulation, data for this study were collected using two different procedures – survey and interviews across various disciplines and backgrounds. For theoretical triangulation, this study used multiple theoretical perspectives during planning and development of the advanced model.

## EXPERTS' OPINIONS

The first qualitative method used in this study consisted of experts' opinions and comments regarding the questionnaire, sentence structure relevant to the type of questions and technical aspects of the questionnaire. These helped to modify the questionnaire and make appropriate changes to the questionnaire items. Experts' opinions were taken prior to the pilot study to confirm and clarify the set of advanced and sophisticated features/applications of Microsoft Outlook, which was the subject of the university-wide survey. This method was used because it provided information relating to the feelings and opinions of people who are knowledgeable and experts in IT areas and helped to modify the questionnaire.

The experts are five members with innovation skills and are familiar with Microsoft Outlook features. These experts are active users of Microsoft Outlook and some of them are responsible for monitoring and development of university-wide email systems. Four experts are professional staff of the university and one expert was a PhD candidate who works at the university and uses UniSA email systems. Although PhD students are not included in the main survey, the researcher chose him because he was an employee and a PhD student, on campus, having work responsibilities, is young and uses the email system extensively. The researcher received valuable and important information from the experts' point of view. The recruitment process for the experts was done by personal familiarity and suggestions by the university's IT department about the people whose specialty in the area could help in this study.

Questionnaires were given to the experts who were provided sufficient time – four to five days – to discuss and freely give their opinions on the issues. Some experts gave their opinions and indicated where changes needed to be made in the questionnaire by direct conversation and underlining in the questionnaire items that the researcher provided them. A few provided written comments and returned them by email. Both direct discussion with experts and written comments from them were helpful in designing the final questionnaire. For example, one of the items under usage was "How many different calendar applications (creating appointment, meeting request, sharing calendar) have you worked with or used?" The options were from nil to more than three. As there are only three applications under calendar, the experts requested that the last option ("more than three") be removed because it would generate a wrong answer. The experts also helped to change the structure of sentences to make them appropriate for the study. For instance, one of the items under incentives was "Use of calendar will increase the opportunity for more meaningful work for me." The experts suggested that the best way to express the sentence would be "Use of calendar is a means of effective self organizing." Similar corrections and modifications were made in many of the items. Experts also helped to make the questionnaire items technically correct. One of the questions under usage was "For each calendar mini feature listed below please indicate your level of usage." There were three sub-questions such as (a) Creating Appointment, (b) Meeting Request and (c) Sharing Calendar. The answer options were: 1. None to 5. Extensive for all three sub-items. For technical purposes the experts suggested modifying the questions and making them into three separate items. For example, one of the items would be "Please indicate your level of usage of Creating Appointment (scheduling and tracking daily activities)". The second item would be "Please indicate your level of usage of Meeting Request (inviting for meeting and tracking responses)." The third item would be "Please indicate your level of usage of Sharing Calendar (giving permission to others to see your calendar)". Answering options would be from 1. Not used at all to 5. Used extensively. To sum up, the major advantage of using experts' opinions lay in studying ways in which individual experts make sense of a phenomenon and construct meaning around it. The experts provided opinions about issues that are of major significance to them. In addition, it provided valuable information and insights that would be difficult to obtain in other ways. The experts drew information from their wealth of experiences in the field, thus providing an excellent device for generating and designing questionnaire items for the subsequent survey.

## PILOT STUDY

The research instruments were pre-tested to identify and modify the items, which respondents tended to misinterpret, skip over or answer improperly. The purpose of the pilot study was to examine the instrument's validity and reliability. Respondents for the pilot study were drawn from the actual study population – academic and administrative staff from University of South Australia's four faculties (divisions) and staff not from a specific division. Questionnaires were distributed to respondents who were asked to complete the questionnaire and return it to the researcher.

The pilot study was conducted to verify the clarity of the questions and solve unforeseen problems with wording, directions, phrasing and sequence of questions. Answers to the pilot study determined the reliability of the survey instrument. A follow-up discussion with respondents helped the researcher adjust and clarify those items that received criticism from respondents. This was to show consistency among items and to ensure respondents' proper comprehension of the questions. Other suggestions for improvement were also accepted and incorporated into the instrument.

The researcher took the responsibility for developing and validating the instrument to be suitable for use and to ensure consistency and reliability of the instrument. For example, a few respondents recommended writing Microsoft Outlook instead of MS Outlook in item no. 1 under usage. Responses for the item nos. 3 to 5 under usage were not clear to many respondents. Based on respondents' suggestions, response rates of items 3 to 5 were changed from 1. None to 5. Extensively to 1. Not used at all, 2. Used rarely, 3. Used regularly, 4. Used frequently and 5. Used extensively. These made the response items clearer. Respondents also misinterpreted item no. 7 under usage. This item was modified, making it simpler and easy for respondents to understand. Suggestions also came to change the response rate from 1. Not used at all, 2. Used rarely, 3. Used regularly, 4. Used frequently and 5. Used extensively instead of 1. Least sophisticated to 5. Highly sophisticated. Corrections to sentence structure were suggested by respondents and appropriate changes were made. For instance, an item under peers was changed to "I learned from my friends how to use calendar successfully" instead of "I learned from my friends how to successfully use calendar." Respondents suggested changing the word "organization" to the word UniSA to specify the answer. For example, this item was modified from "Using calendar improves my image within the organization" to "Using calendar improves my image within UniSA." Several words were deleted from the items to make them more grammatically correct. For example, instead of "more increasingly," the word "more" was deleted. Such advice ensured that the researcher made corrections to the instruments before proceeding with the final study.

## 5.6 Data Collection Process

The primary procedure for obtaining data was through an online survey questionnaire. The researcher used UniSA's TellUs software to collect online data. The questionnaire was sent on 15 August 2006 through a university wide online newsletter called AllStaff@UniSA. Sending the questionnaire through this newsletter was recommended by the university's vice president and pro-vice chancellor of research and innovation. In the newsletter, the principal supervisor briefly explained the purpose of the research and urged university staff to help in the research by completing a five-minute online questionnaire. For ease of access, a link to the questionnaire was given in the message. Details about the research including ethics approval information were provided in another link, which led to the researcher's personal (staff) homepage. Other relevant details such as purpose and benefits of the study as well as the rights of potential participants were included in the information sheet located on the researcher's homepage. Once a participant completed the questionnaire and clicked on submit at the end, it was automatically saved in the TellUs system, which can only be opened and downloaded by the researcher. The TellUs system ensures a person can only answer once.

The readers of AllStaff@UniSA newsletter are relatively low in number and it is not a popular newsletter because it contains very general information about the university's programs and other events. Therefore, it was expected that the response rate would be relatively low. In order to get the required sample size, in the second stage, the researcher contacted school executive officers in all schools in the four faculties (divisions). The researcher explained the significance of the study and requested the posting of the questionnaire in school staff members' email lists. The email message for staff was similar to the principal supervisor's message to all staff at UniSA, which contained brief information about the research and the request to complete the five-minute online questionnaire. A link to the questionnaire and another link to the details about the survey were given. This email was more personalized as it went from the school executive officer to school staff. School executive officers forwarded the email with a brief introduction about the researcher and the research project. A reminder was sent after a week. This process ensured that an adequate sample size to analyze the data would be received. The total data collection procedures took place during August and September 2006. A total 275 completed questionnaires were received.

## 5.7 Data Analysis

Statistical analysis of the data was undertaken using SPSS (Statistical Package for Social Sciences) package. The researcher chose cumulative percentage as a descriptive tool for the findings. Frequency distribution and percentages were calculated. Descriptive statistics outlined the profile of users whereas percentile statistics identified the levels of adoption. Several cross-tabulations were performed to discover the relationship between individual adoption and the demographic characteristics of the respondents such as gender, age, academic division, level of occupation and academic qualifications. Correlation matrix, internal reliability test and test of linearity were performed.

To test the proposed model, multiple regression analysis was performed on the collected data. Multiple regression analysis, a form of general linear modeling, is a multivariate statistical technique that can be used to analyze the relationship between a single dependent (criterion) variable and several independent (predictor) variables (Hair, Anderson, Tatham & Black, 1998). Multiple regression analysis weighted each independent variable to provide a prediction of dependent variable. The weights denote the relative contribution of independent variables to the overall prediction of dependent variable (Hair, Anderson, Tatham & Black, 1998). "The set of weighted independent variables form the regression variate (also referred to as the regression equation or regression model), a linear combination of the independent variables that best predict the dependent variable" (Hair, Anderson, Tatham & Black, 1998, p.149). In the context of this study, with ten independent variables, the regression model can be shown in the following equation:

Y=b0+b1X1+b2X2+b3X3.......+b10X10

Where:

Y=Dependent Variable
b0=Intercept (constant)
b1, b2, b3.........b10=Coefficients
X1, X2, X3.......X10=Independent Variables

Regression analysis provided an objective means of assessing the predictive power of the set of independent variables. It also provided a means of objectively assessing the degree and character of the relationship between dependent and independent variables (Hair, Anderson, Tatham & Black, 1998; Dielman, 2005). The analysis determined the relative importance of each independent variable and the type of relationship in the prediction of the dependent measure. The analysis then provided a means of assessing the magnitude of each independent variable's relationship. In making this simultaneous assessment, the relative importance of each independent variable was determined (Hair, Anderson, Tatham & Black, 1998; Dielman, 2005).

According to Hair, Anderson, Tatham and Black (1998), multiple regression analysis provides an insight into the relationship among independent variables in their prediction of the dependent variable. These interrelationships are important to check because correlation among independent variables may make some variables redundant in the predictive effort. The assessment of multicollinearity was undertaken by identifying the extent of collinearity and the degree to which the estimated coefficients are affected. "The simple and most obvious means of identifying collinearity is an examination of the correlation matrix for independent variables. The presence of high correlations (generally .90 and above) is the first indication of substantial collinearity" (Hair, Anderson, Tatham & Black, 1998, p.191).

The study examined the linearity of the relationship between dependent and independent variables that represent the degree to which change in the dependent variable is associated with the independent variable. The concept of correlation is based on a linear relationship. Linearity was examined through residual plots. The study selected a method for specifying the regression model to be estimated and assessed by statistical significance of the overall model in predicting the dependent variable (Dielman, 2005; Hair, Anderson, Tatham & Black, 1998).

In regression analysis, the study used a confirmatory approach whereby the researcher specified the independent variable to be included in the regression equation (Dielman, 2005; Hair, Anderson, Tatham & Black, 1998). In this situation, confirmatory perspective involved the inclusion of all ten independent variables and all are directly entered into the regression equation at one time. The study examined R-Squared which is the correlation coefficient, also referred to as the coefficient of determination. This value indicates the percentage of total variation of $Y$ (dependent variable) explained by independent variables. The study checked standard error of estimate (SEE), which is another measure of the accuracy of the prediction. The study also reported correlation coefficient ($r$), regression coefficient ($b_n$) (provides a means of assessing the relative importance of individual variables in the overall prediction) of each independent variable and partial $t$ value. To check overall model fit, the study looked at the $F$ ratio. With the model estimation completed, the regression variate specified and the diagnostic tests that confirmed the appropriateness of the result, the researcher then found the equation for individual adoption of innovation. In addition, the regression coefficient also provided a means of assessing the relative importance of individual variables in overall prediction of individual adoption. Finally, this analysis demonstrated the relative importance and contribution of the factors (organizational, individual and social) in individual adoption of innovation. The analyses tested the new model and extended previous research by investigating multiple factors in individual adoption of innovation.

Analysis of variance (ANOVA) tests were conducted to see whether demographic characteristics of employees have any impact on adoption or usage level. In order to test the impact of demographic characteristics on dependent variables, it was necessary to check whether various demographics categories such as male and female, different age groups, different disciplines, academic and administrative staff, full-time and part-time staff and educational qualifications differ significantly in terms of usage level. To find significant differences in demographics, ANOVA tests were conducted. After ANOVA tests, an hierarchical regression analysis was conducted to see what impact these demographic characteristics had on the regression model and how demographic variables affect individual acceptance of innovation.

## 5.8 Qualitative Study

Qualitative study is defined as an inquiry process of understanding a social or human problem. It is "based on building a complex, holistic picture, formed with words, reporting detailed views of informants and conducted in natural settings" (Creswell, 1994, p.2). Qualitative study emphasizes detailed explanations of cases that arise in the natural flow of social life. It tries to present authentic interpretations that are sensitive to specific social or organizational context (Neuman, 2000, p.122). Unlike quantitative study, qualitative study is viewed as subjective and more concerned with non-statistical methods of inquiry and analysis of a phenomenon. The qualitative approach is able to identify patterns and themes as they emerge in order to explain phenomenon and verify information sources. In terms of qualitative method, this study uses interviews that were conducted after the quantitative data has been analyzed, and aimed to support and improve our understanding of quantitative investigation by providing further insights into factors that affect individual adoption of innovation.

### INTERVIEWS

The qualitative research method used in this study consisted of in-depth interviews. In-depth interviews allow the researcher to explore a range of views that respondents have in regard to the study. Applying the interview method allowed the researcher to interact directly with respondents and obtain information from them. Open-ended questions provided an opportunity to obtain rich information from respondents, facilitating a deeper level of understanding.

Interviews were designed to explore ambiguous and apparently contradictory items from the quantitative study. A semi-structured interview format was selected and in-depth interviews were conducted face-to-face. This format allowed flexibility for the researcher to focus on issues of significance in the study. Respondents had opportunities to give reasons and expound on answers they gave to questions. Respondents were free to bring up any aspects of the interview they wished to discuss.

In the selection of respondents, the researcher utilized criterion sampling, which is also called purposive sampling (Creswell, 1994; Miles & Huberman, 1994) to choose respondents who meet some pre-defined criteria. The criteria were: academic divisions (four academic divisions) and employees who were not in the division, gender (male and female), and job classification (academic and administrative staff). This ensured that the interview sample was generally of the same composition as the overall sample. A total of 13 participants were selected. First, respondents were contacted via telephone and then sent an email with an attached information sheet explaining the purpose of the research and inviting them to participate in the study. Permission was also sought and a consent form was signed prior to conducting the actual interview, with an option for the interviewee to withdraw from participating at any time.

A digital recorder was used during the interview. All respondents gave their permission to use the recorder. An informal conversation style was used in all of the interviews. Each interview began with a brief explanation of the aims of the research and an assurance of confidentiality of the information and anonymity as per the university ethics standard protocol. The interview took about 30 to 45 minutes. The actual interview was then saved into a computer and an interview report was written immediately after an interview was conducted. Transcriptions of the recorded interviews were performed to facilitate analysis.

At the start of each interview the researcher provided an interview questionnaire to the respondent and explained the purpose and objectives of the study. This questionnaire sheet helped both interviewee and interviewer to stay focused on the issues set for discussion and allowed respondents to do most of the talking. The interview questions were designed to draw insightful responses and to complement the quantitative survey.

## INTERVIEW DATA ANALYSIS TECHNIQUE

There are several ways to analyze qualitative data (Creswell, 1994). According to Creswell (1994, p.153), the researcher needs to be comfortable with developing categories and making comparisons and contrasts. It also requires that the researcher be open to possibilities and see contrary or alternative explanations for the findings. Miles and Huberman (1994, p.10) define analysis of qualitative data as consisting of three concurrent flow of activity: data reduction, data display and conclusion drawing with verification. The first phase is data reduction. Data reduction is a process of selecting, focusing, simplifying, abstracting and organizing data in such a way that final conclusion can be drawn and verified. Other scholars (Miles & Huberman, 1994) and Neuman (2000, p.428), argue that the researcher focuses on what is common across cases, although other features of the cases may differ.

The second phase of data analysis is data display. Data display is an organized, compressed assembly of information that permits drawing conclusions (Miles & Huberman, 1994). Data display helps the researcher to see and understand what is happening and to do something – either draw justified conclusions or move on to the next step of analysis. The third phase of data analysis is conclusion drawing and verification. In this stage the researcher decides what things mean – noting regularities, patterns, explanations, possible configuration, causal flow and proposition (Miles & Huberman, 1994, p.11). According to Neuman (2000, p.428), "the researcher pinpoints features whereby a set of cases is similar with regards to an outcome and causal feature and another set where the cases differ on outcome and causal feature." For verification, data need to be organized categorically and reviewed repeatedly to verify any emerging conclusion. Miles and Huberman (1994, p.11) state that "the meanings emerging from data have to be tested for their plausibility, their sturdiness, their 'confirmability' – that is validity." For the purpose of this study the researcher sought to identify and describe patterns and themes from the participants' perspectives and then attempted to understand and explain these patterns and themes. The researcher has concluded the analysis by considering what the analyzed data mean and assessing its implications for the research questions in the study. Verifications are made by reviewing data as many times as is deemed necessary to double-check any emerging conclusions.

## 5.9 Conclusion

This chapter discussed the research methodology used in this study. It also discussed research design and the rationale behind the selection of a multi-method approach. After reviewing relevant literature and developing an advanced model, a multi-step methodology was developed. The study used a quantitative method – survey – as the primary procedure for obtaining the data for the study was through an online survey questionnaire. This quantitative study intends to test an extensive list of factors that affect individual adoption of innovation and examine the advanced model of innovation adoption developed in this study. The study used UniSA's TellUs system to collect anonymous online data. The instruments were tested before conducting the actual study. Data were analyzed by using the software known as Statistical Package for Social Sciences (SPSS). Descriptive analysis, frequencies, cross-tabulations, correlations, multiple regressions and ANOVA tests were used to analyze the data. The study was also expanded by adding qualitative data from a series of interviews that were conducted after the survey questionnaire results had been analyzed. The chapter also explained the interview data analysis technique. The rationale for adding interviews was to provide additional information and provide qualitative evidence for the proposed advanced model. The next chapter presents an analysis and discussion of the quantitative data.

# 6

# Impact of Organizational, Individual and Social Factors

## 6.1 Introduction

The purpose of this chapter is to provide a systematic analysis of data collected from an organization's individual employees. In this chapter, the proposed advanced model of innovation adoption (AMIA) is tested statistically using data from the questionnaire survey. The statistical testing assists and supports the development of a theoretical construct that brings individual innovation adoption issues into a coherent model. The chapter discusses the factors that influence employees to adopt innovation and the impact of demographic characteristics on employees' use of innovations. Finally, the chapter discusses the implications of the quantitative results.

For the purpose of clarity, this chapter presents the results of the investigation in 13 sections. The first section is the introduction; the second presents the demographic profile of the respondents and the third addresses the level of usage of the Microsoft Outlook calendar by the respondents. Section 6.4 provides a cross-tabulation for level of usage by demographic characteristics of the respondents and section 6.5 presents correlations among of the study variables. Section 6.6 provides information about the reliability and validity of the instruments. Section 6.7 describes regression analysis usage as a dependent variable and section 6.8 provides the ANOVA (analysis of variance). Section 6.9 provides an hierarchical regression with demographic effects and section 6.10 provides regression analysis for attitude as dependent variable. Section 6.11 discusses the quantitative results, section 6.12 provides implications of the quantitative results and section 6.13 is the conclusion.

## 6.2 Analysis of Demographic Data

This section analyzes the demographic data and explains descriptive statistics concerning a population or sample in the form of a frequency table. Descriptive data constitute important sources of information about employees' adoption of innovation in an organizational context. The study elaborates on the description of respondents' profile in order to identify their basic characteristics concerning the taking up of innovation. Demographic data collected from the questionnaire provide information on the personnel and organizational characteristics of the respondents. Table 6.1 summarizes the respondent demographics, including gender, age, division, classification (academic and administrative), position (employed as full-time or part-time) and academic qualifications.

Males constitute 36% while females represent 64% of the respondent cohort. This distribution of gender reflects the university's total employee distribution in which the female employees outnumber the male employees. Nineteen percent of the total employees belong to the 20- to 30-year age group and 20% belong to the 31- to 40-year age group.

**Table 6.1      Demographic information about the respondents**

| Characteristics | | Frequency | Percentage |
|---|---|---|---|
| Gender | Male | 100 | 36.4 |
| | Female | 175 | 63.6 |
| Age | 20-30 | 53 | 19.3 |
| | 31-40 | 56 | 20.4 |
| | 41-50 | 86 | 31.3 |
| | 51-60 | 67 | 24.4 |
| | 61 and above | 13 | 4.7 |
| Faculty (division) | Business | 66 | 24.0 |
| | Education, Arts and Social Sciences | 69 | 25.1 |
| | Health Science | 71 | 25.8 |
| | IT, Engineering and Environment | 32 | 11.6 |
| | Not in a division | 37 | 13.5 |
| Classification | Academic Staff | 177 | 64.4 |
| | Professional (Administrative) staff | 94 | 34.2 |
| | Missing Values | 4 | 1.5 |
| Employed as | Full-time | 213 | 77.5 |
| | Part-time | 61 | 22.2 |
| | Missing value | 1 | .4 |
| Qualification | PhD or other doctorate | 86 | 31.3 |
| | Master's degree | 56 | 20.4 |

| | | |
|---|---|---|
| Grad. diploma | 29 | 10.5 |
| Bachelor's degree | 60 | 21.8 |
| Undergrad. diploma | 16 | 5.8 |
| Missing values | 28 | 10.2 |
| **Total** | 275 | |

Those aged 41–50 make up 31% of the respondents, whereas respondents aged 51–60 comprise 24% of the respondents. Respondents aged 60 and above make up only 5%. Twenty-four percent of the respondents are from the Division of Business and 25% of them are from the Division of Education, Arts and Social Sciences. The Division of Health Science constitutes 26% of respondents, whereas respondents from the Division of Information Technology, Engineering and Environment comprise 12%. Respondents not in a specific division represent 13%.

The majority of respondents are academic staff (65%), whereas only 35% are professional (administrative) staff. Almost 78% of the respondents are full-time employees and 22% are part-time employees. The survey results reveal that 31% of the respondents are PhD holders and 20% hold a master's degree. Eleven percent of the respondents have graduate diplomas, whereas 22% of the respondents hold bachelor's degrees. Only 6% of the total employees have an undergraduate diploma. This information tells us that most of our respondents are middle aged, moderately to highly educated, academic staff and employed full-time. Goodness of fit Chi-square tests (how well the model actually reflects the data) were conducted and analyses indicate that the sample is representative of the research population regarding gender and academic divisions. Such information may prove significant when the adoption and usage level of these respondents are investigated.

## 6.3 Employees' Level of Using Calendar

Section 6.3 and section 6.4 provide descriptive statistics about the data on level of usage in terms of demographic characteristics. The data analysis and interpretation of results begins in section 6.5 (inter-correlation among study variables).

This section reports on the respondents' level of using the Microsoft Outlook calendar application. These items verified usage in terms of frequency, time spent, different features accessed and number of applications used by the employees. Tables 6.2 to 6.8 summarize data collected from respondents.

These tables show that the selection of calendar is justified. There is a wide range of usage, from nil to quite frequent.

## FREQUENCY OF USE OF CALENDAR FEATURE IN JOB-RELATED ACTIVITIES

Thirteen percent of the respondents use calendar once a month or less, whereas 8% use it a few times a month. Only 9% of respondents use calendar a few times a week. Fourteen percent of the respondents use calendar about once a day while 56% respondents use it several times a day. This confirms their familiarity with the innovation and hence their usage level. Table 6.2 displays the relevant data below.

**Table 6.2    Frequency of use of calendar in job-related activities**

| Frequency of use | Frequency | Percent |
|---|---|---|
| Once a month or less | 36 | 13.1 |
| A few times a month | 22 | 8.0 |
| A few times a week | 25 | 9.1 |
| About once a day | 39 | 14.2 |
| Several times a day | 153 | 55.6 |
| **Total** | 275 | 100.0 |

## AVERAGE TIME SPENT PER WEEK USING CALENDAR FOR JOB-RELATED WORK

Table 6.3 shows data for average time spent per week using calendar. Respondents seem to be moderate users of calendar. The average time spent per week on using it indicates that 38% of them spend less than a 1/2 hour per week, 26% spend a 1/2 hour–1 hour per week, 18% spend 1–2 hours per week, 9% spend 2–3 hours per week and only 10% spend more than 3 hours per week. The respondents who use more than 3 hours are probably administrative staff who have to make regular and ongoing appointments and arrange meetings.

Table 6.3    Average time spent on calendar per week

| Time spent on calendar | Frequency | Percent |
|---|---|---|
| Less than 1/2 hour | 104 | 37.8 |
| From 1/2 hour to 1 hour | 70 | 25.5 |
| 1-2 hours | 50 | 18.2 |
| 2-3 hours | 24 | 8.7 |
| More than 3 hours | 26 | 9.5 |
| Total | 274 | 99.6 |
| Missing value | 1 | .4 |
| **Total** | 275 | 100.0 |

## LEVEL OF USAGE OF CREATING APPOINTMENT (SCHEDULING AND TRACKING DAILY ACTIVITIES)

The response to the question about the level of usage of calendar to create appointments shows that 17% of respondents have not used it for that purpose, whereas 15% of them used it rarely. Twenty-two percent of the respondents used it regularly, while 25% have used it frequently and 21% have used it extensively. Many respondents are not familiar with this specific feature of calendar application. Table 6.4 displays the data regarding level of usage for creating appointments (scheduling and tracking daily activities).

Table 6.4    Level of usage of creating appointment

| Use of creating appointment | Frequency | Percent |
|---|---|---|
| Not used at all | 47 | 17.1 |
| Used rarely | 41 | 14.9 |
| Used regularly | 61 | 22.2 |
| Used frequently | 68 | 24.7 |
| Used extensively | 58 | 21.1 |
| **Total** | 275 | 100.0 |

## LEVEL OF USAGE OF MEETING REQUEST (INVITING FOR MEETING AND TRACKING RESPONSE)

The data on level of usage for meeting request indicate that only 13% of the respondents use it extensively whereas 17% of the respondents use it frequently. Twenty-eight percent of the respondents use meeting request on a regular basis, 20% of them use it rarely while 22% of the respondents have not used this option at all. The data confirms that at that time a large number (22%) of the respondents did not use this feature. This in itself reflects employees' under-adoption of specific applications of an innovation. Table 6.5 displays data for the respondents.

**Table 6.5      Level of usage of meeting request**

| Use of meeting request | Frequency | Percent |
|---|---|---|
| Not used at all | 60 | 21.8 |
| Used rarely | 54 | 19.6 |
| Used regularly | 77 | 28.0 |
| Used frequently | 47 | 17.1 |
| Used extensively | 35 | 12.7 |
| Total | 273 | 99.3 |
| Missing values | 2 | .7 |
| **Total** | 275 | 100.0 |

## LEVEL OF USAGE OF SHARING CALENDAR (GIVING PERMISSION TO OTHERS TO SEE YOUR CALENDAR)

The data in Table 6.6 below shows that 36% of the respondents indicated they have never used sharing calendar whereas 21% of respondents used it only rarely. The responses showed that 18% of respondents use sharing calendar regularly, 11% of the respondents use it frequently and only 12% of the respondents use it extensively. This information confirms the choice of the subjects as being representative of a population that is using calendar application at different levels. Many still have not adopted the system and use it only rarely.

**Table 6.6     Level of usage of sharing calendar**

| Use of sharing calendar | Frequency | Percent |
|---|---|---|
| Not used at all | 100 | 36.4 |
| Used rarely | 58 | 21.1 |
| Used regularly | 50 | 18.2 |
| Used frequently | 31 | 11.3 |
| Used extensively | 34 | 12.4 |
| Total | 273 | 99.3 |
| Missing values | 2 | .7 |
| **Total** | 275 | 100.0 |

## NUMBER OF DIFFERENT CALENDAR APPLICATIONS (CREATING APPOINTMENT, MEETING REQUEST, SHARING CALENDAR) WORKED WITH OR USED

For the questionnaire item concerning the number of different calendar applications worked with or used, such as creating appointment, meeting request and sharing calendar the responses showed that the majority (55%) of the respondents have used three features. Those who indicated that they used two features constitute 23%, whereas those who used only one feature were 11%. Ten percent have not used different calendar applications. This usage level reflects a more "official" use of the system and thus such information confirms the suitability of the respondents as subjects of a study on the uses of calendar applications. However, a significant number of the employees have never used any calendar features other than the core feature of MS Outlook, which is email. Table 6.7 displays the data for the respondents.

**Table 6.7     Number of different calendar applications have worked with or used**

| Number of different calendar applications | Frequency | Percent |
|---|---|---|
| Nil | 28 | 10.2 |
| One feature | 30 | 10.9 |
| Two features | 64 | 23.3 |
| Three features | 151 | 54.9 |
| Total | 273 | 99.3 |
| Missing values | 2 | .7 |
| **Total** | 275 | 100.0 |

## USE OF SOPHISTICATED ELEMENTS OF CALENDAR (RECURRING APPOINTMENT, SHARING AND PERMISSIONS, IMPORT AND EXPORT TO OTHER APPLICATIONS, ETC.)

Table 6.8 shows that 23% of the respondents have not used the sophisticated elements of calendar such as recurring appointment, sharing and permissions, import and export to other applications, etc., whereas 26% of the respondents only used them rarely. Twenty-nine percent of the respondents used sophisticated elements regularly while 17% used them frequently. A minority (6%) said they have used sophisticated elements extensively. This result shows that nearly one quarter of the employees have never used or do not know how to use sophisticated elements of calendar.

Table 6.8     Use of sophisticated elements of calendar (recurring appointment, sharing and permissions, import and export to other applications, etc.)

| Number of different calendar applications | Frequency | Percent |
|---|---|---|
| Nil | 28 | 10.2 |
| One feature | 30 | 10.9 |
| Two features | 64 | 23.3 |
| Three features | 151 | 54.9 |
| Total | 273 | 99.3 |
| Missing values | 2 | .7 |
| **Total** | 275 | 100.0 |

## 6.4 Cross-tabulations for Level of Usage According to Respondents' Demographic Characteristics

This section provides a cross-tabulation for level of usage measured by frequency, time spent, different applications used, number of application used and the sophisticated element used by respondents' demographic characteristics such as gender, age, division, classification, employment status and qualification. Tables 6.9 to 6.24 summarize the relevant respondent data.

## FREQUENCY OF USE OF CALENDAR BY GENDER

The data in Table 6.9 shows that 17% of the male respondents indicated that they use calendar several times a day whereas 39% female respondents mentioned that they use calendar several times a day. Only 4% of male and 6% female respondents indicated that they use calendar a few times a week. It is indicated that 6% of the male respondents and 7% of the female respondents use calendar once a month or less. The study data indicate that females use calendar more frequently than their male counterparts. Figure 6.1 shows the extent of use in terms of gender.

**Table 6.9    Frequency of use of calendar by gender**

| Gender | | Frequency of use of calendar | | | | | Total |
|---|---|---|---|---|---|---|---|
| | | Once a month or less | A few times a month | A few times a week | About once a day | Several times a day | |
| Male | Count | 17 | 10 | 10 | 16 | 47 | 100 |
| | % of total | 6.2% | 3.6% | 3.6% | 5.8% | 17.1% | 36.4% |
| Female | Count | 19 | 12 | 15 | 23 | 106 | 175 |
| | % of Total | 6.9% | 4.4% | 5.5% | 8.4% | 38.5% | 63.6% |
| Total | Count | 36 | 22 | 25 | 39 | 153 | 275 |
| | % of Total | 13.1% | 8.0% | 9.1% | 14.2% | 55.6% | 100.0% |

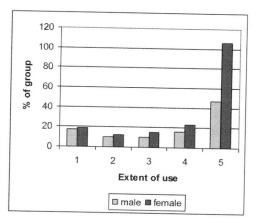

**Figure 6.1    Extent of use by gender**

## AVERAGE TIME SPENT PER WEEK ON USING CALENDAR FOR JOB-RELATED ACTIVITIES BY GENDER

Nearly 21% of female and 17% of male respondents spent an average of less than half an hour per week using calendar. The significance of this information is that while the current level of usage is low the possibility remains that more people will use calendar in the future. Data indicated that only 3% of males and 7% of females spent an average of more than three hours per week using calendar. Table 6.10 displays data for average time spent per week on using calendar according to gender.

**Table 6.10     Average time spent per week on using calendar for job-related activities by gender**

| Gender | | Average time spent per week on using calendar | | | | | Total |
|---|---|---|---|---|---|---|---|
| | | Less than 1/2 hour | From 1/2 hour to 1 hour | 1-2 hours | 2-3 hours | More than 3 hours | |
| Male | Count | 47 | 28 | 10 | 8 | 7 | 100 |
| | % of total | 17.2% | 10.2% | 3.6% | 2.9% | 2.6% | 36.5% |
| Female | Count | 57 | 42 | 40 | 16 | 19 | 174 |
| | % of total | 20.8% | 15.3% | 14.6% | 5.8% | 6.9% | 63.5% |
| Total | Count | 104 | 70 | 50 | 24 | 26 | 274 |
| | % of total | 38.0% | 25.5% | 18.2% | 8.8% | 9.5% | 100.0% |

## USAGE OF NUMBER OF DIFFERENT CALENDAR APPLICATIONS BY GENDER

Data in Table 6.11 shows 39% of the female respondents used three features of calendar, 14% used two features and 6% of them used only one feature. Among the male respondents 17% of them used three features, 9% of them used two features and 5% of them used only one feature. Female employees are more frequent adopters of innovation compared to male employees. Figure 6.2 shows the number of calendar features used according to gender.

Table 6.11    Usage of number of different calendar applications by gender

| Gender | | Usage of number of different applications | | | | Total |
|---|---|---|---|---|---|---|
| | | Nil | One feature | Two features | Three features | |
| Male | Count | 15 | 14 | 25 | 45 | 99 |
| | % of total | 5.5% | 5.1% | 9.2% | 16.5% | 36.3% |
| Female | Count | 13 | 16 | 39 | 106 | 174 |
| | % of total | 4.8% | 5.9% | 14.3% | 38.8% | 63.7% |
| Total | Count | 28 | 30 | 64 | 151 | 273 |
| | % of total | 10.3% | 11.0% | 23.4% | 55.3% | 100.0% |

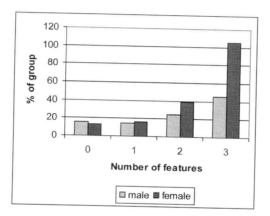

Figure 6.2    Number of calendar features used by gender

## USE OF SOPHISTICATED ELEMENTS OF CALENDAR BY GENDER

When respondents were asked to indicate whether and to what extent they used sophisticated elements of calendar, 12% of female respondents and 11% of male respondents indicated that they have not used them at all. Seventeen percent of the females and 9% of the males pointed out that they used them rarely. Only 2% of male and 4% of female respondents, respectively, indicated that they used sophisticated elements extensively. This result confirms that most employees have not explored the advanced features of calendar and the organization will have to improve and provide better service and/or training in this regard. Table 6.12 displays data for the respondents.

**Table 6.12     Use of sophisticated elements of calendar by gender**

| Gender | | Use of sophisticated elements of calendar | | | | | Total |
|---|---|---|---|---|---|---|---|
| | | Not used at all | Used rarely | Used regularly | Used frequently | Used extensively | |
| Male | Count | 29 | 24 | 29 | 13 | 5 | 100 |
| | % of total | 10.5% | 8.7% | 10.5% | 4.7% | 1.8% | 36.4% |
| Female | Count | 33 | 47 | 51 | 33 | 11 | 175 |
| | % of total | 12.0% | 17.1% | 18.5% | 12.0% | 4.0% | 63.6% |
| Total | Count | 62 | 71 | 80 | 46 | 16 | 275 |
| | % of total | 22.5% | 25.8% | 29.1% | 16.7% | 5.8% | 100.0% |

## FREQUENCY OF USE OF CALENDAR BY DIVISION

The data in Table 6.13 below shows that 16% of the respondents in the Division of Health Science use calendar several times a day while 11% of the respondents in the Division of Business and 11% of the respondents who are not in a division indicated that they also use calendar several times a day. Similarly, 10% of the respondents in the Division of Education, Art and Social Sciences and nearly 7% of the respondents in the Division of IT, Engineering and Environment indicated that they use calendar several times a day. These data indicate that respondents in the Division of Health Science are frequent users of calendar.

**Table 6.13     Frequency of use of calendar by faculty (division)**

| Faculty (division) | | Frequency of use of calendar | | | | | Total |
|---|---|---|---|---|---|---|---|
| | | Once a month or less | A few times a month | A few times a week | About once a day | Several times a day | |
| Business | Count | 9 | 10 | 7 | 9 | 31 | 66 |
| | % of total | 3.3% | 3.6% | 2.5% | 3.3% | 11.3% | 24.0% |
| Education, Arts and SS | Count | 19 | 5 | 7 | 10 | 28 | 69 |
| | % of total | 6.9% | 1.8% | 2.5% | 3.6% | 10.2% | 25.1% |
| HealthScience | Count | 4 | 5 | 6 | 12 | 44 | 71 |
| | % of total | 1.5% | 1.8% | 2.2% | 4.4% | 16.0% | 25.8% |
| IT, Eng. and Environment | Count | 3 | 2 | 3 | 5 | 19 | 32 |
| | % of total | 1.1% | .7% | 1.1% | 1.8% | 6.9% | 11.6% |

| Not in a division | Count | 1 | 0 | 2 | 3 | 31 | 37 |
| | % of total | .4% | .0% | .7% | 1.1% | 11.3% | 13.5% |
| **Total** | Count | 36 | 22 | 25 | 39 | 153 | 275 |
| | % of total | 13.1% | 8.0% | 9.1% | 14.2% | 55.6% | 100.0% |

## AVERAGE TIME SPENT PER WEEK ON USING CALENDAR FOR JOB-RELATED ACTIVITIES BY FACULTY (DIVISION)

It was found that 8% of respondents in the Division of Health Science use calendar from a 1/2 hour–1 hour per week followed by the Divisions of Business (6%), Education, Art and Social Sciences (5%), those not in a division (4%) and then the Division of IT, Engineering and Environment (3%). Only 1% of respondents who are not in a division use calendar less than a 1/2 hour per week (see Table 6.14). The data indicate that people who are not in a division spend more time using calendar, as most of them are administrative staff and they access it more often than academic staff.

**Table 6.14**    Average time spent per week on using calendar for job-related activities by division

| Division | | Average time spent per week on using calendar | | | | | Total |
| | | Less than 1/2 hour | From 1/2 hour to 1 hour | 1-2 hours | 2-3 hours | More than 3 hours | |
| Business | Count | 30 | 16 | 9 | 6 | 4 | 65 |
| | % of total | 10.9% | 5.8% | 3.3% | 2.2% | 1.5% | 23.7% |
| Education, Arts and SS | Count | 36 | 14 | 11 | 4 | 4 | 69 |
| | % of total | 13.1% | 5.1% | 4.0% | 1.5% | 1.5% | 25.2% |
| Health Science | Count | 23 | 21 | 13 | 6 | 8 | 71 |
| | % of total | 8.4% | 7.7% | 4.7% | 2.2% | 2.9% | 25.9% |
| IT, Eng and Environment | Count | 12 | 7 | 7 | 1 | 5 | 32 |
| | % of total | 4.4% | 2.6% | 2.6% | .4% | 1.8% | 11.7% |
| Not in a division | Count | 3 | 12 | 10 | 7 | 5 | 37 |
| | % of total | 1.1% | 4.4% | 3.6% | 2.6% | 1.8% | 13.5% |
| **Total** | Count | 104 | 70 | 50 | 24 | 26 | 274 |
| | % of total | 38.0% | 25.5% | 18.2% | 8.8% | 9.5% | 100.0% |

## USAGE OF NUMBER OF DIFFERENT CALENDAR APPLICATIONS BY DIVISION

The results of the study indicate that nearly 12% of respondents in the Division of Business use three features of calendar while 5% use two features and 4% use only one feature. Likewise 14% of respondents in Health Science use three features, 8% use two features and 2% use only one feature. Respondents who are not in a division (11%) mention that they use three features while Education, Art and Social Sciences (10%) and IT, Engineering and Environment (8%) use three features. Data show that a very small number of respondents use none or only one feature of calendar. These results indicate that the Division of Health Sciences has the highest percentage of using three features followed by Business, employees not in a division, Education, Art and Social Sciences and IT, Engineering and Environment. Table 6.15 displays data for usage of number of different calendar applications by division.

**Table 6.15     Usage of number of different calendar applications by division**

| Division | | Nil | One feature | Two features | Three features | Total |
|---|---|---|---|---|---|---|
| | | **Usage of number of different applications** | | | | **Total** |
| Business | Count | 8 | 12 | 13 | 32 | 65 |
| | % of Total | 2.9% | 4.4% | 4.8% | 11.7% | 23.8% |
| Education, Arts and SS | Count | 13 | 7 | 21 | 28 | 69 |
| | % of Total | 4.8% | 2.6% | 7.7% | 10.3% | 25.3% |
| Health Science | Count | 4 | 6 | 21 | 39 | 70 |
| | % of Total | 1.5% | 2.2% | 7.7% | 14.3% | 25.6% |
| IT, Eng. and Environment | Count | 3 | 3 | 5 | 21 | 32 |
| | % of Total | 1.1% | 1.1% | 1.8% | 7.7% | 11.7% |
| Not in a division | Count | 0 | 2 | 4 | 31 | 37 |
| | % of Total | .0% | .7% | 1.5% | 11.4% | 13.6% |
| Total | Count | 28 | 30 | 64 | 151 | 273 |
| | % of Total | 10.3% | 11.0% | 23.4% | 55.3% | 100.0% |

## USE OF SOPHISTICATED ELEMENTS OF CALENDAR BY DIVISION

Concerning the use of calendar's more sophisticated elements, 8% of the respondents in Education, Art and Social Sciences and 7% of the respondents in Business indicated that they have not used them. Similarly, 4% of the respondents in Health Science and only 3% of respondents in IT, Engineering and Environment mentioned that they have not used these elements (see Table 6.16). These data indicate that the IT division probably can use the sophisticated elements of calendar much better while staff in the Education, Art and Social Sciences division are probably less acquainted with sophisticated elements of calendar. Only 8% of the respondents in Health Science and 7% of the respondents in Business have used them rarely. Data indicated that 6% of the respondents in Education, Art and Social Sciences, 3% of the respondents not in the division and 2% of the respondents in IT, Engineering and Environment have used the sophisticated elements rarely. Three of the disciplines – Health Science, IT, Engineering and Environment and not in the division – indicated (1%) and Business and Education, Art and Social Sciences indicated that less than 1% of the respondents use sophisticated elements extensively. These data show that people in various divisions probably do not know how to use the advanced elements of calendar.

**Table. 6.16    Use of sophisticated elements of calendar by division**

| Division | | Use of sophisticated elements of calendar | | | | | Total |
|---|---|---|---|---|---|---|---|
| | | Not used at all | Used rarely | Used regularly | Used frequently | Used extensively | |
| Business | Count | 20 | 19 | 16 | 9 | 2 | 66 |
| | % of total | 7.3% | 6.9% | 5.8% | 3.3% | .7% | 24.0% |
| Education, Arts and SS | Count | 23 | 16 | 18 | 10 | 2 | 69 |
| | % of total | 8.4% | 5.8% | 6.5% | 3.6% | .7% | 25.1% |
| Health Science | Count | 12 | 21 | 25 | 9 | 4 | 71 |
| | % of total | 4.4% | 7.6% | 9.1% | 3.3% | 1.5% | 25.8% |
| IT, Eng. and Environment | Count | 7 | 6 | 6 | 9 | 4 | 32 |
| | % of total | 2.5% | 2.2% | 2.2% | 3.3% | 1.5% | 11.6% |
| Not in a division | Count | 0 | 9 | 15 | 9 | 4 | 37 |
| | % of Total | .0% | 3.3% | 5.5% | 3.3% | 1.5% | 13.5% |
| Total | Count | 62 | 71 | 80 | 46 | 16 | 275 |
| | % of Total | 22.5% | 25.8% | 29.1% | 16.7% | 5.8% | 100.0% |

## FREQUENCY OF USE OF CALENDAR BY ACADEMIC AND PROFESSIONAL STAFF

Data in Table 6.17 show that 12% of the academic respondents indicated they use calendar once a month or less. In contrast less than 1% of professional respondents mentioned that they use calendar once a month or less. Results indicate that 28% of the respondents in both academic and administrative staff use calendar several times a day. These data show that both academic and administrative staff use calendar to a moderate extent. However, data indicate that some of the academic employees use it less frequently than professional staff. This is probably because of the nature of job requirements and timing of the year, as academic staff have longer semester breaks compared to administrative staff. Figure 6.3 shows extent of use by academic and professional staff.

**Table 6.17**   **Frequency of use of calendar by academic and administrative staff**

| Classify | | Once a month or less | A few times a month | A few times a week | About once a day | Several times a day | Total |
|---|---|---|---|---|---|---|---|
| | | **Frequency of use of calendar** | | | | | **Total** |
| Academic staff | Count | 34 | 21 | 20 | 26 | 76 | 177 |
| | % of total | 12.5% | 7.7% | 7.4% | 9.6% | 28.0% | 65.3% |
| Professional staff | Count | 1 | 1 | 4 | 12 | 76 | 94 |
| | % of total | .4% | .4% | 1.5% | 4.4% | 28.0% | 34.7% |
| **Total** | Count | 35 | 22 | 24 | 38 | 152 | 271 |
| | % of total | 12.9% | 8.1% | 8.9% | 14.0% | 56.1% | 100.0% |

## AVERAGE TIME SPENT PER WEEK ON USING CALENDAR FOR JOB-RELATED ACTIVITIES BY ACADEMIC AND ADMINISTRATIVE STAFF

According to Table 6.18 about one-third (33%) of the academic staff spent an average of less than a 1/2 hour per week using calendar while only 5% of professional staff use it an average of less than a 1/2 hour per week. Data indicate that 4% of the academic staff and 5% of the professional staff use calendar an average of more than 3 hours per week. The results show that about 8% of the academic staff and about 11% of administrative staff use calendar an average of 1–2 hours per week. It makes sense that administrative staff use calendar more than academic staff.

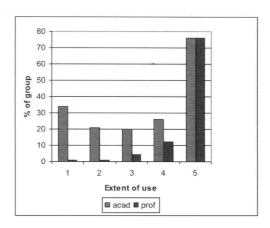

**Figure 6.3    Extent of use by academic and professional staff**

**Table 6.18    Average time spent per week on using calendar for job-related activities by academic and administrative staff**

| Classify | | Average time spent per week on using calendar | | | | | Total |
|---|---|---|---|---|---|---|---|
| | | Less than 1/2 hour | From 1/2 hour to 1 hour | 1-2 hours | 2-3 hours | More than 3 hours | |
| Academic staff | Count | 88 | 44 | 21 | 12 | 12 | 177 |
| | % of total | 32.6% | 16.3% | 7.8% | 4.4% | 4.4% | 65.6% |
| Professional staff | Count | 14 | 25 | 29 | 11 | 14 | 93 |
| | % of total | 5.2% | 9.3% | 10.7% | 4.1% | 5.2% | 34.4% |
| Total | Count | 102 | 69 | 50 | 23 | 26 | 270 |
| | % of total | 37.8% | 25.6% | 18.5% | 8.5% | 9.6% | 100.0% |

## USAGE OF NUMBER OF DIFFERENT CALENDAR APPLICATIONS BY ACADEMIC AND ADMINISTRATIVE STAFF

Data in Table 6.19 indicates that 29% of administrative respondents and 27% of academic respondents use three features of calendar. Among the academic staff 10% use one feature while 18% use two features. Less than 1% of administrative staff use one feature of calendar and 6% use two features. Results show that most administrative staff members use more features of calendar compared to academic personnel. Figure 6.4 shows the differences between academic and administrative staff in terms of numbers of features used.

Table 6.19      Usage of number of different calendar applications by
                academic and administrative staff

| Classify | | Usage of number of different applications | | | | Total |
|---|---|---|---|---|---|---|
| | | Nil | One feature | Two features | Three features | |
| Academic staff | Count | 27 | 28 | 48 | 72 | 175 |
| | % of Total | 10.0% | 10.4% | 17.8% | 26.8% | 65.1% |
| Professional staff | Count | 0 | 1 | 16 | 77 | 94 |
| | % of Total | .0% | .4% | 5.9% | 28.6% | 34.9% |
| Total | Count | 27 | 29 | 64 | 149 | 269 |
| | % of Total | 10.0% | 10.8% | 23.8% | 55.4% | 100.0% |

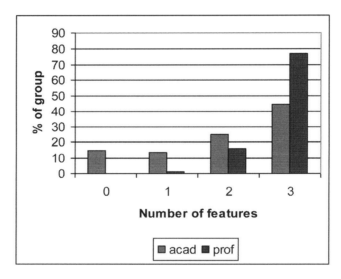

Figure 6.4      Number of features used by academic and administrative
                staff

## USE OF SOPHISTICATED ELEMENTS OF CALENDAR BY ACADEMIC
## AND ADMINISTRATIVE STAFF

When respondents were asked to indicate whether and to what extent they
used sophisticated elements of calendar, 21% of academic and only 1% of
professional respondents indicated that they have not used them at all.

Data in Table 6.20 show that 6% of the academic staff and 11% of the professional staff used sophisticated elements frequently. Only 4% of the academic staff and 2% of the professional staff have used sophisticated elements extensively. The results show that many academic staff have not used sophisticated elements of calendar while professional staff are frequent users, although an insignificant number of staff (2%) used sophisticated elements extensively.

**Table 6.20    Use of sophisticated elements of calendar by academic and administrative staff**

| Classify | | Use of sophisticated elements of calendar | | | | | Total |
|---|---|---|---|---|---|---|---|
| | | Not used at all | Used rarely | Used regularly | Used frequently | Used extensively | |
| Academic staff | Count | 56 | 48 | 46 | 17 | 10 | 177 |
| | % of total | 20.7% | 17.7% | 17.0% | 6.3% | 3.7% | 65.3% |
| Professional staff | Count | 4 | 22 | 33 | 29 | 6 | 94 |
| | % of total | 1.5% | 8.1% | 12.2% | 10.7% | 2.2% | 34.7% |
| Total | Count | 60 | 70 | 79 | 46 | 16 | 271 |
| | % of total | 22.1% | 25.8% | 29.2% | 17.0% | 5.9% | 100.0% |

## FREQUENCY OF USE OF CALENDAR BY FULL-TIME AND PART-TIME EMPLOYEES

Virtually half (49%) of the full-time employee respondents indicated that they use calendar several time a day while only 7% of the part-time employee respondents indicated that they use calendar several time a day. Data showed that 11% of full-time employee and 3% of part-time employee respondents indicated that they use calendar about once a day. The study indicated that 7% of the full-time employee respondents and 6% of the part-time employee respondents use calendar once a month or less. This data indicate that full-time staff have more commitment to the university and they use calendar more compared to part-time staff who have less obligation to the university activities. Table 6.21 shows data for frequency of use of calendar by full-time and part-time employees.

Table 6.21     Frequency of use of calendar by full-time and part-time employees

| Employed as | | Frequency of use of calendar | | | | | Total |
|---|---|---|---|---|---|---|---|
| | | Once a month or less | A few times a month | A few times a week | About once a day | Several times a day | |
| Full-time | Count | 19 | 10 | 19 | 31 | 134 | 213 |
| | % of total | 6.9% | 3.6% | 6.9% | 11.3% | 48.9% | 77.7% |
| Part-time | Count | 16 | 12 | 6 | 8 | 19 | 61 |
| | % of total | 5.8% | 4.4% | 2.2% | 2.9% | 6.9% | 22.3% |
| Total | Count | 35 | 22 | 25 | 39 | 153 | 274 |
| | % of total | 12.8% | 8.0% | 9.1% | 14.2% | 55.8% | 100.0% |

## AVERAGE TIME SPENT PER WEEK ON USING CALENDAR FOR JOB-RELATED ACTIVITIES BY FULL-TIME AND PART-TIME EMPLOYEES

To assess the impact of employment status on usage level, respondents were asked the average amount of time spent per week on using calendar for job-related activities. Interestingly, 15% of the full-time employee respondents indicated that they use calendar 1–2 hours per week whereas only 3% of the part-time respondents indicated that they use calendar 1–2 hours per week for job-related activities. Nineteen percent of the full-time employee respondents and 6% of the part-time employee respondents spent an average of from 1/2–1 hour per week using calendar. Data in Table 6.22 indicates higher time spent with calendar by full-time employees.

Table 6.22     Average time spent per week on using calendar for job-related activities by full-time and part-time employees

| Employed as | | Average time spent per week on using calendar | | | | | Total |
|---|---|---|---|---|---|---|---|
| | | Less than 1/2 hour | From 1/2 hour to 1 hour | 1-2 hours | 2-3 hours | More than 3 hours | |
| Full-time | Count | 69 | 53 | 43 | 22 | 25 | 212 |
| | % of total | 25.3% | 19.4% | 15.8% | 8.1% | 9.2% | 77.7% |
| Part-time | Count | 34 | 17 | 7 | 2 | 1 | 61 |
| | % of total | 12.5% | 6.2% | 2.6% | .7% | .4% | 22.3% |
| Total | Count | 103 | 70 | 50 | 24 | 26 | 273 |
| | % of total | 37.7% | 25.6% | 18.3% | 8.8% | 9.5% | 100.0% |

## USAGE OF NUMBER OF DIFFERENT CALENDAR APPLICATIONS BY FULL-TIME AND PART-TIME EMPLOYEES

The result of the study indicated that 50% of the full-time employees use three features of calendar compared to 6% of part-time employees who use three features of calendar. Among the full-time employees 16% of them use two features and 6% use one feature while 7% of part-time employees use two features and 5% use one feature. Data indicate that full-time employees uses more calendar applications compared to part-time employees. Table 6.23 displays data for the respondents.

**Table 6.23    Usage of number of different calendar applications by full-time and part-time employees**

| Employed as | | Usage of number of different applications | | | | Total |
|---|---|---|---|---|---|---|
| | | Nil | One feature | Two features | Three features | |
| Full-time | Count | 16 | 16 | 44 | 136 | 212 |
| | % of total | 5.9% | 5.9% | 16.2% | 50.0% | 77.9% |
| Part-time | Count | 11 | 14 | 20 | 15 | 60 |
| | % of total | 4.0% | 5.1% | 7.4% | 5.5% | 22.1% |
| **Total** | Count | 27 | 30 | 64 | 151 | 272 |
| | % of total | 9.9% | 11.0% | 23.5% | 55.5% | 100.0% |

## USE OF SOPHISTICATED ELEMENTS OF CALENDAR BY FULL-TIME AND PART-TIME EMPLOYEES

In a question that asked respondents to indicate whether and to what extent they used sophisticated elements of calendar, 19% of the full-time employees and only 7% of the part-time employees indicated that they rarely used calendar's sophisticated elements. The results show that 25% of the full-time employees and 4% of the part-time employees used them regularly. Only 5% of the full-time employees and 1% of the part-time employees have used sophisticated elements extensively (see Table 6.24). Data shows that full-time employees used more sophisticated elements compared to part-time employees.

**Table 6.24     Use of sophisticated elements of calendar by full-time and part-time employees**

| Employed as | | Use of sophisticated elements of calendar | | | | | Total |
|---|---|---|---|---|---|---|---|
| | | Not used at all | Used rarely | Used regularly | Used frequently | Used extensively | |
| Full-time | Count | 37 | 52 | 68 | 43 | 13 | 213 |
| | % of total | 13.5% | 19.0% | 24.8% | 15.7% | 4.7% | 77.7% |
| Part-time | Count | 24 | 19 | 12 | 3 | 3 | 61 |
| | % of total | 8.8% | 6.9% | 4.4% | 1.1% | 1.1% | 22.3% |
| Total | Count | 61 | 71 | 80 | 46 | 16 | 274 |
| | % of total | 22.3% | 25.9% | 29.2% | 16.8% | 5.8% | 100.0% |

## 6.5 Inter-correlations Among Study Variables

The study set out to determine what relationships exist between two or more variables in the advanced model. A correlation is a measure of the linear relationship between variables. A Pearson correlation analysis (measure of the strength of relationship between two variables) was conducted to discover the relationships among the study variables. The correlations among all research variables are presented in Table 6.25. Pearson's correlation coefficients ($r$) of the variables were significant at level of 0.01. From the Pearson's $r$ analysis, the correlation matrix table shows that there is a significant, positive correlation between dependent and independent variables. The table shows that usage is significantly and positively related to three organizational variables: training ($r = 0.196$, $p < 0.01$), managerial support ($r = 0.475$, $p < 0.01$) and incentives ($r = 0.624$, $p < 0.01$). The data also show that the level of adoption or usage is significant and positively related to five individual or personal factors: perceived usefulness ($r = 0.658$, $p < 0.01$), personal innovativeness ($r = 0.331$, $p < 0.01$), prior experience ($r = 0.279$, $p < 0.01$), image ($r = 0.528$, $p < 0.01$) and enjoyment with innovation ($r = 0.546$, $p < 0.01$). The analysis demonstrates that usage is also significant and positively related to two social factors: peers ($r = 0.215$, $p < 0.01$) and social network ($r = 0.367$, $p < 0.01$). There is also a strong positive correlation between attitude and usage ($r = 0.727$, $p < 0.01$). Table 5.25 shows that correlations among dependent and independent variables ranged from $r = 0.196$ to $r = 0.658$ and correlations among all variables ranged from $r = 0.053$ to $r = 0.809$, indicating no multicollinearity problems among the variables. "The simplest and most obvious means of identifying collinearity is an examination of the correlation matrix for the independent variables and the presence of high correlations (generally .90 and above) is the first indication of substantial collinearity" (Hair, Anderson, Tatham & Black, 1998, p.191).

## RELATIONSHIP BETWEEN USAGE AND OTHER VARIABLES

Testing for linearity is based on co-relational measures of association. Correlations represent linear associations between variables. It is important to examine all relationships in order to identify any departures from linearity that may impact on correlation. The most common way to assess linearity is to examine scatterplots of the variables and to identify any non-linear patterns in the data. Scatterplots show that there are linear relationships between dependent and independent variables. Figure 6.5 illustrates that there are clear linear relationships between: usage and managerial support; usage and incentive; usage and perceived usefulness; usage and image and usage and enjoyment with innovation. However, relationships between usage and training, usage and personal innovativeness, usage and prior experience, usage and peers and usage and social network are not very clear. Although the linear relationships are in some cases not very clear, there was no evidence that supported non-linear relationships. Table 6.25 shows the strength of the relationship. There is also a strong linear association between usage and attitude. This result suggests that individual employees' level of use is also influenced by their attitude toward innovation adoption and usage.

## 6.6 Reliability and Validity of the Instruments

A reliability test was performed to determine the internal consistency of the instruments. The reliability coefficient in the form of Cronbach's alpha for dependent and independent variables is presented. Table 6.26 presents means, standard deviations and reliability coefficients for all independent and dependent variables, for which the reliability scores range from 0.70 to 0.96. The scales show good reliability with Cronbach's alpha greater than 0.70. The higher reliability range indicates the collected data maintains a high internal consistency. As Hair, Anderson, Tatham and Black (1998, p.118) state, "the diagnostic measure is the reliability coefficient that assesses the consistency of the entire scale, with Cronbach's alpha being the most widely used measure." They claimed "the generally agreed upon lower limit for Cronbach's alpha is .70, although it may decrease to .60 in exploratory

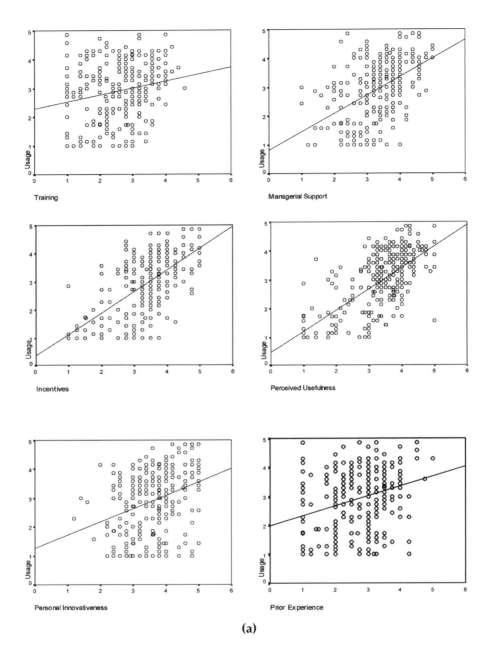

(a)

**Figure 6.5(a) and (b)    Relationship between usage with other variables**

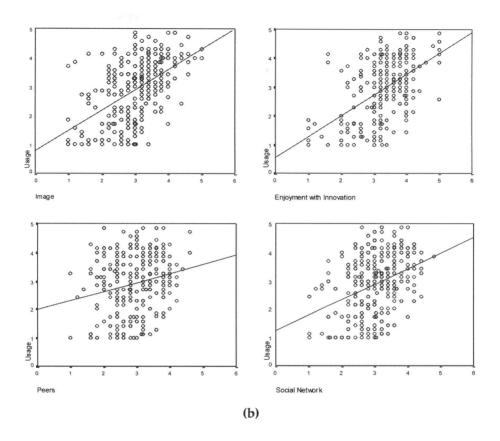

**(b)**

research" (Hair, Anderson, Tatham & Black, 1998, p.118). According to DeVellis (2003) reliability values between 0.70 and 0.80 are considered "respectable" while reliability values between 0.80 and 0.90 are considered "very good." When all of the reliability scores for the independent and dependent variables exceed 0.70, the instruments are regarded as reliable in measuring an individual's adoption of innovation across independent variables. Data shows that instruments have strong reliability. These instruments have been used to collect data for measuring the proposed advanced model of innovation adoption.

Table 6.25    Inter-correlations among study variables

| Study variables | Usage | Train. | Man. | Incent. | Useful. | Innov. | Exper. | Image | Enjoy. | Peers | Social. |
|---|---|---|---|---|---|---|---|---|---|---|---|
| 1. Usage | 1 | | | | | | | | | | |
| 2. Training | .196** | 1 | | | | | | | | | |
| 3.Managerial support | .475** | .569** | 1 | | | | | | | | |
| 4. Incentive | .624** | .191** | .423** | 1 | | | | | | | |
| 5. Usefulness | .658** | .253** | .424** | .809** | 1 | | | | | | |
| 6. Innovativeness | .331** | .053 | .059 | .289** | .313** | 1 | | | | | |
| 7. Experience | .279** | .229** | .157** | .318** | .332** | .348** | 1 | | | | |
| 8. Image | .528** | .352** | .504** | .627** | .622** | .230** | .290** | 1 | | | |
| 9. Enjoyment | .546** | .230** | .360** | .726** | .707** | .255** | .274*** | .616** | 1 | | |
| 10. Peers | .215** | .259** | .385** | .331** | .300** | -.066 | .104 | .359** | .333** | 1 | |
| 11. Social net | .367** | .326** | .496** | .471** | .438** | .055 | .281** | .596** | .458** | .547** | 1 |

**Table 6.26    Variable means, standard deviations and scale reliability**

| Variables | Mean | SD | Cronbach's alpha |
|---|---|---|---|
| **Organizational factors** | | | |
| Training | 2.59 | .86 | .88 |
| Managerial support | 3.28 | .79 | .82 |
| Incentive | 3.33 | .86 | .82 |
| | | | |
| **Individual factors** | | | |
| Perceived usefulness | 3.31 | .94 | .96 |
| Personal innovativeness | 3.62 | .76 | .85 |
| Prior experience | 2.69 | .87 | .70 |
| Image | 3.02 | .79 | .86 |
| Enjoyment with innovation | 3.26 | .79 | .92 |
| | | | |
| **Social influence** | | | |
| Peers | 2.89 | .70 | .76 |
| Social network | 3.03 | .71 | .75 |
| | | | |
| **Usage (Dependent variable)** | 2.91 | 1.06 | .91 |

## TEST FOR MULTICOLLINEARITY

Collinearity was tested before conducting regression analysis and finding the regression model, by examining the collinearity statistics – the variance inflation factor (VIF) and the tolerance level. "Collinearity is the expression of the relationship between two (collinearity) or more (multicollinearity) independent variables. Multicollinearity occurs when any single independent variable is highly correlated with a set of other independent variables" (Hair, Anderson, Tatham & Black, 1998, p.143). Furthermore, "Tolerance is the amount of variability of the selected independent variable not explained by the other independent variables. Thus very small tolerance values (and thus large VIF values because VIF = 1/tolerance) denote high collinearity" (Hair, Anderson, Tatham & Black, 1998, p.193). As a rule of thumb, if the tolerance level is less than 0.10, then there is a problem of multicollinearity or when the tolerance level is more than 0.10 then there is no multicollinearity problem. If the VIF of a variable exceeds 10, that variable is said to be highly collinear and will pose a problem for regression analysis (Hair, Anderson, Tatham & Black, 1998, p.193). Although several variables showed significant correlations, their tolerance values ranged from 0.276 to 0.789 and VIF values ranged from only 1.268 to

3.628, indicating that multicollinearity is not likely a threat to the parameter estimates in this study. Table 6.27 shows the collinearity statistics.

**Table 6.27    Test for multicollinearity**

|  | Unstandardized coefficients | | Standardized coefficients | t | Sig. | Collinearity statistics | |
|---|---|---|---|---|---|---|---|
|  | B | Std. error | Beta (β) |  |  | Tolerance | VIF |
| Training | -.149 | .065 | -.122 | -2.304 | .022 | .630 | 1.587 |
| Managerial support | .401 | .080 | .299 | 5.035 | .000 | .504 | 1.984 |
| Incentive | .158 | .098 | .129 | 1.602 | .110 | .276 | 3.628 |
| Usefulness | .367 | .087 | .327 | 4.213 | .000 | .295 | 3.386 |
| Innovativeness | .180 | .066 | .130 | 2.738 | .007 | .789 | 1.268 |
| Experience | .039 | .058 | .032 | .662 | .508 | .764 | 1.309 |
| Image | .102 | .086 | .077 | 1.186 | .237 | .422 | 2.368 |
| Enjoyment | .100 | .089 | .075 | 1.129 | .260 | .398 | 2.513 |
| Peers | -.072 | .078 | -.048 | -.924 | .357 | .659 | 1.518 |
| Social Net | -.022 | .091 | -.015 | -.245 | .807 | .477 | 2.094 |

## TEST FOR OUTLIERS

Both univariate and multivariate outliers have been checked. For the univariate outliers, Z-scores for individuals of each variable were checked to see if the score is less than -3.00 or greater than +3.00, which needs to be deleted. For the multivariate outliers, Mahalanobis distance scores (measure the influence of a case by examining the distance of cases from the mean of predictor variables) for individuals have been checked. Scores in excess of the critical value (determined by Chi-squire critical value at p<0.001, where df = number of variables) need to be deleted. Both results show that there is no significant problem of outliers.

## 6.7 Multiple Regressions with Usage as Dependent Variable

The researcher is interested in more accurately predicting the level of innovation to be used by individual employees in an organization. This would enable the development of a theoretical construct that brings individual innovation adoption issues into a coherent model; a model that improves theoretical foundations, promotes management awareness, understanding and support in innovation adoption. To this end, a multiple regression analysis provided an objective means of assessing the predictive power of a set of independent variables. In the procedure each independent variable was weighted by the regression analysis to ensure maximum prediction from the set of independent variables. The weights denote the relative contribution of the independent variables and facilitate interpretation as to the influence of each variable in the model.

To apply regression procedures usage level is considered to be a dependent variable that is predicted by independent variables representing the perception of individual employees in an organizational context. The following ten variables were classified as independent variables: training, managerial support, incentive, perceived usefulness, personal innovativeness, image, prior experience, enjoyment with innovation, peers and social network. The sample of 275 observations meets the proposed guideline for the ratio of observations to independent variables with a ratio of fifteen to one (Hair, Anderson, Tatham & Black, 1998, p.166). This ensures that the sample will not be in danger of overfitting the results and helps to validate the results to ensure the findings' generalizability to the entire population in the study.

When meeting the assumptions of regression analysis it is essential to ensure that the result obtained will be truly representative of the sample and the analysis obtained is the best result possible. The data were tested to see if there are any serious violations of the assumptions that could be detected and corrected. Several assumptions addressed for the variables are linearity, outliers, normality, multicollinearity, homoscedasticity/heteroscedasticity and independence of residuals. For linearity, scatterplots of the individual variables did not indicate any non-linear relationships between the dependent and independent variables. The test for multicollinearity shows that there is no problem with multicollinearity. Furthermore, multicollinearity, normality and homoscedasticity were tested during regression analysis.

## ESTIMATION OF THE REGRESSION MODEL AND ASSESSMENT OF OVERALL MODEL FIT

The following section deals with the regression model and overall assessment of the model fit. With the regression analysis specified in terms of dependent and independent variables, the sample is regarded as adequate and the assumptions for the individual variables are met. Now the model building process will proceed to an estimation of the regression model and assessment of the overall model fit. From the regression analysis we can see descriptive statistics in Table 6.28, which tell us the mean and standard deviation of each variable in our data set. This table is not necessary for interpreting the regression model but it is a useful summary of the data.

**Table 6.28     Descriptive statistics**

|                    | Mean   | Std. deviation | N   |
|--------------------|--------|----------------|-----|
| Training           | 2.5921 | .86890         | 275 |
| Managerial support | 3.2863 | .79018         | 275 |
| Incentive          | 3.3331 | .86441         | 275 |
| Usefulness         | 3.3165 | .94480         | 275 |
| Innovativeness     | 3.6207 | .76743         | 275 |
| Experience         | 2.6974 | .87430         | 275 |
| Image              | 3.0235 | .79591         | 275 |
| Enjoyment          | 3.2629 | .79748         | 275 |
| Peers              | 2.8984 | .70875         | 275 |
| Social Net         | 3.0321 | .71307         | 275 |
| Usage              | 2.9107 | 1.06032        | 275 |

The following output describes the overall model and provides very important information about the model: the values of R, $R^2$ and the adjusted $R^2$. In the column labeled R are values of multiple correlation coefficients between the predictor and the outcome. R square ($R^2$) is the correlation coefficient squired ($0.729^2 = 0.531$) also referred to as the coefficient of determination. This value indicates the percentage of total variation of Y (dependent variable) that is explained by the independent variables or predictor variables. In this case, 53.1% of the variance in usage or the individual acceptance can be explained by training, managerial support, incentive, perceived usefulness, personal innovativeness, image, prior experience, enjoyment with innovation, peers and social network variables. Cohen (1988) suggests that an $R^2$ of 0.15 indicates moderate variance and an $R^2$ of 0.35 indicates a large amount of variance explained (as cited in Ahuja & Thatcher, 2005, p.450). The standard error of the estimate is another measure of the predictions' accuracy. It represents an estimate of the standard deviation of the actual dependent values around the regression line. It is a measure of variation around the regression line. Finally, the last column shows Durbin-Watson statistics, which inform us there is no problem regarding autocorrelation. As a rule of thumb, values less than 1 or greater than 3 are definitely cause for concern (Field, 2005, p.189) and for these data the value is 1.627, so the assumption has been met. Table 6.29 summarizes the regression model.

**Table 6.29   Regression model summary**

| R | R Square | Adjusted R square | Std. error of the estimate | Durbin-Watson |
|---|---|---|---|---|
| .729 | .531 | .515 | .73831 | 1.627 |

The next part of the output contains an analysis of variance (ANOVA) that tests whether the model is significantly predicting the outcome. Specifically the F-test represents the contribution to prediction accuracy as a result of fitting the model relative to the inaccuracy that still exists in the model. The output explains the value of the sum of squires for the model (SSm) that represents the improvement in prediction resulting from fitting a regression line to the data rather than using the mean as an estimate of the outcome. The model is a significantly better predictor of dependent variable than intercept alone: $F_{(10, 264)} = 29.912$, $p<0.001$. From the data it can be concluded that the model is highly significant ($p<0.001$) in predicting the outcome variable. Table 6.30 shows results of ANOVA tests.

**Table 6.30   ANOVA**

| | Sum of squares | df | Mean square | F | Significance |
|---|---|---|---|---|---|
| Regression | 163.631 | 10 | 16.363 | 29.912 | .000 |
| Residual | 144.421 | 264 | .547 | | |
| Total | 308.052 | 274 | | | |

Table 6.31 below (coefficients) indicates B-values (unstandardized coefficient) and constant for regression equation and significance of each independent variable in the model predicting the dependent variable. Unstandardized

coefficient B-values indicate the individual contribution of each predictor to the model. If the significant B-values are replaced into the equation

$(Y = b_0 + b_1X_1 + b_2X_2 + b_3X_3 \ldots\ldots + b_{10}X_{10})$, then the empirical model can be written as:

$$U = b_0 + b_1TR + b_2MS + b_3IN + b_4PU + b_5PI + b_6PE + b_7IM + b_8EI + b_9PR + b_{10}SN$$

Where:

U = Usage                          PE = Prior experience
TR = Training                      IM = Image
MS = Managerial support            EI = Enjoyment with innovation
IN = Incentives                    PR = Peers
PU = Perceived usefulness          SN = Social network
PI = Personal innovativeness

**Table 6.31     Coefficients**

| Variables | Unstandardized coefficients | | Standardized coefficients | t | Sig. |
|---|---|---|---|---|---|
| | B | Std. error | Beta (β) | | |
| (Constant) | -.879 | .320 | | -2.744 | .006 |
| Training | -.149 | .065 | -.122 | -2.304 | .022 |
| Managerial sup | .401 | .080 | .299 | 5.035 | .000 |
| Incentive | .158 | .098 | .129 | 1.602 | .110 |
| Usefulness | .367 | .087 | .327 | 4.213 | .000 |
| Innovativeness | .180 | .066 | .130 | 2.738 | .007 |
| Experience | .039 | .058 | .032 | .662 | .508 |
| Image | .102 | .086 | .077 | 1.186 | .237 |
| Enjoyment | .100 | .089 | .075 | 1.129 | .260 |
| Peers | -.072 | .078 | -.048 | -.924 | .357 |
| Social Network | -.022 | .091 | -.015 | -.245 | .807 |

The variables whose impact on usage is statistically significant are: training, managerial support, perceived usefulness and personal innovativeness. Incentives and enjoyment with innovation are not significant variables in the first stage of analysis. However if enjoyment with innovation is taken away from the analysis, as it is not a significant and is highly related with incentives

($r = 0.726$, $p<0.01$) then incentives becomes significant and $R^2$ remains almost unchanged ($R^2 = 0.529$).

The relevance of "incentives" as they influence behavior deserves further attention. There is a hierarchy and progressive stages of statistical analysis that emanate from descriptive statistics through to correlation and then to multiple regressions. While descriptive statistics are used to summarize the data either numerically or graphically to describe features of the sample, correlation analysis measures the degree to which two variables are linearly related. On the other hand, multiple regression analysis aims to find a linear relationship between a dependent variable and several possible predictor variables. Such analysis takes into account several predictive variables simultaneously, thus modeling the property more accurately (Field, 2005).

In the initial correlation analysis, "incentives" shows a positive and significant relationship with usage. The researcher wanted to conduct higher-level statistical analysis in regards to incentives and other variables. The multiple regression analysis shows that "incentives" was not significant. Further analysis indicated that this was due to a close relationship between the two factors "incentives" and "enjoyment with innovation." Although the standard measure of collinearity showed that they did not meet the 0.9 level needed to demonstrate collinearity, the correlation between them of 0.7 indicates a degree of consistency (Hair, Anderson, Tatham & Black, 1998, p.191).

Stepwise regression provided a method of further examining this relationship, as it allows independent variables to be added to the model one by one until the addition of further variables causes the confidence level of the model to fall below 95% (0.05 significance level). That stepwise analysis shows that "incentives" is among the five independent variables included in the model.

The initial correlation analysis and the stepwise regression support the conclusion that "incentives" is significant, even though some analyses show "incentives" is not significant.

The unstandardized coefficient B-values show the relationship between adoption and each predictor. If the value is positive we can tell that there is a positive relationship between the predictor and the outcome whereas a negative coefficient represents a negative relationship. For these data three significant predictors have positive B-values indicating positive relationships and one has negative B-values indicating negative relationships. Therefore, as the managerial support increases, the individual adoption increases; as the individual perceived usefulness increases, so does usage. As individual innovativeness increases the usage level also increases; as incentive increases the level of usage also increases. Training has a negative relationship. However, from the correlation matrix it can be seen that training is positively correlated with usage ($r = +0.196$, $p<0.01$). The training factor in personal interviews will be discussed in a later section.

The unstandardized coefficient B-values also tell us to what degree each predictor affects the outcome if the effects of all other predictors are held constant.

Training ($B = -0.149$): This value indicates that as training increases by one unit, individual adoption is negatively affected by 0.149 units. This interpretation is true only if the effects of all other predictors are held constant. However, training is positively correlated with usage ($r = +0.196$) at significant level of 0.01. Further discussion will be provided in in the chapter discussing qualitative analysis.

Managerial Support ($B = 0.401$): This value indicates that as managerial support increases by one unit, individual adoption increases by 0.401 units. This interpretation is true only if the effects of all other predictors are held constant.

Incentives ($B = 0.192$): This value indicates that as incentives increases by one unit, the individual usage level also increase by 0.192 units. Incentives positively influence the adoption and usage by individual employees. This interpretation is true only if the effects of all other predictors are held constant.

Perceived usefulness ($B = 0.367$): This value indicates that as the perceived usefulness increases by one unit, the individual usage level increases by 0.367 units. Perceived usefulness by individual employees is associated with the increase of innovation usage. This interpretation is true only if the effects of all other predictors are held constant.

Personal innovativeness ($B = 0.180$): This value indicates that as personal innovativeness increased by one unit, the individual usage level increases by 0.180 units. The willingness of an individual to experiment with innovation increases the rate of adoption. This interpretation is true only if the effects of all other predictors are held constant.

Each of these B-values has an associated standard error indicating to what extent these values would vary across different samples and these standard errors are used to determine whether or not the B-values differ significantly from zero. A t-statistic can be derived that tests whether a B-value is significantly different from zero. In this case, as in multiple regression analysis, the t-test measures whether the predictor is making a significant contribution to the model. Therefore, if the t-test associated with a B-value is significant then the predictor is making a significant contribution to the model. The smaller the value of significance (and the larger the value of t), the greater the contribution of the predictor. For this model, training (t (275) = -2.304, p<0.022); managerial support (t (275) = 5.035, P<0.001); incentives (t (275) = 2.041, p<0.042); perceived usefulness (t (275) = 4.213, p<0.001); and personal innovativeness (t (275) = 2.738, p<0.007) are all significant predictors of individual acceptance of innovation.

In addition to providing a basis for predicting individual usage level, the regression coefficients also provide a means of assessing the relative importance of individual variables in the overall prediction of individual usage. The beta coefficients ($\beta$) are used to compare the variables. From the magnitude of the beta-statistics we can see the perceived usefulness has a higher impact, followed by managerial support, incentives, personal innovativeness and training. However, training has the lowest impact on the contributing variables. It emerges that usefulness is a more important factor followed by managerial support, incentives and personal innovativeness. Training has the lowest importance. The weight of the predictors is shown in the standardized beta value. Higher beta values indicate more importance and lower beta values indicate the predictors' low importance.

## ASSESSING THE ASSUMPTION OF NO MULTICOLLINEARITY

The assumption of multicollinearity is not violated as tolerance values are greater than 0.10 and VIF (variance inflation factor) values are less than 10. Multicollinearity is a concern when tolerance values are less than 0.10 or the VIF values are greater than 10 (Hair, Anderson, Tatham & Black, 1998, p.193). Table 6.32 displays collinearity statistics below.

**Table 6.32    Collinearity statistics**

| Collinearity statistics | | |
|---|---|---|
| **Variables** | **Tolerance** | **VIF** |
| Training | .630 | 1.587 |
| Managerial support | .504 | 1.984 |
| Incentive | .276 | 3.628 |
| Usefulness | .295 | 3.386 |
| Innovativeness | .789 | 1.268 |
| Experience | .764 | 1.309 |
| Image | .422 | 2.368 |
| Enjoyment | .398 | 2.513 |
| Peers | .659 | 1.518 |
| Social Network | .477 | 2.094 |

## CHECKING ASSUMPTIONS

In the final stage of the analysis, the assumptions of the model need to be checked. The statistical results identified that there is: no problem regarding outliers; no problem with multicollinearity and Durbin-Watson statistics prove that no autocorrelation exists. The researcher investigated the plot of *ZRESID (standardized residuals) against *ZPRED (standardized predicted values); the histogram and the normal probability plot of the residuals. The scatterplots show relationships between predicted values of dependent variables and residuals. This plot allows testing of linearity and homoscedasticity of residuals assumptions to occur. The graph of *ZRESID against *ZPRED should look like a random array of dots evenly dispersed around zero. If this graph funnels out, the chances are that there is heteroscedasticity in the data. If there is any sort of curve in this graph then the chances are that the data has broken the assumption of linearity. Figure 6.6 shows the plot of standardized residuals against standardized predicted values. The points are randomly and evenly dispersed throughout the plot. Most of the points are evenly dispersed around zero. There is no clear relationship between residuals and predicted values so linearity is evident. It also seems not to have violated the assumption of homoscedasticity, although there are few residuals around the plots. The points do not form the shape of a funnel and there is no curvilinear relationship in the plots. This pattern is indicative of a situation in which the assumptions of linearity and homoscedasticity have been met.

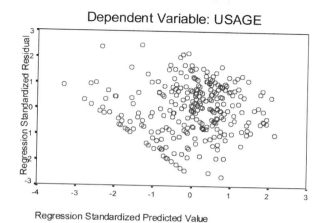

**Figure 6.6     Plot of standardized residuals against standardized predicted values**

To test the normality of residuals, it is necessary to check the histogram and normal probability plots. Histogram and normal probability plots show whether residuals are normally distributed. The histogram should look like a normal distribution (a bell-shaped curve). A non-normal histogram shows distribution as skewed or unsymmetrical. The SPSS (statistical package for social sciences) draws a curve on the histogram to show the shape of the distribution. For this data, a histogram shows that distribution is roughly normal although there is a slight deficiency of residuals in the middle. Therefore, the histogram shows that data are normally distributed. Further, to check the normality assumption, the researcher examined normal probability plots. The straight line in a normal probability plot represents a normal distribution and the points represent residuals. In a perfectly normally distributed data set, all points would lie on the line. This is what we see for this study data. In this case both the histogram and normal probability plots show relatively normal distribution, hence assumption is not violated. Figure 6.7 shows a histogram of normally distributed residuals and Figure 6.8 shows normal P-P plot of regression standardized residuals.

The standard multiple regression indicated that ten independent variables accounted for 53.1% of the variance in the individual acceptance of innovation ($F (10, 264) = 29.912$, $p<0.001$). Perceived usefulness was an important predictor ($\beta = 0.327$, $t (275) = 4.213$, $p<0.001$) followed by managerial support ($\beta = 0.299$, $t (275) = 5.035$, $P<0.001$), incentives ($\beta = 0.156$, $t (275) = 2.041$, $p<0.042$), personal

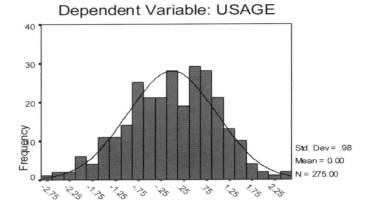

Figure 6.7     **Histogram of normally distributed residuals**

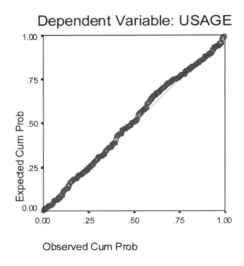

Figure 6.8     **Normal P-P plot of regression standardized residuals**

innovativeness ($\beta = 0.130$, t (275) = 2.738, p<0.007) and training ($\beta = -0.122$, t (275) = -2.304, p<0.022). All are statistically significant. Other independent variables are not statistically significant and they do not contribute much to the overall prediction. All the assumptions have been met and the model can be generalized to the population in this study. The non-significant variables were investigated by using in-depth interviews, which are discussed in more detail in Chapter 7.

It now remains to be seen whether the demographic characteristics of the employees have any impact on adoption or usage level. In order to test the impact of demographic characteristics on the dependent variable, it is first necessary to check whether various demographic categories – male and female; different age groups; different disciplines; academic and professional staff; full-time and part-time staff and educational qualifications – have significant differences in usage level. To find significant differences in demographic characteristics ANOVA tests were conducted and the results are shown in the next section.

## 6.8 The Impact of Respondents' Demographic Characteristics on Usage

Demographic characteristics in the form of gender, age, academic divisions, classifications, employment status and qualifications may make a significant impact on employee adoption and usage of innovation. The ANOVA test is conducted to find significance differences in the respondents' demographic characteristics. The following section describes the results of ANOVA tests.

### ANOVA TEST FOR USAGE LEVEL BY GENDER

An ANOVA test was conducted to determine whether there is a significant difference in usage according to gender. Descriptive statistics (see Table 6.33) shows that mean usage of female respondents is higher (mean = 3.06, standard deviation = 1.03) than the male respondents (mean = 2.64, standard deviation = 1.05). A test of homogeneity of variances (see Table 6.34) indicates that assumption is not violated (Sig = 0.620). The result of a one-way ANOVA shown in Table 6.35, F (1, 273) = 10.322, is significant at the 0.001 level. This implies that there are significant differences between usages by gender. Figure 6.9 shows mean usage in terms of gender.

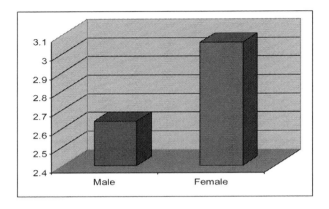

**Figure 6.9**    **Mean usage level by gender**

**Table 6.33**    **Summary Statistics of Gender Distribution**

| Gender | N | Mean | Std. dev. | Std. error | 95% Confidence interval for mean | | Min. | Max. |
|---|---|---|---|---|---|---|---|---|
| | | | | | Lower bound | Upper bound | | |
| Male | 100 | 2.6435 | 1.05507 | .10551 | 2.4341 | 2.8528 | 1.00 | 4.71 |
| Female | 175 | 3.0634 | 1.03564 | .07829 | 2.9089 | 3.2179 | 1.00 | 4.86 |
| Total | 275 | 2.9107 | 1.06032 | .06394 | 2.7848 | 3.0366 | 1.00 | 4.86 |

**Table 6.34**    **Test of homogeneity of variances between types of gender**

| Levene statistic | Df1 | df2 | Sig. |
|---|---|---|---|
| .246 | 1 | 273 | .620 |

**Table 6.35**    **Oneway ANOVA test for usage level by gender**

| | Sum of squares | Df | Mean square | F | Sig. |
|---|---|---|---|---|---|
| Between groups | 11.223 | 1 | 11.223 | 10.322 | .001 |
| Within groups | 296.829 | 273 | 1.087 | | |
| Total | 308.052 | 274 | | | |

## ANOVA TEST FOR USAGE LEVEL BY AGE GROUP

An ANOVA test was conducted to determine whether there is a significant difference in usage by age groups. The results of descriptive statistics (see Table 6.36) shows that mean usage of age group between 41–50 is the highest (mean = 3.06, standard deviation = 0.96); followed by age group 20–30 (mean = 2.95, standard deviation = 1.04); age group 51–60 (mean = 2.88, standard deviation = 1.18); age group 31–40 (mean = 2.86, standard deviation = 1.04) and age group 61 and above (mean = 2.40, standard deviation = 1.16). There seems to be little difference in mean usage by various age groups. Figure 6.10 displays mean usage level by age. Homogeneity of variance tests in Table 6.37 indicates that assumption is not violated (Sig = 0.143). The result of a one-way ANOVA shown in Table 6.38, $F_{(4, 270)} = 0.980$ is not significant (p<0.419). The result implies that there are no significant differences between various age groups' usage levels. Further post hoc tests show there are no mean differences in respondents' different age groups.

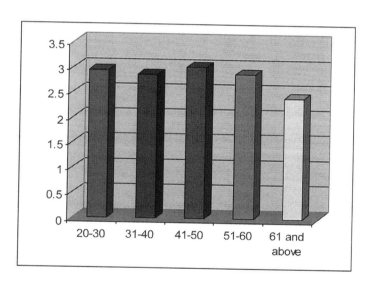

**Figure 6.10    Mean usage level by age**

Table 6.36     Summary statistics of age distributions

| Age | N | Mean | Std. dev. | Std. error | 95% Confidence interval for mean | | Min. | Max. |
|---|---|---|---|---|---|---|---|---|
| | | | | | Lower bound | Upper bound | | |
| 20-30 | 53 | 2.9564 | 1.04598 | .14368 | 2.6681 | 3.2447 | 1.00 | 4.57 |
| 31-40 | 56 | 2.8622 | 1.04268 | .13933 | 2.5830 | 3.1415 | 1.00 | 4.29 |
| 41-50 | 86 | 3.0100 | .96232 | .10377 | 2.8037 | 3.2164 | 1.00 | 4.86 |
| 51-60 | 67 | 2.8849 | 1.18098 | .14428 | 2.5968 | 3.1729 | 1.00 | 4.86 |
| 61 and above | 13 | 2.4091 | 1.16168 | .32219 | 1.7071 | 3.1111 | 1.00 | 4.29 |
| Total | 275 | 2.9107 | 1.06032 | .06394 | 2.7848 | 3.0366 | 1.00 | 4.86 |

Table 6.37     Test of homogeneity of variances among age group

| Levene statistic | Df1 | df2 | Sig. |
|---|---|---|---|
| 1.731 | 4 | 270 | .143 |

Table 6.38     Oneway ANOVA test for usage level by age group

| | Sum of squares | df | Mean square | F | Sig. |
|---|---|---|---|---|---|
| Between groups | 4.407 | 4 | 1.102 | .980 | .419 |
| Within groups | 303.645 | 270 | 1.125 | | |
| Total | 308.052 | 274 | | | |

## ANOVA TEST FOR USAGE LEVEL BY DIVISION

An ANOVA test was conducted to determine whether there is a significant difference in usage in different divisions. The result for descriptive statistics in Table 6.39 shows that the highest mean usage is among the respondents who are not in a division (mean = 3.66, standard deviation = 0.77); followed by the divisions of Information Technology, Engineering and Environment (mean = 3.15, standard deviation = 1.04); Health Science (mean = 3.04, standard deviation = 0.92); Business (mean = 2.67, standard deviation = 1.06) and Education, Arts and Social Sciences (mean = 2.47, standard deviation = 1.07). There are differences in mean usage by various disciplines. Figure 6.11 shows mean usage level by divisions. Homogeneity of variance tests in Table 6.40

indicate that assumption is violated (Sig = 0.013). The result of a one-way ANOVA shown in table 5.41, $F_{(4, 270)} = 10.305$ is significant at 0.001 level. The result implies that there are significant differences in usage levels by various disciplines. Further post hoc tests shows there are mean differences in different disciplines. Table 6.42 shows respondents who are not in a faculty (division) have a strongly significant difference in usage than others, followed by Education, Arts and Social Sciences. This implies that professional staff in various units at the university, such as Chancellery and the Flexible Learning Center, need to use calendar applications more extensively. The Division of Education, Arts and Social Sciences deals with social science activities and staff who work there probably use innovation less compared to other divisions.

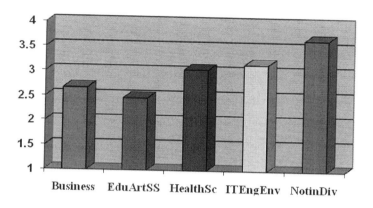

**Figure 6.11    Mean usage level by divisions**

**Table 6.39    Summary statistics of divisions distribution**

| Division | N | Mean | Std. dev. | Std. error | 95% Confidence interval for mean | | Min. | Max. |
|---|---|---|---|---|---|---|---|---|
| | | | | | Lower bound | Upper bound | | |
| Business | 66 | 2.6742 | 1.06166 | .13068 | 2.4132 | 2.9352 | 1.00 | 4.86 |
| Education, Arts and Social Sciences | 69 | 2.4799 | 1.07682 | .12963 | 2.2212 | 2.7386 | 1.00 | 4.71 |
| Health Science | 71 | 3.0451 | .92280 | .10952 | 2.8267 | 3.2636 | 1.00 | 4.86 |
| IT, Engineering and Environment | 32 | 3.1562 | 1.04498 | .18473 | 2.7795 | 3.5330 | 1.00 | 4.86 |
| Not in a division | 37 | 3.6657 | .77603 | .12758 | 3.4069 | 3.9244 | 1.43 | 4.86 |
| Total | 275 | 2.9107 | 1.06032 | .06394 | 2.7848 | 3.0366 | 1.00 | 4.86 |

Table 6.40     Test of homogeneity of variances among divisions

| Levene statistic | df1 | df2 | Sig. |
|---|---|---|---|
| 3.234 | 4 | 270 | .013 |

Table 6.41     Oneway ANOVA test for usage level by division

| | Sum of squares | df | Mean square | F | Sig. |
|---|---|---|---|---|---|
| Between groups | 40.799 | 4 | 10.200 | 10.305 | .000 |
| Within groups | 267.253 | 270 | .990 | | |
| Total | 308.052 | 274 | | | |

Table 6.42     Oneway ANOVA post hoc (Tamhane) test for usage level by division

| (I) DIVISION | (J) DIVISION | Mean difference (I-J) | Std. error | Sig. | 95% Confidence interval | |
|---|---|---|---|---|---|---|
| | | | | | Lower bound | Upper bound |
| Business | Education, Arts and Social Sciences | .1943 | .18407 | .969 | -.3297 | .7184 |
| | Health Science | -.3709 | .17050 | .273 | -.8566 | .1147 |
| | IT, Engineering and Environment | -.4820 | .22628 | .315 | -1.1387 | .1747 |
| | Not in a division | -.9915(*) | .18263 | .000 | -1.5150 | -.4679 |
| Education, Arts and Social Sciences | Business | -.1943 | .18407 | .969 | -.7184 | .3297 |
| | Health Science | -.5652(*) | .16970 | .011 | -1.0483 | -.0822 |
| | IT, Engineering and Environment | -.6764(*) | .22568 | .038 | -1.3314 | -.0213 |
| | Not in a division | -1.1858(*) | .18188 | .000 | -1.7071 | -.6645 |
| Health Science | Business | .3709 | .17050 | .273 | -.1147 | .8566 |
| | Education, Arts and Social Sciences | .5652(*) | .16970 | .011 | .0822 | 1.0483 |
| | IT, Engineering and Environment | -.1111 | .21475 | 1.000 | -.7381 | .5158 |
| | Not in a division | -.6205(*) | .16814 | .004 | -1.1038 | -.1373 |

| | | | | | | |
|---|---|---|---|---|---|---|
| IT, Engineering and Environment | Business | .4820 | .22628 | .315 | -.1747 | 1.1387 |
| | Education, Arts and Social Sciences | .6764(*) | .22568 | .038 | .0213 | 1.3314 |
| | Health Science | .1111 | .21475 | 1.000 | -.5158 | .7381 |
| | Not in a division | -.5094 | .22450 | .240 | -1.1634 | .1446 |
| Not in a division | Business | .9915(*) | .18263 | .000 | .4679 | 1.5150 |
| | Education, Arts and Social Sciences | 1.1858(*) | .18188 | .000 | .6645 | 1.7071 |
| | Health Science | .6205(*) | .16814 | .004 | .1373 | 1.1038 |
| | IT, Engineering and Environment | .5094 | .22450 | .240 | -.1446 | 1.1634 |

## ANOVA TEST FOR USAGE LEVEL BY CLASSIFICATION

An ANOVA test was conducted to determine whether there is significant difference in usage by employees classified as academic and administrative (professional) staff. Descriptive statistics in Table 6.43 shows that mean usage of professional staff is higher (mean = 3.56, standard deviation = 0.68) than the academic staff (mean = 2.57, standard deviation = 1.06). Figure 6.12 shows mean usage according to employees' classification (academic staff and professional staff). Test of homogeneity of variances in Table 6.44 indicates that assumption is violated (Sig = 0.000). The result of Oneway ANOVA shown in Table 6.45, $F(1, 269) = 66.520$ is significant at the 0.001 level. This implies that there are significant differences between academic and professional staff's use of innovation. Professional staff use it more because they need to manage various administrative activities more efficiently than academic staff.

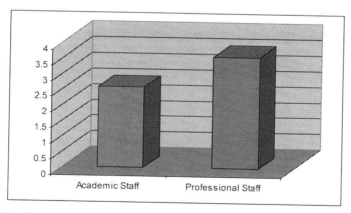

**Figure 6.12    Mean usage by classification of employees**

**Table 6.43    Summary statistics of classification of employees**

| Classification | N | Mean | Std. dev. | Std. error | 95% Confidence interval for mean | | Min. | Max. |
|---|---|---|---|---|---|---|---|---|
| | | | | | Lower bound | Upper bound | | |
| Academic staff | 177 | 2.5745 | 1.06332 | .07992 | 2.4168 | 2.7323 | 1.00 | 4.86 |
| Professional staff | 94 | 3.5642 | .68926 | .07109 | 3.4231 | 3.7054 | 1.43 | 4.86 |
| Total | 271 | 2.9178 | 1.05990 | .06438 | 2.7911 | 3.0446 | 1.00 | 4.86 |

**Table 6.44    Test of homogeneity of variances between classifications of employees**

| Levene statistic | df1 | df2 | Sig. |
|---|---|---|---|
| 32.904 | 1 | 269 | .000 |

**Table 6.45    Oneway ANOVA test for usage level by classification of employees**

| | Sum of squares | Df | Mean square | F | Sig. |
|---|---|---|---|---|---|
| Between groups | 60.134 | 1 | 60.134 | 66.520 | .000 |
| Within groups | 243.178 | 269 | .904 | | |
| Total | 303.312 | 270 | | | |

## ANOVA TEST FOR USAGE LEVEL BY EMPLOYMENT STATUS

An ANOVA test was conducted to determine whether there is any significant difference in usage by full-time and part-time employees. Descriptive statistics in Table 6.46 show that mean usage of full-time staff is higher (mean = 3.10, standard deviation = 1.00) than the part-time staff (mean = 2.25, standard deviation = 0.95). Figure 6.13 shows mean usage level by employed as (full-time and part-time employees). The test of homogeneity of variances Table 6.47 indicates that assumption is not violated (Sig = 0.780). The result of a one-way ANOVA shown in Table 6.48, F (1, 272) = 34.792 is significant at the 0.001 level. This implies that there are significant differences between usages by full-time and part-time staff. Full-time employees are obliged to use university standard system and are more likely to spend more time on campus; whereas part-time employees stay on campus for a limited time and hence their usage level is less as they have fewer responsibilities for work activities on campus.

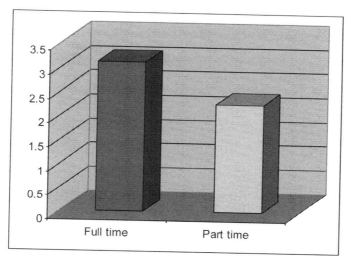

Figure 6.13    **Mean usage level by employed as full-time and part-time employees**

Table 6.46    **Summary statistics of employment status (full-time and part-time employees)**

| Employed as | N | Mean | Std. dev. | Std. error | 95% Confidence interval for mean | | Min | Max |
|---|---|---|---|---|---|---|---|---|
| | | | | | Lower bound | Upper bound | | |
| Full-time | 213 | 3.1076 | 1.00855 | .06910 | 2.9714 | 3.2439 | 1.00 | 4.86 |
| Part-time | 61 | 2.2544 | .95067 | .12172 | 2.0109 | 2.4979 | 1.00 | 3.86 |
| Total | 274 | 2.9177 | 1.05592 | .06379 | 2.7921 | 3.0433 | 1.00 | 4.86 |

Table 6.47    **Test of homogeneity of variances between employment status (full-time and part-time employees)**

| Levene statistic | df1 | df2 | Sig. |
|---|---|---|---|
| .078 | 1 | 272 | .780 |

**Table 6.48     Oneway ANOVA test for usage level by employment status**

|  | Sum of squares | Df | Mean square | F | Sig. |
|---|---|---|---|---|---|
| Between groups | 34.520 | 1 | 34.520 | 34.792 | .000 |
| Within groups | 269.868 | 272 | .992 |  |  |
| Total | 304.387 | 273 |  |  |  |

## ANOVA TEST FOR USAGE LEVEL BY QUALIFICATIONS

An ANOVA test was conducted to determine whether there is significant difference in usage with different qualifications. The results of descriptive statistics in Table 6.49 shows that people who have an undergraduate diploma are the highest users of the system (mean = 3.43, standard deviation = 0.771); followed by respondents who have a graduate diploma (mean = 3.03, standard deviation = 1.104); respondents who have a PhD or other doctorate (mean = 2.83, standard deviation = 1.053); respondents who have a bachelor's degree (mean = 2.78, standard deviation = 1.08) and respondents who have a master's degree have the lowest usage mean (mean = 2.61, standard deviation = 1.038). Figure 6.14 shows mean usage level by academic qualifications. There are differences in mean usage for different qualifications, with highest usages by the respondents who have an undergraduate graduate diploma. This is probably because many administrative staff are in this category in terms of qualifications and need to use the system more compared to other employees. However, data indicate that the mean differences of usage are closer to each

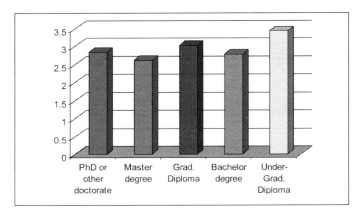

**Figure 6.14     Mean usage level by academic qualifications**

other. The homogeneity of variance test in Table 6.50 indicates that assumption is not violated (Sig = 0.090). The result of the one-way ANOVA shown in Table 6.51, F (4, 242) = 2.204 indicates that it is not significant (p<0.069). The result implies that there are no significant differences in usage by various education levels. Calendar is used almost equally by all staff despite their different levels of educational qualification.

**Table 6.49     Summary statistics of academic qualifications**

| | N | Mean | Std. dev. | Std. error | 95% Confidence interval for mean | | Min. | Max. |
|---|---|---|---|---|---|---|---|---|
| | | | | | Lower bound | Upper bound | | |
| PhD or other doctorate | 86 | 2.8379 | 1.05334 | .11359 | 2.6121 | 3.0638 | 1.00 | 4.86 |
| Master's degree | 56 | 2.6168 | 1.03846 | .13877 | 2.3387 | 2.8949 | 1.00 | 4.43 |
| Grad. diploma | 29 | 3.0376 | 1.10413 | .20503 | 2.6176 | 3.4576 | 1.00 | 4.86 |
| Bachelor's degree | 60 | 2.7863 | 1.10813 | .14306 | 2.5001 | 3.0726 | 1.00 | 4.43 |
| Undergrad. Diploma | 16 | 3.4375 | .77102 | .19276 | 3.0267 | 3.8483 | 1.57 | 4.57 |
| Total | 247 | 2.8375 | 1.06483 | .06775 | 2.7041 | 2.9710 | 1.00 | 4.86 |

**Table 6.50     Test of homogeneity of variances among academic qualifications**

| Levene statistic | df1 | df2 | Sig. |
|---|---|---|---|
| 2.037 | 4 | 242 | .090 |

**Table 6.51     Oneway ANOVA test for usage level by academic qualifications**

| | Sum of squares | df | Mean square | F | Sig. |
|---|---|---|---|---|---|
| Between groups | 9.806 | 4 | 2.452 | 2.204 | .069 |
| Within groups | 269.124 | 242 | 1.112 | | |
| Total | 278.930 | 246 | | | |

The ANOVA tests concluded that there are significant differences in usage level by gender (male and female), divisions (various disciplines), classifications of staff (academic and professional) and employment category (full-time and part-time). Age and qualifications do not make any significant difference in terms of usage. This information is useful to further analyze how these significant demographic factors affect overall usage of innovation. The next section will investigate how these demographic characteristics affect individuals' adoption of innovation.

## 6.9 Hierarchical Regression Model for Impact of Demographic Variables

From the ANOVA tests it was identified that gender (male and female), division (various disciplines), classification (academic and administrative) and employment category (full-time and part-time) have significant differences in usage level. The following tests will show what impact these demographic characteristics have on the regression model and how demographic variables affect individual acceptance of innovation. The analysis of multiple regressions with demographic variables, which are also called control variables, will show whether gender, division, classification and employment category predict individual adoption and whether other independent variables still improve prediction of individual adoption when demographic variables are included in the model.

The following section describes the overall model and informs whether the model is successful in predicting usage level. Table 6.52 shows that there are two models and how well each model fits the data. R-squared change shows how much more variance the second model is explained compared to the first model and whether that is significant. Model 1 refers to the first stage in the analysis where all the demographics are used as predictors. All categorical variables (demographics) were recorded as a dichotomous variable (0 and 1) before they were entered into the regression model. Model 2 refers to when all demographics and other independent variables are used as predictors. In the column labeled R are the values of the multiple correlation coefficients between the predictors and the outcome. The next column gives values of $R^2$ which measure how much variability in the outcome is accounted for by the predictors. For the first model $R^2$ value is 0.332, which means demographic variables such as gender, classification, employment status and division account for 33.2% of variation in usage. However, when other independent predictors are also included in the analysis (Model 2), this value increases to 0.606 or 60.6% of the variance in usage. Therefore, if demographics account for 33.2%, other independent variables account for an additional 27.4%. Therefore, inclusion of other independent variables has explained a very large amount of the variation in usage. Model 1 is significant at F (7, 263) = 18.705, p<0.001. Model 2 is significant at F (10, 253) = 17.617, p<0.001. These statistics show the significant difference made by adding other predictors to the model.

**Table 6.52    Model summary**

| Model | R | R square | Adjusted R square | Std. error of the estimate | Change statistics | | | | |
|-------|---|----------|-------------------|----------------------------|-------------------|---|---|---|---|
| | | | | | R square change | F change | df1 | df2 | Sig. F change |
| 1 | .577 | .332 | .315 | .87747 | .332 | 18.705 | 7 | 263 | .000 |
| 2 | .779 | .606 | .580 | .68690 | .274 | 17.617 | 10 | 253 | .000 |

The next part of the output in Table 6.53 contains an ANOVA that tests whether the model is significantly better at predicting the outcome than intercept alone. F ratio represents the ratio of improvement in prediction as a result of fitting the model. For the first model the F-ratio is 18.705 (F (7, 263) = 18.705) which is significant at p<0.001 level. The model shows the impact of demographic variables on usage. In other words, this model shows how demographics predict usage level. For the second model the F-ratio is 22.932 (F (17,253) = 22.932) which is significant at p<0.001 level. We can see that the second model significantly improves our ability to predict the outcome and this model with other independent predictors is better because the F-ratio is significantly higher. This model shows the improvement in prediction for usage when a combination of demographic and independent variables are included.

Table 6.53     Analysis of variance (ANOVA)

| Model | | Sum of squares | df | Mean square | F | Sig. |
|---|---|---|---|---|---|---|
| 1 | Regression | 100.814 | 7 | 14.402 | 18.705 | .000 |
| | Residual | 202.498 | 263 | .770 | | |
| | Total | 303.312 | 270 | | | |
| 2 | Regression | 183.939 | 17 | 10.820 | 22.932 | .000 |
| | Residual | 119.374 | 253 | .472 | | |
| | Total | 303.312 | 270 | | | |

Table 6.54 represents coefficients of the regression models which indicates B-values (unstandardized coefficient) and constants for regression equations and significance of the variables in each model predicting the usage. In Model 1, gender (male and female), classification (academic and professional staff), employed as full-time or part-time, and the divisions of Business and Education, Arts and Social Sciences were significant. These variables do not significantly affect the usage level when other independent variables are not considered.

Table 6.54     Coefficients

| Model | | Unstandardized coefficients | | Standardized coefficients | t | Sig. |
|---|---|---|---|---|---|---|
| | | B | Std. error | Beta (β) | | |
| 1 | (Constant) | 3.058 | .177 | | 17.308 | .000 |
| | Gender | .299 | .118 | .136 | 2.529 | .012 |
| | Classification | .678 | .128 | .305 | 5.312 | .000 |
| | Employed as | -.601 | .132 | -.236 | -4.555 | .000 |
| | Business | -.527 | .190 | -.211 | -2.773 | .006 |
| | EduArt and SS | -.814 | .192 | -.335 | -4.245 | .000 |
| | Health Science | -.253 | .191 | -.104 | -1.324 | .187 |
| | ITEndEnv | -.306 | .214 | -.093 | -1.432 | .153 |
| 2 | (Constant) | .068 | .352 | | .193 | .847 |
| | Gender | .212 | .098 | .097 | 2.173 | .031 |
| | Classification | .244 | .110 | .110 | 2.218 | .027 |
| | Employed as | -.417 | .106 | -.164 | -3.933 | .000 |
| | Business | -.375 | .153 | -.150 | -2.448 | .015 |
| | EduArt and SS | -.528 | .156 | -.217 | -3.391 | .001 |
| | Health Science | -.143 | .152 | -.059 | -.937 | .350 |
| | ITEndEnv | -.297 | .173 | -.091 | -1.719 | .087 |

| | | | | | |
|---|---|---|---|---|---|
| Training | -.108 | .061 | -.088 | -1.757 | .080 |
| Managerial sup | .220 | .079 | .164 | 2.780 | .006 |
| Incentive | .111 | .094 | .090 | 1.180 | .239 |
| Usefulness | .362 | .085 | .325 | 4.260 | .000 |
| Innovativeness | .225 | .062 | .164 | 3.639 | .000 |
| Experience | .007 | .056 | .006 | .121 | .904 |
| Image | .062 | .082 | .047 | .753 | .452 |
| Enjoyment | .070 | .084 | .053 | .835 | .404 |
| Peers | -.052 | .073 | -.035 | -.708 | .480 |
| Social Net | -.032 | .085 | -.022 | -.373 | .709 |

In Model 2, when all ten independent variables are regressed with demographic variables (moderating or controlled variables), Table 6.54 shows that gender (male and female), classification (academic and professional staff), whether employed as full-time and part-time, and the Division of Business and Division of Education, Arts and Social Sciences were significant, as well as the four independent variables such as training, managerial support, perceived usefulness and personal innovativeness. Unstandardized coefficient B-values indicate the individual contribution of each predictor to the model.

From the hierarchical regression analysis we can see that the impact of demographic variables on usage – gender (male and female), classification (academic and professional staff), whether employed as full-time or part-time, and the Divisions of Business, Education, Arts and Social Sciences, were significant. As the researcher converted these categorical variables (demographics) to dummy (0 and 1) variables and based on the direction (positive or negative) of the B coefficient, it was easy to identify that females were significantly higher users than their male counterparts. The results identified professional (administrative) staff as having a higher impact on usage than academic staff. Administrative staff need to use the system extensively to manage administrative activities. Furthermore, most of the administrative staff are female and as we have seen, women have higher usage rates then male employees. Therefore, it makes sense that administrative staff are higher users of the systems compared to academic staff. The results showed that full-time employees are significantly higher users than part-time employees. Full-time employees have more duties on campus and they need to attend many activities and programs. Therefore, they tend to use the system more than part-time employees who only work on campus for limited hours and participate in limited university activities.

Regarding the usage level in various divisions, results indicated that employees who are not in a division have a significantly higher effect on usage than people who are in the Division of Business and Division of Education, Arts and Social Sciences. Employees who are not in a division are professional (administrative) staff and they tend to use the system more than academic staff. They need to use the system to maintain various programs, manage schedules and arrange meetings and appointments. The Division of IT, Engineering and Environment and Division of Health Sciences have higher rates of usage compared to the Division of Business and Division of Education, Arts and Social Sciences. These are discussed further in the discussion section. The contributing independent variables are training, managerial support, perceived usefulness and personal innovativeness.

## CHECKING ASSUMPTIONS

Finally, the study checked the assumptions of the model by investigating outliers and multicollinearity. It analyzed the plot of *ZRESID against *ZPRED; histogram and normal probability plot of the residuals. Scatterplots show relationships between predicted values of dependent variables and residuals. This plot allows testing of linearity and homoscedasticity of residual assumptions. The graph of *ZRESID against *ZPRED should look like a random array of dots evenly dispersed around zero. If this graph funnels out, the chances are that there is heteroscedasticity in the data. If there is any sort of curve in this graph then the chances are that the data has broken the assumption of linearity. Figure 6.15 shows the plot of standardized residuals against standardized predicted values. The points are randomly and evenly dispersed throughout the plot. Most of the points are evenly dispersed around zero. There is no clear relationship between residuals and predicted values, so they have linearity. It also seems not to have violated the assumption of homoscedasticity although there are few residuals around the plots. The points do not form the shape of a funnel and there is no curvilinear relationship in the plots. This pattern is indicative of a situation in which the assumptions of linearity and homoscedasticity have been met.

To test the normality of residuals, the researcher checked the histogram and normal probability plots. Histogram and normal probability plots show whether residuals are normally distributed. The histogram should look like a normal distribution (a bell-shaped curve). A non-normal histogram shows distribution is skewed or unsymmetrical. The SPSS draws a curve on the histogram to show the shape of the distribution. For this data, the histogram shows distribution is

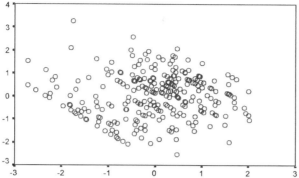

Dependent Variable: USAGE

Regression Standardized Predicted Value

**Figure 6.15**    **Plot of standardized residuals against standardized predicted values**

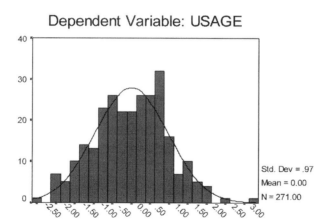

Dependent Variable: USAGE

Std. Dev = .97
Mean = 0.00
N = 271.00

Regression Standardized Residual

**Figure 6.16**    **Histogram of normally distributed residuals**

roughly normal although there is a slight deficiency of residuals in the middle. Therefore, the histogram shows that data are normally distributed. To check the normality assumption, the researcher examined normal probability plot. The straight line in the normal probability plot represents a normal distribution and the points represent residuals. In a perfect, normally distributed data set, all points will lie on the line. This is what we generally see for this study's data. In this case, both the histogram and the normal probability plot show relatively normal distribution, hence assumptions are not violated. Figure 6.16 shows a histogram of normally distributed residuals and Figure 6.17 shows normal P-P plot of regression standardized residuals.

Hierarchical regressions with categorical predictors identified two models. The first model, which used only demographic characteristics, accounted for 33.2% of the variance in the individual acceptance of innovation ($F_{(7, 263)} = 18.705$, $p < 0.001$). In the second model demographics were used as a controlled variable and, together with other independent variables, accounted for 60.6% of variance in the individual acceptance of innovation ($F_{(17, 253)} = 22.932$, $p < 0.001$). In this model perceived usefulness was an important

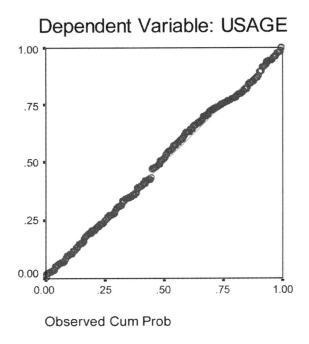

**Figure 6.17    Normal P-P plot of regression standardized residuals**

predictor $\beta = 0.325$, t (275) = 4.260, p<0.001) followed by the Division of Education, Art and Social Science ($\beta = -0.217$, t (275) = -3.391, p<0.001); employment status ($\beta = -0.164$, t (275) = -3.933, p<0.001); personal innovativeness ($\beta = 0.164$, t (275) = 3.639, p<0.001); managerial support ($\beta = 0.164$, t (275) = 2.780, p<0.006); Business ($\beta = -0.150$, t (275) = -2.448, p<0.015); classification ($\beta = 0.110$, t (275) = 2.218, p<0.027) and gender ($\beta = 0.097$, t (275) = 2.173, p<0.031); and Training ($\beta = -0.088$, t (275) = -1.757, p<0.080). All these variables are statistically significant. The variables which were not statistically significant will be discussed in greater detail in qualitative analysis of data in Chapter 7. All the assumptions have been met and the model would be generalizable to the population in this study.

## 6.10 Regression Analysis for Attitude with Organizational, Individual and Social Factors

Two major regression analyses (multiple regression and hierarchical regression) are shown in sections 6.7 and 6.9. These two analyses were conducted using 'Usage' as the dependent variable. In this section, the researcher conducted several additional regression analyses to see how organizational, individual and social factors affect individuals' attitudes toward the adoption of innovation.

The following section explains how individuals' attitudes concerning the acceptance of innovation are affected by organizational, individual and social factors.

### REGRESSION ANALYSIS FOR ORGANIZATIONAL FACTORS WITH ATTITUDE AS DEPENDENT VARIABLE

Regression analysis was performed for organizational factors with attitude as the dependent variable and the result of the regression model is shown in Table 6.55. The model explained 63.9% of the variance in attitude and its associated F statistics indicated that it was significant at the p<0.001 level. Managerial support and incentive are shown as significant at the p<0.001 level. However, training was not significant. Incentive was found to be the most important predictor variable in the model ($\beta = 0.700$, t (275) = 17.335, p<0.001) followed by managerial support ($\beta = 0.181$, t (275) = 3.765, p<0.001). The variables are positively related. The model implies that incentives and managerial support do influence individual attitudes about accepting the innovation.

**Table 6.55      Regression model for organizational factors**

| Variables | Unstand. coef. B | Stand. coef. β | T | R square | F | Sig. |
|---|---|---|---|---|---|---|
|  |  |  |  | .639 | 160.043 | .000 |
| (Constant) | .628 |  | 3.975 |  |  | .000 |
| Training | .019 | .019 | .433 |  |  | .666 |
| Managerial Support | .201 | .181 | 3.765 |  |  | .000 |
| Incentive | .708 | .700 | 17.335 |  |  | .000 |

## REGRESSION FOR INDIVIDUAL FACTORS WITH ATTITUDE AS DEPENDENT VARIABLE

Regression analysis was conducted for individual factors with attitude as the dependent variable and the result of the regression model is shown in Table 6.56. The result of the regression model explains 75.1% of the variance in attitude and its associated F statistics indicated that it was significant at the p<0.001 level. Perceived usefulness, image and enjoyment with innovation were shown as significant at the p<0.001 level. However, personal innovativeness and prior experience were not significant in regression analysis but in correlation matrix where attitude shows a significant correlation with innovativeness and prior experience (r = 0.227 and r = 0.305, respectively). The result indicated that perceived usefulness and enjoyment with innovation were the top two significant predictors in the model (β = 0.397, t (275) = 8.516, p<0.001 and β = 0.386, t (275) = 8.500, p<0.001 respectively). Image was the next significant predictor (β = 0.203, t (275) = 4.926, p<0.001). The variables are positively related. The model implies that perceived usefulness, image and enjoyment with innovation wield a strong influence on individual attitude concerning the acceptance of innovation.

**Table 6.56      Regression model for individual factors**

| Variables | Unstand. coef. B | Stand. coef. β | T | R square | F | Sig. |
|---|---|---|---|---|---|---|
|  |  |  |  | .751 | 162.616 | .000 |
| (Constant) | .563 |  | 3.606 |  |  | .000 |
| Usefulness | .368 | .397 | 8.516 |  |  | .000 |
| Innovativeness | -.058 | -.051 | -1.531 |  |  | .127 |
| Prior Experience | .026 | .026 | .767 |  |  | .443 |
| Image | .223 | .203 | 4.926 |  |  | .000 |
| Enjoyment | .423 | .386 | 8.500 |  |  | .000 |

## REGRESSION FOR SOCIAL FACTORS WITH ATTITUDE AS DEPENDENT VARIABLE

Regression analysis was carried out for social factors with attitude as the dependent variable and the result of the model is shown in Table 6.57. It explained 29.1% of the variance in attitude and its associated F statistics indicated that it was significant at the $p<0.001$ level. Social network is the only variable significant at the $p<0.001$ level. However, peer importance was not significant. This also consistent with correlation matrix where attitude had a moderately high correlation with social network ($r = 0.533$) but low with peers ($r = 0.361$). The result indicated that social network is the only significant predictor of the model ($\beta = 0.479$, t (275) = 7.842, $p<0.001$). Social network is thus positively related with attitude. The model implies that social network can positively influence an individual's attitude toward accepting innovation.

**Table 6.57    Regression model for social factors**

| Variables | Unstand. coef. B | Stand. coef. β | T | R square | F | Sig. |
|---|---|---|---|---|---|---|
| | | | | .291 | 55.720 | .000 |
| (Constant) | 1.564 | | 7.218 | | | .000 |
| Peers | .122 | .099 | 1.621 | | | .106 |
| Social Network | .587 | .479 | 7.842 | | | .000 |

## REGRESSION FOR ORGANIZATIONAL, INDIVIDUAL AND SOCIAL FACTORS WITH ATTITUDE AS DEPENDENT VARIABLE

Regression analysis was conducted for combined organizational, individual and social factors with attitude as a dependent variable and the result of the regression model is shown in Table 6.58. The result of the regression model explained 77.4% of the variance in attitude and its associated F statistics indicated that it was significant at the $p<0.001$ level. Managerial support, incentive, perceived usefulness, image and enjoyment with innovation were shown as significant at the $p<0.01$ level. Enjoyment with innovation therefore emerged as the strongest significant predictor in the model ($\beta = 0.336$, t (275) = 7.244, $p<0.001$ followed by perceived usefulness ($\beta = 0.282$, t (275) = 5.246, $p<0.001$), incentive ($\beta = 0.168$, t (275) = 3.017, $p<0.01$), image ($\beta = 0.124$, t (275) = 2.762, $p<0.01$) and managerial support ($\beta = 0.116$, t (275) = 2.818, $p<0.01$). The variables are positively related. The model implies that enjoyment with innovation, perceived usefulness, incentives, image and managerial support influence individual attitude regarding any acceptance of innovation.

**Table 6.58    Regression model for organizational, individual and social factors**

| Variables | Unstand. coef. B | Stand. coef. β | t | R square | F | Sig. |
|---|---|---|---|---|---|---|
|  |  |  |  | .774 | 90.389 | .000 |
| (Constant) | .263 |  | 1.433 |  |  | .153 |
| Training | -.057 | -.057 | -1.534 |  |  | .126 |
| Managerial Support | .129 | .116 | 2.818 |  |  | .005 |
| Incentive | .170 | .168 | 3.017 |  |  | .003 |
| Usefulness | .262 | .282 | 5.246 |  |  | .000 |
| Innovativeness | -.044 | -.039 | -1.169 |  |  | .244 |
| Prior Experience | .020 | .020 | .607 |  |  | .545 |
| Image | .137 | .124 | 2.762 |  |  | .006 |
| Enjoyment | .369 | .336 | 7.244 |  |  | .000 |
| Peers | -.006 | -.005 | -.127 |  |  | .899 |
| Social Network | .076 | .062 | 1.458 |  |  | .146 |

Discussion and implications of the quantitative data analysis are presented in the next section.

## 6.11 Discussion of Quantitative Results

The study proposed and tested an advanced model of innovation adoption and examined the role of three different categories of factors – namely organizational, individual and social factors in affecting employees' system-use. The results provide substantial support for the advanced model for innovation adoption and demonstrate the relative contribution of the independent variables to variations in individuals' acceptance of innovation.

The results show in three different regression analyses (usage as dependent variable, usage as dependent variable with demographics as control variable and attitude as dependent variable) that managerial support and incentive have a significant effect on attitude and usage model. Although training was a significant predictor in usage model, it shows a negative relationship with usage. However, in the analysis of inter-correlation of the variables, training was significantly and positively correlated with usage ($r = 0.196$, $p<0.01$). Encouragement to use the system, offering educational and training programs, applying innovation to support a wider variety of business tasks and encouraging experimentation with the system would stimulate extensive usage among employees (Igbaria, Parasuraman & Baroudi, 1996). With high organizational support, when employees view innovation as being useful, they will use it. Lee, Lee and Kwon (2005) mention that employees' perception and managerial support would interact with each other to influence employees' intention to use innovation. The organization may nurture in their employees a positive intention to use the innovation via preplanned support activities such as allocating sufficient resources and qualified support technicians. By providing proper managerial support, training and incentives, an organization can generate acceptance of innovation.

An analysis showed that perceived usefulness is a significant predictor in all three regression analyses. Individuals are likely to have a favorable attitude about using a system if they believe that using it will improve their performance and productivity.

Personal innovativeness was significant in two analyses (usage as dependent variable and usage as dependent variable with demographics as the control variable), but was not significant in the regression analysis with attitude as dependent variable. The study found that personal innovativeness does influence adoption. There are many employees who use innovation because they want to explore a new system. Prior experience was not significantly affecting either attitude or usage models. During the analysis for inter-correlation among study variables, prior experience has shown that prior experience was positively and significantly correlated with usage. Prior experience will be further investigated in the qualitative study in Chapter 7.

Image has a significant effect on attitude as shown in the regression analysis with attitude as dependent variable. Image is also positively and significantly correlated with usage, as we can see in the analysis for inter-correlations among study variables. When an individual feels that use of innovation or a new system enhances one's image or status within the organization, she or he will possess a positive attitude. Employees often act in response to the factors that create or sustain a favorable image within a reference group. Enjoying innovation was significant in the attitude model but not in the two other models despite it being positively and significantly correlated with usage. Enjoyment can create a positive attitude toward usage of innovation. There are individuals who like to play with innovation and discover new things. On the contrary, there are people who dislike doing this. Although innovation is in front of them, they never try it, or if they do try it once, never try to explore or use it again. The qualitative analysis in the next chapter will discuss enjoyment of innovation in more detail.

Peers and social network did not show any significant impact on attitude or usage models. The technology acceptance model did not include social norms (perceived expectations of specific referent individuals or group and his or her motivation to comply with these expectations) as determinants of behavioral intention since Ajzen and Fishbein (1980) acknowledged that social norms is one of the least understood aspects of the theory of reasoned action. These variables also were not significant in the study conducted by Lewis, Agarwal and Sambamurthy (2003). Although the findings of this study revealed that both variables are not significant, the researcher believes that peers and social network have a strong impact on attitude and adoption, as friends, social groups and people in different disciplines or people in or outside the organization can affect attitude and usage. Receiving encouragement or suggestions can affect attitudes about using innovation. For example, I have used many new technologies because my friends used them and they helped me to use them. However, the variables that were not significant in the quantitative analysis suggested the need for additional investigation. The non-significant factors in this study will be further investigated in the qualitative analysis.

Among the demographic variables, gender (male and female), classification (academic and administrative staff), full-time or part-time employee status, and employees who are not in a division compared to employees who are in the Division of Business and the Division of Education, Art, and Social Sciences, have significant impact on usage. Female employees are using the system more than male employees because the university has more female employees and many of the administrative (professional) staff are female. Administrative (professional) staff need to use the system more than academic staff because administrative staff maintain appointments, arrange and track meetings, share calendars with their managers and do office activities. Full-time employees need to use the system at a much higher rate than part-time employees. Full-time employees have more responsibilities and they are involved in more activities, programs and meetings than part-time employees. Part-time employees have limited duties on campus and they are on campus for a limited time only, and therefore their usage level is less.

Considering the divisions, employees who are not in one have a significant and greater usage rate than employees who are. This set includes employees who work in the Chancellery, Flexible Learning Centre, library and other administrative units. They are professional (administrative) staff and as we have seen earlier professional staff have a significantly greater usage rate than academic staff. In particular professional staff have significantly higher usage rates compared to staff who work in the Division of Business and Division of Education, Arts and Social Sciences. The Division of Information Technology, Engineering and Environment and Division of Health Sciences have higher usage of innovation than the Division of Business and Division of Education, Arts and Social Sciences. The employees in the Division of Information Technology, Engineering and Environment and the Division of Health Sciences have a higher usage rate compared to employees in the Division of Business and Division of Education, Arts and Social Sciences. Employees in the Division of Education, Arts and Social Sciences might use more manual and traditional systems such as writing memos or making appointments by telephone instead of using calendar. The employees in the Division of Education, Arts and Social Sciences have the lowest usage rate compared to the other divisions.

## 6.12 Implications of Quantitative Results

The advanced model was tested empirically in this chapter. The study investigated factors that influence employees' attitude toward acceptance of innovation as they make adoption and usage decisions. The study examined the simultaneous effects of three critical sets of factors – organizational, individual and social factors. The theoretical rationale for these factors draws on multiple streams of research and the study integrated the construct of the theory of reasoned action (TRA), the technology acceptance model (TAM) and the conceptual framework provided by Frambach and Schillewaert (2002).

Findings of the study contribute to a better theoretical understanding of the factors that influence individual adoption of innovation and provide practical implications for management in the organization. The research's posited predictors explained between 53–77% of the variance in attitude and usage, suggesting that the model serves as an adequate conceptualization of the phenomenon of interest. This research involves combining multiple variables found in different innovation adoption-related studies into a single study. In addition, this study addressed a long list of factors identified by Frambach and Schillewaert (2002), tested their significance and assessed the difference between the factors.

Findings of the study provide insights into relative effects of organizational, individual and social factors on usage. These predictors influence individuals' attitudes toward the innovation, which consequently lead to its adoption. Four out of five individual factors – perceived usefulness, personal innovativeness, image and enjoyment with innovation, which were introduced and placed corresponding to the main belief constructs of the technology acceptance model and the theory of reasoned action, showed significant impact on attitude regarding the acceptance of innovation. The fifth variable, prior experience, was significant neither on attitude nor on usage. Prior experience will be further investigated in the qualitative analysis. Three organizational factors – training, managerial support and incentives – were incorporated into the model as external factors since the theory of reasoned action, the technology acceptance model and Frambach and Schillewaert (2002) suggested external factors in their models would affect the attitude and usage. These three external variables significantly affected attitudes toward adoption. Two subjective norms – peers and social network – were tested, but both proved not to be significant. The technology acceptance model did not include the theory of reasoned action's subjective norms since it was not significant and was one of the least understood aspects of the theory of reasoned action. However, social factors will be further investigated in the qualitative study.

Testing the effects of demographic variables in this study is another contribution of the model. Most IT-related studies did not include demographic characteristics in their models and they did not examine the effect of these moderating or controlled variables on usage. Frambach and Schillewaert (2002) provided a conceptual framework that includes demographic characteristics as a controlled variable and they proposed more research to be done. The theory of reasoned action also acknowledges the importance of demographic variables. Ajzen and Fishbein (1980, p.8) state that "our analysis of behavior has made no reference to various factors other than attitudes toward targets that social and behavioral scientists have invoked to explain behavior. Among these factors are personality characteristics such as demographic variables and external variables." There is much evidence to suggest that such factors are sometimes related to the behavior of interests (Ajzen & Fishbein, 1980). This study included demographic variables in the research model and assessed their relative contribution toward adoption. The results indicate that these variables, such as gender (male and female), classification (academic and professional staff), employment status (full-time and part-time) and academic divisions significantly affect individuals' attitudes concerning acceptance of innovation.

The study has important implications for management in the organization. When an organization plans to implement a new system, it would like to predict whether the system will be acceptable to employees. If the new system is not likely to be fully adopted, then the organization needs to take corrective action to increase the acceptability of the system. Organizations need to make an implementation plan carefully in order to enhance the business impact resulting from the large investments in time and money associated with introducing innovation. The present study is relevant to these concerns and would help management develop strategies to implement innovation successfully in the organization.

The result of this study confirms that perceived usefulness has a strong effect on usage. This suggests that the functionality of a system must be emphasized to potential users. The model indicates that efforts should focus initially on greater management support and incentives. The organization should aim to increase awareness of potential applications and emphasize the benefits and advantages of using the system. Findings suggest that managers need to focus their attention on exhibiting commitment to innovation for a smooth process of adoption. Unless individual employees perceive strong support, specific resources and some kind of incentives behind the use of innovation, they are unlikely to develop a positive attitude toward the innovation. Providing training to employees and support when they encounter technical problems may enhance adoption and level of usage. Individuals learn an innovation much more effectively when a personal trainer or technical assistant helps them directly and shows them how to use it.

It is also important for an organization to assist employees in developing positive perceptions about their ability to use the innovation. Individual employees who are personally more innovative are more inclined to use the innovation. Management can develop these employees as integral agents of change because they are likely to exhibit favorable attitudes toward adoption and can influence others in this regard. Organizational activities and strategies which are aimed at promoting more extensive use of innovation should emphasize not only the positive impact of productivity by adopting the innovation, but also highlight features that make the individual employee's use of innovation more enjoyable. The creation of opportunities through innovation, in order to gain knowledge, experience and image could enhance an individual's attitude toward the innovation and thereby, encourage adoption.

## 6.13 Conclusion

This chapter discussed empirical tests for the proposed advanced model of innovation adoption. The advanced model was developed by integrating the construct of the theory of reasoned action, the technology acceptance model and the conceptual framework of Frambach and Schillewaert (2002). Furthermore, the advanced model introduced several modifications that were not present in these models. The main theoretical contribution of this research is the development of an advanced model of innovation adoption (AMIA) and theoretical construct that brings individual innovation adoption issues into a coherent model.

The quantitative data analysis shows that the proposed model contributes to a better understanding of the factors that determine the individual acceptance of innovation in an organizational context. The model explains 53.1% of the variance in overall usage, 60.6% of the variance in the hierarchical regression model (usage as dependent variable with demographics as control variable) and 77.4% of the variance in the attitude model. The proposed advanced model of innovation adoption predicted well compared to TAM and TRA in predicting behavioral intention ($R^2$ for TAM was 0.50–0.70 while $R^2$ for TRA was between 0.30–0.60) (Davis, Bagozzi & Warshaw, 1989, p.996; Taylor & Todd, 1995, p.167).

The empirical study investigated effects of organizational, individual and social factors on usage of innovation. These factors affect individuals' attitudes toward the innovation leading to its adoption. Three organizational factors, namely training, managerial support and incentives, were incorporated into the model because external factors affect attitudes about innovation and usage. The theory of reasoned action, the technology acceptance model and that of Frambach and Schillewaert (2002) suggested external factors in their models would affect the attitude and usage. Empirical results show that all three variables did significantly affect individual attitudes toward adoption and usage.

Five individual factors – perceived usefulness, personal innovativeness, prior experience, image, and enjoyment of innovation – were introduced and placed corresponding to the main belief constructs of the technology acceptance model and the theory of reasoned action. Excepting prior experience, four other variables were shown to be significant. Prior experience will be further investigated in the next chapter.

The theory of reasoned action and the technology acceptance model did not include demographic characteristics but did acknowledge the importance of demographic variables. Frambach and Schillewaert (2002) provided a conceptual framework that includes demographic characteristics as a controlled variable and proposed empirical testing. The advanced model has incorporated those authors' demographic variables into the model. Testing the effects of demographic variables in this study is another contribution of the model. This study included demographic variables in the research model and assessed their relative contribution toward adoption.

To further investigate the impact of social factors and to substantiate and supplement the result obtained from the quantitative study, a qualitative study was conducted using in-depth interviews. This additional study provides further insights into the proposed advanced model. The next chapter will present the qualitative data analysis and discussion.

# 7

# Perception of Professionals and Management Personnel

## 7.1 Introduction

The study uses qualitative data developed from a series of interviews conducted after the questionnaire results had been analyzed. A semi-structured interview format was selected, which allowed flexibility for both the researcher and respondents to focus on major issues. Although the protocol for the interviews depended on the actual results of the quantitative analysis, the interviewer sought deep analysis of the factors that turned out to be problematic and insignificant. This qualitative study supports the development of an advanced model and helps further understanding of the factors that affect adoption and continuous usage of innovation. The results of the interviews assisted in the validation of the quantitative results and confirmation of the advanced model. Finally, the qualitative study identified critical and problematic issues, while at the same time verifying the results of the overall study. There are four sections in this chapter: introduction, analysis of interview findings, summary of interviews and conclusion.

## 7.2 Analysis of Interview Findings

Detailed understanding of the qualitative results is important for fine-tuning the theoretical framework and for developing the advanced model of innovation adoption (AMIA). The interview questions related to the factors in the research model, specifically training, managerial support, incentives, perceived usefulness, personal innovativeness, prior experience, image, enjoyment with innovation, peers and social network. Interviews will also relate to the issues arising from the quantitative data analysis. Detailed analysis of the interview data is presented in the following section.

## When asked, "How do you think training can help employees to learn and understand a new system or an innovation?"

All respondents agreed that training helps employees to understand a new system and learn about innovation. If there is no training then employees will not be able to make maximum use of innovation. They believe that training improves employees' efficiency, effectiveness, productivity and their understanding about innovation. They strongly feel that training is essential and needs to be more effective in the organization. They argued that if employees do not know about innovation then it becomes difficult for them to adopt and use it. Consequently, training is essential in order to understand innovation. Although training will cost the organization financially, the organization will benefit because employees are likely to work more efficiently. Arguably, training has great value for employees and for the organization. The following are representative comments made by respondents in regards to training:

*"Training demystifies the fear that people have with new technology. The new software we bought here recently, no one in this office embraced it and used it although fairly easy to use, but because there was no training about it."*

*"When I have any new software, I try it myself. But it makes very difficult and consumes a lot of time and I am not comfortable. But when I get training to do all those things it becomes easier for me to use. So, I believe that training is important."*

*"In my previous office the oldest designer could not use a computer and then we gave him training and then he became one of the best designers using computers."*

Respondents pointed out that training can help users to understand knowledge about a certain innovation or system and provide ideas of how to use them properly. The respondents indicated that training does make them more comfortable with using innovation. Training helps them learn and use different features. When they go back to their desks they can use the system more confidently. As one respondent remarked:

*"Recently I had training for a new system and I was scared to use it without training. It was really helpful."*

Respondents feel that there are many technologies or systems that they are currently using only for certain applications. Although there are many applications that they believe they could be used for, which would be good for them and for their job, they do not know how to use them. Training could definitely help in this regard. Several respondents mentioned that training helped them to understand more about Microsoft Outlook and its features. A few examples are as follows:

*"I use several calendar applications but believe there are many other applications and they may be very helpful for me, but I just do not know how to use them."*

*"I use calendar for only basic things such as email and making appointments. I did not have training about it. I saw that some people can check whether others are busy or not but I do not know how to check it. I do not know Sharing calendar or many other applications. If I had training it would be much better."*

*"Working every day I taught myself how to use calendar. But there are a lot of applications that I do not use and no one has shown me what to do with those features. Training would be very helpful for learning those features."*

However, the respondents differed on how this could be achieved, whether through individual or group training. Most of the respondents mentioned that individual training works much better than group training. In group training you may get an introduction to and basic functions of an innovation, but frustration occurs when you try to use it alone. In individual training you learn quickly. As stated by some respondents:

*"To provide individual attention, I think it is better to have individual training. In individual training you may find help according to your need. But if there is a standard application then probably group training can provide it."*

*"One-to-one is the best training. The advanced features are not that difficult for employees to learn once it is shown to them. They just do not know where to start and once someone shows them, then they are able to use it."*

Some respondents said that individual training is much more effective but group training is also useful. The group training where most of the time is spent with individuals to show them how to use the technology is also helpful. They stated:

*"When it is new technology probably group training is better as everyone will be facing the same problems. When you learn basic things in groups then you have an individual needs and in group training that individual need cannot be fulfilled. So individual training becomes essential to address individual goals."*

*"For me individual training is more effective. I have also done some group training. Group training is okay but one needs individual attention within a group session. I appreciated individual attention during group sessions."*

One respondent mentioned that it is not a matter whether it is group or individual training but the trainer who is important. One person said:

*"Personal training is much more important and effective because when you encountered a problem they can show you how to solve it. The trainer needs good interpersonal skills and should be able to sit down with you quietly and show, slowly, everything you need."*

Such comments reflect the findings of Yuan, Fulk, Shumate, Monge, Bryant and Matsaganis (2005) who said that individual adoption of innovation is positively influenced by the amount of relevant formal training. Such training enhances an individual's belief, possession of skills and knowledge that lead to the successful execution of tasks. Instructional procedures that are more individualized and focus on the relative amount of learning and progress are likely to enhance the adoption process. However, there are employees who feel that they do not have enough time to go to training. As one respondent said:

*"One of the main worries is time. To find enough time to go for training is quite difficult. The main problem is finding the extra time for training."*

## When asked, "How does managerial support (providing resources) affect you in accepting a new system or innovation?"

Respondents believed that managerial support is important in accepting an innovation or system because it will be difficult to learn it without their support. This support is financial, technical or the provision of time to learn and understand an innovation. As stated by the respondents:

*"If you have managerial support and resources and you have training then your level of acceptance will be greater and you will be ready for changes."*

*"Sometimes it is difficult to get resources and it is expensive to buy them myself. So, if management helps me to buy the technology, then it will facilitate the adoption and usage of the new technology."*

*"With our previous software it used to take up to three days to process a job and now with our recent technology it takes about one and one-half hours to complete the same job. I looked for the software and management bought it, and now we need to go for some training. Managerial support was essential for buying the software."*

Managerial support gives the employees confidence about using an innovation. Without managerial help and support employees are not inclined to adopt and use a new system. Respondents put it this way:

*"Managerial support makes you much more confident, by getting managerial help in training, finding time and other resources."*

*"If you get managerial support then it will make it easier to embrace new technology. If you do not have enough managerial support then you decline to adopt it."*

Managerial support is needed to equip users with innovation and resources for training and other support. Two respondents stated:

*"We thought of buying a new software called SharePoint. We have asked management to provide us support to buy the software. If we have to pay much money by ourselves then we are not going to buy it, but if management helps us then we are going to have it and adopt it here."*

*"Managerial help would make things easier. If there is no managerial support then I will have to find my own resources which make it a lot harder."*

As indicated by most of the respondents, time to learn and understand an innovation or system is a critical factor. Management should allocate enough time so that they can manage their own work and, at the same time, become acquainted with innovation. Respondents argued that:

*"It is time that I need to learn the technology. So, time must be built into my workload. To learn a new system or technology a person needs time and that is the frustration because I do not have enough time. I am too busy with my teaching or projects. Providing time would be crucial for adoption of new technology."*

*"If management gives you support, providing time to learn during the business hours then you are going to be much happier to try out new technology. If you have to learn after office hours then it would be difficult."*

*"To learn and understand the new system I need to go for training. So management must reduce my work hours or provide me time so that I can go for training and learn new technology."*

A few respondents argued that employees should not be forced to adopt an innovation or system because if they are forced to then they will just accept it but will not explore its full potential. Management needs to provide enough training and other support to enable employees to understand the advantages of the innovation in their jobs. Management also needs to provide quick responses to employees' needs and requirements in using a new system. One respondent put in this way:

*"If management takes a long time to provide support then I lose motivation and use the manual system. If management is quicker to provide resources then it will be helpful to adopt new technology."*

Lee, Lee and Kwon (2005) highlight the importance of managerial support and mention that managerial support is associated with greater adoption and usage, while lack of organizational support is considered problematic. Management support significantly affects individuals' adoption decisions and usage of innovation in the organization.

## When asked, "To what extent do you think incentives are a factor for employees to adopt an innovation?"

Respondents agreed that incentives have a tremendous impact on adoption of innovation. Incentives encourage individual employees to accept new innovation. If there are incentives employees may be motivated to try it. As some respondents stated:

*"I think such incentives are a very important factor. If management wants employees to use new technology then they need to support it and incentives can be a very useful way of gaining motivation for employees."*

*"If I am promised new advantages, promotion, facilities or financial incentives then it would motivate me to accept new technology."*

*"We told a certain employee that if she learns this software to create timetable then she would be promoted as permanent employee. Because of this reason she undertook the training and learned it despite that it was difficult software. She did it because she knew that if she had these skills she would be promoted as a permanent employee."*

Many respondents feel that time is another important factor and that it could be a good incentive for employees to adopt an innovation. They argued that:

*"Incentives do not have to be money. Time would be a good incentive. If you are given technology and you do not have time to learn it then you will not use it. When management provides you time then you will have motivation to engage with technology and explore it."*

*"There is a certain technology here and we were encouraged to use it, but I said I don't want to use it because it needs a certain amount of time and I have never felt that I have that amount of time to go there and use it. I am willing to try it and use it occasionally but not extensively because it will take too much time to use it regularly."*

A few respondents mentioned that they do not think the money incentive is effective or necessary for employees in their adoption of innovation. According to them, individual employees want to keep pace with innovation and they know that they have to learn new things continuously in order to stay employed. One interviewee stated at length that:

*"In this era, new technology is a way of life. It is probably not necessary to provide incentives just because they have adopted it, but there is a cost for keeping the job. This is because companies are continuously improving and one of the elements is continuously adopting new technology. The world is moving too fast and to keep you marketable and employed, you need to embrace new technology. So, the reward is continuous employment and maybe a better salary because of increased productivity, which also creates efficiency so the company needs less people to pay for and consequently provides a savings for the company."*

Many respondents felt that incentives will certainly be helpful in encouraging them to adopt innovation. They believed that if such adoption benefits the organization then it should reward employees accordingly. By using innovation employees can do much better than those who do not use it. Some interviewees thought that if innovation adoption makes life easier, then there is more time to do other things such as being with one's family more often. One interviewee put it this way:

> "Most of the people work with technology if that makes their job easier, more efficient and saves time. If it is not cumbersome and effective then they will use it and it gives them more time to do research plus other things."

According to Bhattacherjee (1998) employees value individual benefits such as career advancement, personal facilities, formal and informal recognition, increased autonomy, self worth, achievement and greater job security. To encourage adoption and assist continuous use of innovation, management must provide individual employees with incentives such as commissions, recognition and praise.

## When asked, "How do you investigate the usefulness of a new system or innovation before adopting it?"

The respondents were unanimous in that they investigate usefulness before adopting any innovation, because when you start a new system or innovation you may encounter many problems. One interviewee noted:

> "Before using any technology I always check the purpose of the technology, its advantages and find out what I can do with it."

There are various strategies individual employees use to investigate the usefulness of innovation. Most of them experiment with it and test it, and ask friends or peers for their opinions. If they feel that the innovation is going to be useful then they will use it. As two respondents remarked:

> "For any new technology that I am considering, I spend about a week to find out a decent amount of information about it and then I give an initial trial to check the technology and finally, I decide whether to use it or not."

> "I use the technology in the testing process and find out its benefits upon using it. Then I form an opinion about its usefulness and make a decision whether to accept it or not."

Some respondents use the most advanced techniques to investigate the usefulness of a system. Others use the Internet to find information about the innovation:

*"I use APQP, which is Advanced Product Quality Planning. This is the best practice used by automotive weapon manufacturing. You can use this analysis to predict the entire thing that could go wrong, how likely they could go wrong, what controls are, what the risk is and what the benefits are. From these you can make plans and decision."*

*"I do some research about the new technology online – look for comments and online discussions – and if I know someone who uses it, I ask about it. I usually check online to see what they have to say as to who used it."*

*"When we have something new we check it with a mailing group or online group. We want to see how it works and how much it will benefit us."*

Many respondents felt that they need to see whether the innovation that they are going to adopt will provide much value and will be worth considering the time that they will spend on it. Several respondents stated:

*"Other deciding factors would be whether it would be valuable considering the time I spend. I always think of whether it would be worth it and valuable using it."*

*"We have a team of people who see whether we could use it, how we are going to use it, how does it work and what are the benefits, etc. If we feel that it is going to be useful then we plan to adopt it."*

Many respondents ask other people or co-workers who use the system and seek recommendation from their colleagues. As respondents put it:

*"All new technology I use, I try first myself and show a couple of friends and ask them how they feel about it."*

*"I try and check it myself and I ask other friends for their recommendations. I get more interested in using certain technologies when I see other friends recommend it to me."*

*"I usually talk to other people about the system or technology. Sometimes it is by word-of-mouth. I normally ask other people about it and for their recommendations."*

There are employees who also check any possible problems that they may face during innovation use. One respondent said:

*"I inquire about possible floors that may frustrate me and how to overcome if I encounter any problem. I spend some time with people who know the system and have contacts so that I can say: 'Hey, I got this problem,' and 'how can I go around it?'"*

For others the importance lies in the social impact of the innovation. One respondent stated:

*"Social impact of technology is what is important to me. What does it mean for the people who are using it, what does it mean for the product at the end, what does it mean for educational purposes, because so often people only look at the financial cost of the technology – buying it and installing it, but they do not look for long term education, development and consequences. So, what is important is to look at the education, benefits and the social impacts of the technology."*

These comments also reflect the findings of Kim, Chan and Gupta (2007, p.116), who stated that individual employees evaluate the consequences of their behavior in terms of usefulness and base their choice of behavior on the desirability of the innovation. When an individual employee realizes that the innovation usage will lead to greater efficiency and effectiveness in the job or offer greater control over the job, the innovation is more likely to be adopted.

## When asked, "How do you think personal innovativeness (initiative) is a factor that affects individuals to explore a new system or innovation?"

Respondents indicated that a degree of initiative is needed in exploring a new system. They thought that personal innovativeness has a huge impact in discovering new things. They felt that personal initiative and interest in innovation are essential for individual employees. Respondents said:

*"Individuals who are innovative are willing to adopt new technology. I think you have to be innovative to explore new technology."*

*"Almost everything I do is based on my own interest. Individual interest is a big factor for me. I find I am comfortable with new technology and it is a lot of fun for me."*

A few respondents felt that it is the age that makes individual employees innovative. They mentioned that young people are probably more inclined toward innovation because their childhood has been one of long exposure to innovation, unlike previous generations. One interviewee stated:

> *"Age has a large impact. Some people just do not try new things. The younger people, people aged below 30 who grew up with computers and technology are most excited if you show them something new and are easy to engage with new things. It has a lot to do with age."*

Some respondents stated that they explore innovation for the sake of finding personal benefits. If the innovation significantly improves their job then they become interested in innovation. Respondents had this to say:

> *"For me it is practical benefits. I know there are some people who are interested in technology because of the technology and they constantly learn different programs. I only use the technology if it can make my life easier and help me doing something faster and better. Technology has to significantly improve my job."*

> *"People will have interest for the technology which relates to their work and helps their job. I do not like Endnotes software but I knew it would be good for my research. The interest in facilitating my work made me want to engage with that technology."*

There are many people who do not want to learn a new system and are happy using older ones. They do not want to change and they are worried about new systems and they fight and resist them. As one interviewee put it:

> *"I have a colleague who is less positive to change and does not see technology as a way forward but as another annoying thing in a list of things that have to be done in a day."*

Some employees are skeptical about learning new things. But others feel that they need to be up-to-date with innovation. Accordingly, they stated:

> *"There are people who want to know anything about technology; but some other people think that they have to learn a new thing again. So, it depends on personality, likes and dislikes and initiative is part of that."*

> *"You need to keep up with various systems and need to keep up-to-date with technology. Exploring something new is important to me."*

Others emphasized the time factor, in that time is needed to explore the new system. Respondents argued that despite their intention to use innovation, they do not have enough time to explore it fully. Therefore they prefer to use the old technology. According to some respondents:

*"Personally I like to use a new system but I do not have enough time to learn the system and learning a new system does take time."*

*"Management always gives you a lot of things to do and you do not have much time left to learn something new and use it. Instead, you tend to go for old habits, what you already know, to do your things."*

*"Most of the time people are busy and they do not have the time, but obviously, there are some people who like to take initiative."*

There are people who are interested and have less fear in using a new system. These types of people are more inclined to try innovation:

*"I have been in the IT business for last 30 years and I observed that people with initiative operate differently. They take chances more, they hit the keyboard just to see what happens and they have less fear. They try to solve problem using new technology."*

*"I think personal initiative has lot to do with trying new technology because some people think, 'I am working with this system and it is good for my job and the next system would be more efficient and better.'"*

*"You have training, you have incentives and you have support, but if you do not have interest, then you will not adopt it."*

Personal innovativeness is the innate tendency of an individual to adopt an innovation (Frambach & Schillewaert, 2002). Individuals with higher personal innovativeness are expected to develop a more positive attitude toward innovation adoption and usage.

## When asked, "How do you feel that prior experience with similar innovation or technology can help to adopt a new technology?"

According to the respondents, prior experience with similar technology is obviously helpful. If you have used similar technology then you will be able to compare it with previous ones and see which features represent substantial improvements. Prior experience helps to make the transition from one system to another. As some respondents stated:

*"Similar technology makes reasonable impact on beginning something. To try out a new technology, it is not necessary to have prior experience but it would be better if you had experience."*

*"Previously, I used a software called Account Soft but now I use similar software called Account Pack. I found that there are a lot of similarities between these two softwares and it was easy for me to understand the new software because I had a similar sort of experience."*

*"I think that prior experience is a very important factor. If I have prior experience with a certain technology, then it will help me to explore the new one."*

Respondents thought that prior experience will help in understanding the similarities between technologies. Several interviewees stated:

*"Absolutely, experience with similar technology gives you the street ahead. You will know the style of things, working processes, and similarities, which make a world of difference compared to the person who does not know. It makes a big difference."*

*"I feel that it is very important. If someone has prior experience with similar technology and similar use then they will adopt it quite easily. They will be comfortable with the product and familiarity of the system."*

*"Being master of a particular brand makes it a lot easier to adopt a new one because many terms and function are the same. So, prior experience has a big impact."*

*"Certainly, prior experience makes it easier to adopt new technology. If you have used the last version of a software then the fundamentals will be the same with new version. So, it will be much easier to use it. You may not have seen the new machine before but you may know what to do with it."*

There are respondents who thought that it is not necessary to have prior experience when adopting an innovation. They felt that they are willing to try something completely new. As one respondent put it:

*"I do not think that prior experience would be required to adopt a new system but certainly it is useful. Personally, I am quite happy to explore something I have never heard about and I enjoy exploring it. If it is completely new I am still willing to try and I do not think lack of prior experience would stop me trying something completely new. But prior experience would make it easier and it would make it more likely to be tried."*

Several respondents pointed out that prior experience made them comfortable about innovation. If individuals are comfortable then they are most likely to use it. On the other hand, bad experiences with innovation may have the opposite effect. As one respondent remarked:

*"Prior experience has a large impact for me. If I feel something is similar then I will feel comfortable. However, if I have had a bad experience with the system then I will be less enthusiastic. I think a comfort zone is really important for learning a new thing."*

Some respondents think that prior experience will in fact obstruct the adoption of innovation. They think that people always like to compare things with what they had previously and if it is not according to their mindset then they tend to refuse to use it. As one respondent said:

*"Most of the time people think that if you know something beforehand, it would be easier to adopt a similar thing. But I think differently. If you have used similar technology before then you tend to close out the new perspective. When you have new technology you immediately compare it with a previous one and if it does not meet the basic standards with the old one you are used to, then automatically you reject it. Innovation adoption would be better if the person has never seen it before."*

Prior experience and familiarity with innovation reduce anxiety and provide confidence to use innovation. Prior experience can have a positive effect on employees' use of new technical upgrades.

## When asked, "How do you feel when you know that you can do something with innovation that your co-workers cannot do?"

Respondents agreed that if they know something that their co-workers do not know then it would create a positive image in the organization and would give them a special sense of pride. It gives them a sense of achievement and feeling of power and authority. If the individual is the only one who knows about the system or the innovation then she or he may get some kind of advantages in the organization, for example a special position in the organization, status and authority. As some respondents suggested:

*"It makes me feel quite special, and if someone has a problem then they will say, 'Go to her.' It makes me kind of proud."*

*"I feel proud of myself as a human being. You know you have knowledge for mastering something."*

*"I like to have that knowledge. If I know something others do not know, I feel that I have achieved something. It gives me particular pride for something. It has a considerable deal of pride."*

Other respondents, however, thought that they had good and bad feelings. They felt good because they knew things that others did not. On the other hand, they knew they had a responsibility to teach and show others how to do use it. They felt that they did not have extra time to spend and do not want to have the burden of extra work. According to these people:

*"I think it gives good and bad feelings. If you know something others do not know you feel proud and feel great that you can do something but the problem is that you get sole responsibility of having that knowledge and you will be asked to explain that."*

*"It feels good that you can share knowledge with others who might need help but the downside is that you will find people will always come to you for help and you are the only one who has such knowledge."*

*"If you know something then other people will be asking you about it. If many of them do not know about new technology, then it is frustrating and you have to teach them, which may cost you time and effort."*

Most of the respondents feel that they want to share the knowledge with others and would like to help others who do not know the system. Respondents said:

*"I feel that I should share the idea with others. If I know something and others do not know I would like to share with them and let them know as well."*

*"I feel that I should not keep it to myself but rather share it without being smart or arrogant about it. I do not feel that I am a better person; rather, I feel if I can help then it is my responsibility to do so."*

Respondents felt that there are many people who did not want to learn new things. There are people who are technophobic and others who are just not interested. As one interviewee stated:

*"I know I have done extra training and I have knowledge about it and others have not. Sometimes they are technophobic and do not want to learn. However, if you show them how simple it is then they can learn relatively easily. Sometimes it is their thinking that frightens them. If you simplify what is being learned then they may find it easy to learn."*

People who have special knowledge and treat it as a form of power would feel their position is threatened if they have to share it. As one respondent put it:

*"My experience is that there are people who work so well and have promoted themselves but they do not tell others what made them so good because that might threaten their job."*

One major problem that does occur is the situation where you are the only one who knows about an innovation but others do not. This requires other people needing to use the same innovation. For instance, if there was only one person using calendar and others did not use it, then it is not helpful because users will not be able to interact with each other and could not make appointments or meeting requests. Consequently, the full benefits that the innovation provides will not be realized. As two respondents stated:

*"Many technologies require that they should be used by many people in order to realize full advantages. For example, if I am the only one using calendar application the value would be seriously limited. So, it is a problem if I am the one only use it and I would be actively seeking other people to use it."*

*"It is interesting and in one sense it feels good if you know something others do not know. But it also can be frustrating because you may have to bring many co-workers up-to-speed."*

Having innovation skills means that many employees will see you as capable and knowledgeable and there is a certain amount of status and prestige that is associated with being an expert. However, if interpersonal skills do not go along with it then status does not last long. There are some people who do have innovation know-how but they lack people skills, are rude and put other people down. They have very little status. Individuals need to possess both innovation and interpersonal skills to have status and respect from their colleagues. An employee will try to adopt a new system when he or she feel that using the system or innovation will lead to improvements in his or her image. "An individual may believe that a system is useful because the system enhances their image and social status" (Yi, Jackson, Park & Probst, 2006, p.355).

## When asked, "To what extent do you think that people who work with computer innovation and enjoy it, are the early adopters of innovation or new systems?"

Respondents agreed that people who work with innovation and enjoy it are the early adopters, such as people who enjoy working with computers. They indicated that playfulness and having fun are important in trying out a new thing. Respondents said:

*"People who enjoy it tend to be early adopters. Most of the people I know working with computer technology do enjoy it and all of become early adopters. Enjoyment plays a major part."*

*"That is very true. People who enjoy it live around the technology, and they are the first to find about it and use it. It is almost like a hobby."*

*"There are people who use their time and find out the new system and play with it. They like to play with the computer and enjoy it. So, enjoyment is very important."*

A few respondents stated that if innovation seems familiar to them then they enjoy it, become more confident and are inclined to use it more often. However, if it is totally new then they do not feel much enjoyment. They may even be scared of using it. As one respondent said:

*"I feel good and bad depending on who I am with because whole prior knowledge has a big impact on that. If I see something new and I have prior experience and then I feel I will do excellent work, this creates enjoyment for me. However, if it is totally foreign and I have never come across it before then I may be a bit scared."*

There are individuals who just like to discover things. They like to explore innovation. It is not because of pressure from management, but it is because they enjoy it. As they said:

*"There are people who get excited to do something with computers and enjoy working and doing so. They enjoy the time using it and they love to discover new things."*

Van der Heijden (2004) emphasized that entertainment and pleasure have a strong influence on adoption decisions and these avenues provide an opportunity to escape reality and become absorbed in a new world.

## When asked, "To what extent do you think that peers can help you to understand and use a new system or innovation?"

Respondents agreed that peers can help to a great extent to understand and use an innovation. For any innovation peers are the first people to whom you can go and ask how to do things with it. For example, peers can show you directly how to use certain applications. Respondents said:

*"It does not matter how much you know, what you know, peers can help you to a great extent. Peers can show you very important applications which even IT experts did not show you. I have received a great deal of help from peers."*

*"In a friendly environment peers are quite important. They normally help each other to understand new things. I have a lot of experience in this aspect because when first I came here I found new technologies which I have not used before. I got help from peers and they were very helpful."*

The encouragement from peers is crucial, as respondents indicated. Individuals are highly influenced by the support and suggestions provided by peers. Respondents put it this way:

*"The help from peers is crucial and very important, and encouragement from peers is also very important. If I did not have peers to support me it would be very difficult to manage. I got not only direct help but also encouragement from them. They provided me with direction and guidance."*

*"Peers have a very strong influence. If peers use a certain technology such as calendar then you almost automatically have to use it so that you will be able to interact with them. If you hear praise from other people and recommendations from peers then that will influence you as well."*

Good peers are essential and they always help others without putting someone down and do not undermine co-workers for their lack of knowledge. A healthy and friendly environment is essential for providing help to and receiving encouragement from peers. As one respondent said:

*"It is very important to have good co-workers or peers who can help you willingly without putting you down."*

Respondents agreed that assistance from peers is much quicker and easy to follow due to its very informality. This is more efficient and effective than reading guidelines or handbooks, online material or going to official training sessions. As several respondents stated:

*"Peers can help you with a problem and show you how to solve it in a way that you cannot read in the book. When peers show you how to do things you learn much more easily. Many industries put new employees with peers so that they can learn faster."*

*"It is good when peers help you. Peers can show you how to do it and they probably know pros and cons and how to handle the technology."*

*"I do not want to go to do a course for half a day. I would rather go to my colleague in the next office and ask for their help, which may only take few minutes for them to show me."*

Several interviewees mentioned that peers should be able and willing to help others. They should be able to explain things to their colleagues. Respondents noted:

*"It depends on who your co-worker is and their skills for interpretation and explanation of things. I know there are certain people in this office who are very good at explaining things. They use easy to understand language, which makes it easy to follow their instructions."*

*"Yes, in every situation co-workers can really help but it depends on who the co-worker is? It also depends on whether they understand what I am talking about and whether they have time and are willing to help. They need to be patient and ... sit down with you and show you what you need to know."*

Respondents agreed that help from peers really saves time. Rather than wasting your time searching for secondary sources, it is much better asking and getting help from people who are nearby. As interviewees said:

*"Peers can help to a great extent. It would be much easier to use a technology when I get help from peers if I encounter any problem. So, I will not have to figure out how to solve it. I can just go to my colleague next door and say 'Look I've got this problem, can you show me how to do it please?' I personally received a lot of help from peers. Some peers have certain skills which I do not have."*

*"If you are struggling with using the computer or applications then you are not enjoying it and you are going to feel like a fool whereas if someone can come along and help you and show you the simple things then you feel it is not a daunting task."*

Employees are influenced by peers to adopt innovation in that their moral support, motivation and encouragement have an influence (Yuan, et al., 2005). Frambach and Schillewaert (2002) claimed that the adoption of innovation by peers may provide an indication as to its importance. Individuals normally try to reproduce by looking at their peers and imitating them.

## When asked, "How do you think your social networks influence you to adopt a new system or innovation?"

Respondents indicated that social network has a strong influence on employees in the adoption of innovation. Social networks provide information about new technologies and how to use them. Employees also give much value to a network's advice and recommendations because other people in the network are also using the same innovation. As two respondents said:

*"Social networks have huge influence. I found different new technologies from the people I worked before and from the people whom I know. Often I hear about new technologies from outside and adopt them because I know other universities are using those technologies."*

*"I always follow social networks. I ask different people and take into account what they suggest to me about new technology."*

A significant number of respondents indicated that they use the Internet and communicate online, receiving information about new technologies and their usage. Sometimes to get proper and reliable information about a certain innovation they depend on virtual communities through which they get ideas about innovation from the users worldwide. As they put it:

*"With an emerging new technology you need to have a network of people who are using similar technology globally because it is so easier to communicate."*

*"If you are in a leading organization, which means you are using state-of-the-art technology, probably you are the only person using it in the region, so you need to have virtual networks to communicate with other people who are using similar technology."*

In general social networks demonstrate a positive influence on adopting something new. However, there are negative aspects as well. For example, if you hear negative views from networks then you will reconsider whether to use it or not. As two respondents stated:

*"If I start using something and start hearing negative views from outside people, then I think whether I should keep using it."*

*"The reverse is also true. If people in the network say no, do not use it because of such problems, then it will make you to think whether you are going to use it or not. A social network's influence is very powerful especially if the organization is not forcing you to adopt."*

Respondents pointed out that a social network's influence is at its highest when individuals feel that the particular innovation will benefit them and increase their work efficiency and other performance-related duties. Respondents put it this way:

*"If I am interested in learning something which is going to make my job easier then I would be more influenced by social networks and their opinions."*

According to respondents, social networks can provide a sense of inadequacy and can be a strong motivator. Many times you will hear people in your network talking about new technologies or systems that you have no idea about. This could influence you to investigate those technologies further. Hearing from friends you will feel that you do not want to be left behind and want to be knowledgeable about any innovation. As respondents said:

*"Talking to other people and hearing about new technologies you do get a sense of having something to adopt and a feeling of inadequacy. That can be a motivator. I think social networks are quite important. I get information from outside of my department and from people working in different schools."*

Respondents agreed that sometimes they adopt innovation due to pressure from social networks even though they were not thinking about adopting it. According to respondents:

*"Social network is quite an influential factor. If other universities or organizations are using a system then there is pressure to use a similar system."*

*"I was influenced by a social network in Outlook usage because all people around me were using Outlook and all the messages I was receiving were using Outlook calendar. I was in the middle of a network where all others were using calendar and I had to use it although I had not used it before."*

From the above interviews it became clear that social networks do exert an influence on employees to adopt and use innovation. However, this influence depends on whether you really need it and whether it will improve your efficiency. Employees may adopt an innovation based on information that other employees in interrelated organizations in their market environment have (Brown & Venkatesh, 2005; Kraut, Rice, Cool & Fish, 1998). External influences are therefore an important factor in the adoption of innovation (Khoumbati, Themistocleous & Irani, 2006).

## 7.3 Summary of Interviews

The in-depth interviews support the development of the advanced model and assist further understanding of the factors that affect adoption of innovation by employees in an organization. The results of the qualitative study validate the quantitative results. Furthermore, the qualitative study provides additional information and further insights into the variables that were insignificant in the quantitative study. The findings of the qualitative study strengthen the outcome of the overall study.

The findings showed that training is vital for employees. Training enhances individuals' beliefs, possession of skills and knowledge that allow tasks to be completed successfully. However, many employees feel that they do not have enough time to go to training or to spend extra time learning something new. It has been noted that managerial support is an important aspect of enabling employees to accept innovation. Managerial support is essential in terms of financial, technical or providing time to learn an innovation and in other resources. Management needs to provide quick responses to employees' needs and requirements. Quick responses and appropriate support may encourage employees to use innovation. Lack of support is considered a critical barrier to the adoption and effective utilization of innovation.

The results found that incentives have tremendous impact and strong influence on individuals' adoption of innovation. Promise of advantages, promotion, facilities or financial incentives motivate employees to adopt and use innovation. Employees are concerned about personal benefits such as career advancement, personal facilities, formal and informal recognition, increased autonomy, beliefs about self worth and achievement and greater job security. To encourage adoption and assist continuous use of innovation, management must provide incentives to employees in the form of commissions, recognition and praise. Incentives do not necessarily have to be financial, if innovation adoption makes life easier and frees up time to do other things.

The findings showed that employees investigate usefulness of innovation by experimenting and testing it, asking friends for their opinions and when they feel that innovation is going to be useful to them. However, before adopting any innovation employees feel that they need to see whether the innovation that they are going to adopt will provide much value and will be worth the time that they will spend on it. Employees must therefore check for any possible problems that may arise.

The qualitative data showed that personal innovativeness wields a strong influence on discovering new things and a degree of personal initiative is needed when exploring innovation. Some individuals have an innate tendency to experiment with innovation. However, others explore innovation for the sake of personal benefit. If innovation significantly improves their job then they become interested and involved in exploring the innovation. Some employees are skeptical about learning new things but others feel that they need to be up-to-date with it. Employees with higher personal innovativeness are more likely to develop a positive attitude toward innovation adoption and use.

The results demonstrate that prior experience with similar innovation is helpful for adopting innovation. Prior experience makes employees comfortable and familiarity makes it easy to adopt new ideas and innovation. Employees develop more sophisticated knowledge about the innovation and this is a major advantage. Prior experience reduces anxiety, provides confidence and positively influences employees to use innovation. However, there are employees who feel that it is not necessary to have prior experience to adopt innovation and they are willing to try something new. It is possible that prior experience may obstruct adoption because people like to compare things with what they had previously and if innovation does not fit their mindset they will not use it.

The findings show that image is an important factor that affects employees' adoption of innovation. If employees know something that their co-workers do not know then they feel positive about it gets a special sense of pride and achievement. If the individual is the only one who knows about the innovation then he or she may obtain some advantage. These may include a special position in the organization, status or authority. Employees feel that they want to share knowledge with others and would like to help others who do not know the system. Employees adopt innovation when they feel that using it will improve their work and standing in the company or organization. In a typical work situation where there is a high degree of interdependence with other employees in carrying out one's duties, increased image and status within the group is important to many employees.

Employees who work with innovation and enjoy it are early adopters. Playfulness and having fun are important factors in adopting innovation. If innovation is familiar to individuals then they enjoy it, become more confident and are inclined to use it. There are individuals who enjoy using innovation and they adopt innovation not because of pressure from management but because they enjoy it. Entertainment and the need for pleasure have a strong influence on adoption decisions.

Peers can help others understand and use innovation because they can show directly how to use certain applications. Peers are the first people to whom an employee can go and ask how to do things with innovation. Employees are very much influenced by moral support, suggestions and encouragement provided by peers. Their assistance and advice is much quicker, easier to follow and more effective than reading guidelines, directories or handbooks, online material or going to official training sessions. In short, help from peers saves time. Fellow workers' adoption of innovation may indicate its importance and advantages, which eventually motivate individual employees to adopt the innovation.

Although there is no doubt that to a large extent peers can help, they must also be able and willing to help others. A healthy and friendly environment is essential for receiving help from peers.

Social networks therefore do exert an influence on employees when the adoption of innovation is being considered because people in the network provide information about new technologies. A business organization's employees may adopt innovation based on the fact that employees in other similar organizations have taken up the same innovation. Social networks may generate feelings of inadequacy in people when they hear talking about new technologies or systems about which one has no idea. This could influence people to investigate those technologies in more detail. People generally do not want to be left behind when new technologies are such an important part of the workplace. Individuals may adopt innovation due to pressure from or out of deference to social networks even though they may not have been thinking about adopting it. While social networks can lead to the adoption of something that is new, they can also create problems. If people hear negative views and opinions from their social networks then they may decide not to use it.

## 7.4 Conclusion

This chapter has presented a qualitative data analysis of the study. The qualitative data supports the development of an advanced model of innovation adoption by employees who work for an organization. The qualitative data also validates and proves the proposed advanced model. In addition, qualitative results provide additional information about the factors that were non-significant in the quantitative study.

The qualitative study was conducted through in-depth interviews to further investigate the effect of organizational, individual and social factors on individual attitude toward adoption and usage. In the qualitative study three organizational factors – training, managerial support and incentives – were investigated. These variables were incorporated in the advanced model as external factors affecting attitude toward adoption and consequently usage. Data analyses showed that these variables were positively and significantly affecting individual attitude toward adoption and usage.

The qualitative study investigated five individual factors: perceived usefulness, personal innovativeness, prior experience, image and enjoyment with innovation. These variables were introduced and placed corresponding to the main belief construct of the technology acceptance model and the theory of reasoned action model as affecting individual attitude toward adoption and usage. The findings show that these variables have positive and significant influence on individuals' attitude toward adoption.

The qualitative study also investigated two social factors – peers and social network. The technology adoption model did not include social factors as subjective norms constructs of the theory of reasoned action was not significant and one of the least understood aspect of the theory of reasoned action. The advanced model in this study incorporated social factors as affecting individual attitude toward adoption and usage. The findings from qualitative data show that both factors positively and significantly affect individual's attitude toward adoption and usage.

Note that these social factors were insignificant in the quantitative study but were found to be highly important and significant in the qualitative study. Although it is difficult to clarify the discrepancies between the findings of the two methodologies, the possible explanations are outlined below.

In the qualitative study participants were more open and free in providing information regarding the factors that affect their attitude towards adoption and use of innovation. Participants were able to explain more in face-to-face communication. They could provide information about personal feelings, perceptions and opinions regarding the factors affecting their attitude and use of innovative ideas. It allowed participants to describe what is meaningful to them. Participants were able to provide more explanation on a wide range of issues.

In the qualitative study, the researcher was able to adapt the questions as required to clarify and ensure that responses were properly understood by repeating or rephrasing the questions. Alternatively, if some responses were not clear the researcher asked them to clarify and provide further information. This helped to produce detailed information and ensure that participants interpreted questions correctly. It also helped to discover how individuals think and feel about a particular issue and why they hold certain opinions.

Conversely, the quantitative study depends on how individual respondents interpret the survey questions and provide responses to particular questions. In the quantitative study respondents did not take much time to think and respond. They tended to respond as quickly as possible with answers that fitted their personal interpretation of the question. To collect the quantitative data this study used a five-point Likert-type scale. Using a seven- or even nine-point scale could provide a wider spread of data and those variables may have become even more significant.

In regression analysis, training was negatively affecting usage although correlation showed that training is positively correlated with attitude and usage. Qualitative results showed that training has a vital role in innovation adoption and usage and positively affect individual attitude toward adoption and continuous usage of innovation. Similarly, prior experience was non-significant in quantitative study but qualitative study showed that prior experience is an important factor affecting individual attitude toward adoption of innovation.

Further research could be conducted in regards to social factors and other factors, which were non-significant in the quantitative study. Conducting research in different types of organizations and testing the advanced model could be another avenue for future research.

The next and final chapter, Chapter 8, will discuss the overall summary of the study, conclusions, research contributions, limitations and future research.

# 8

# Conclusion and Implications

## 8.1 Introduction

This study provides a new theoretical construct and develops an advanced model of innovation adoption (AMIA) by investigating a wide range of factors that affect individuals' adoption of innovation in an organizational context. The proposed advanced model was tested via a variety of methods consisting chiefly of a questionnaire survey and in-depth interviews. The research process was reviewed and assessed in conjunction with the findings. This chapter presents the summary, conclusions and implications, the contribution to knowledge, research limitations and ideas for future research.

## 8.2 Summary of Research

This study investigated the adoption of innovation by employees in an organization. Innovation must be appropriately used by employees in order for them and their organization or business to obtain the benefits. The current literature shows that we know relatively little about the ways in which or reasons why individuals adopt innovation. Although innovation adoption has been studied extensively, drivers of adoption and research on individual innovation acceptance in the organizational context remains limited (Frambach & Schillewaert, 2002). Organizational innovations that need to be incorporated in work processes of an organization are of little value if they are not used or complied with by employees. Therefore, it is important to examine the adoption of innovations by employees within organizations, which this study seeks to address.

Three questions were proposed in an attempt to explain the factors which affect and determine the adoption and continued use of innovation by individual employees: (1) What is the impact of organizational factors – training, managerial support and incentives – on individual adoption of innovation? (2) Do individual factors – perceived usefulness, personal innovativeness, prior experience, image and enjoyment with innovation – affect individuals' adoption of innovation? (3) What is the impact of social factors – peers and social network – on the individual adoption of innovation?

A literature review was undertaken from which a new theoretical construct was proposed and an advanced model for innovation adoption was developed. It took into consideration the strength and limitations of other existing models. The theoretical framework of this study is based on the theory of reasoned action (TRA), the technology acceptance model (TAM) and Frambach and Schillewaert's (2002) conceptual framework of individual innovation acceptance. The model in this study maintains the basic structure of the TRA and incorporates the elements of the TAM and Frambach and Schillewaert's list of factors. They recommended a study be undertaken to test these factors while introducing several modifications. In addition, the model added a few other variables found in various innovation adoption-related research and added demographic factors to the advanced model that were lacking in the TAM or TRA.

Several avenues of data collection were employed to test the relevance of the proposed advanced model: (1) a primary questionnaire survey – to test the proposed advanced model, and (2) interviews – to get further insight about the factors that affect adoption and usage. Statistical analysis of data was done using the SPSS (statistical package for social sciences) package. Frequency distribution and percentages were calculated and several cross-tabulations were performed. Correlation matrix, test for reliability and ANOVA (analysis of variance) tests were carried out. To test the proposed model, multiple regression analysis was performed on the collected data. The analyses tested the advanced model and the findings supported it.

The study was expanded by adding qualitative data from a series of interviews conducted after the questionnaire results had been analyzed. Results from the interviews further supported the quantitative analysis of the study. This qualitative study helped further understand of the factors that affect adoption and continuous usage of innovation. The results of the interviews also assisted in the validation of the quantitative results. The interview study identified critical and problematic issues while at the same time strengthening the results of the overall study.

## 8.3 Conclusions and Implications for Innovation Adoption

From a theoretical point of view, this research has served to broaden one's understanding of the factors affecting innovation adoption. This research is a response to the call for a more in-depth and comprehensive research on ways in which individuals adopt innovation, and factors that influence employees' decision to take on innovation. The main theoretical contribution of this research is the development of an advanced model of innovation adoption. Such a model is particularly useful for understanding the adoption of innovation by employees in comparison with TRA, TAM or Frambach and Schillewaert's (2002) model. This is because it examines a more complete and wider range of factors impacting individuals' adoption of innovation.

The theory of reasoned action was first introduced in 1967 by Ajzen and Fishbein (1980), a widely studied model which is concerned with the determinants of conscious intended behavior. However, their analysis of behavior did not make any reference to various factors such as personality characteristics (demographic variables) or external factors and there is evidence that these factors influence the behavior (Ajzen & Fishbein, 1980).

The technology acceptance model, which was introduced in 1986 by Davis (1989), is an adaptation of the theory of reasoned action specifically tailored to explain determinants of technology acceptance. The model tested only two variables – perceived usefulness and ease of use. Thompson, Higgins and Howell (1991) argue that the model should drop behavioral intention and link attitude to actual behavior because we are interested in actual behavior. Similarly, Yi, Jackson, Park and Probst (2006) suggest that the innovation acceptance model should be integrated into a more inclusive model incorporating variables related to both human and social processes. Further, TAM also did not include demographic factors as suggested by TRA and did not test as many variables compared to the more recent model of technology acceptance provided by Frambach and Schillewaert (2002).

In 2002 a more comprehensive theoretical framework was provided by Frambach and Schillewaert (2002) to assess individual adoption of innovation and recommended a study to test the model. However, this model did not include several important variables, which have been used in other innovation adoption research using TRA or TAM.

The proposed advanced model is clear, simpler and consists of three processes. The model is directly linked to attitude and adoption because organizational, individual and social factors affect attitude, which consequently influences adoption. This model is better and more comprehensive than TRA, TAM or Frambach and Schillewaert's model in explaining individuals' adoption of innovation because it has ten independent variables and five moderating variables compared to two variables in both TRA and TAM. In addition, the researcher has removed some unnecessary complexity compared to previous models and this model will consequently provide greater explanatory power in practical settings. The proposed advanced model will move the innovation acceptance and adoption model into the next generation. It is possible that this model will remain for a long period of time testing innovation acceptance and adoption in the organization. This is because as organizational, individual and social factors or demographics characteristics change over time and new factors emerge in the future, they can easily be added and fitted into boxes identified as organizational, individual, social factors or demographics characteristics and test them in any organizational context at any location around the globe.

The literature has made it clear that for a long period of time most of the research on innovation acceptance has used either TRA or TAM for the theoretical framework. However, a few studies have extended these models by adding one or two variables (Chang & Cheung, 2001, p.2; Huang, 2005). Despite those models having some problems or shortcomings, innovation acceptance-related studies continue to use them because there has been no alternative. The advanced model developed in this study provides a new approach that will advance research in the field of innovation acceptance.

By identifying a comprehensive list of organizational, individual and social factors as well as demographics in individuals' adoption of innovation, this study departs from traditional innovation acceptance research that used only a few factors. Furthermore, most of the previous research emphasized the organizational point of view rather than that of employees, who in fact use the innovation. By employing a combination of quantitative and qualitative data, this study creates a better understanding of the different factors that play a role in affecting individuals' adoption of innovation.

The analysis of quantitative and qualitative data has resulted in an empirical model that can be written as follows:

$$U = -0.879 - 0.149\ TR + 0.401\ MS + 0.158\ IN + 0.367\ PU + 0.180\ PI + 0.039\ PE + 0.102\ IM + 0.100\ EI - 0.072\ PR - 0.022\ SN$$

Where:

U = Usage
TR = Training
MS = Managerial support
IN = Incentives
PU = Perceived usefulness
PI = Personal innovativeness

PE = Prior experience
IM = Image
EI = Enjoyment with innovation
PR = Peers
SN = Social network

The multiple regressions indicated that ten independent variables accounted for 53.1% of the variance in the individual acceptance of innovation. Table 6.31 illustrated the coefficients and constant for regression equation and significance of each independent variable in the model predicting the dependent variable. The correlations among independent and dependent variables in Table 6.25 show that independent variables are positively and significantly related to dependent variable usage. The models concerning TRA and the TAM did not include external factors but did mention that external factors are important in affecting individuals' behavior. The researcher has incorporated three external organizational factors and used the previous models as the basis of developing an advanced model. Based on the findings, this study has shown the importance of external factors in explaining the adoption of innovation by individual employees in the organization.

The data from the regression analysis indicated that training is significant but it was negatively related. The data from the Pearson correlation analysis shows that training has a positive and significant relationship with usage. It means training significantly affects usage and if training increases the level of usage also increases. There could be several reasons for a negative relationship emerging. Training is important for some individuals but not to others. Some individuals do not to need training but they still adopt or accept an innovation. There are employees who may prefer to implement the innovation and feel that they do not need training. This discrepancy in the results was highlighted in the qualitative study, which revealed that training does influence employees' adoption of innovation. Training helps employees to understand and learn about an innovation and its features. Training also assists individual users in encouraging them to use innovation in their daily work. Findings indicated that training and educational programs should aim to increase awareness of potential applications and benefits in using the innovation. Training should be provided for employees, especially during the early stages of implementation of innovation or systems in an organization.

The study found that senior management support and incentives are important factors in a smooth process of innovation adoption. When individuals perceive strong managerial support, allocation of sufficient resources and some kind of personal benefits, they are likely to develop a positive attitude toward the innovation. Findings suggest that managers need to focus careful attention on showing their commitment to innovation. Unless individuals perceive that management is strongly behind the use of an innovation, they are unlikely to develop favorable attitudes toward the innovation. A business organization may nurture in their employees a positive attitude to use an innovation by implementing preplanned support activities such as allocating resources and providing incentives such as recognition, increased autonomy and greater job security.

Unlike TRA or TAM, which have used only one to two variables under belief construct in their models, this study tested five variables under belief construct defined as individual factors and found significant support for those variables. The result of this study found that perceived usefulness has a strong effect on usage. It also revealed that there is a strong positive relationship between usefulness and usage because individuals adopt an innovation or system when they see that it will give them much value. In order to increase the adoption of a new system or innovation, an organization should emphasize its benefits, functionality and advantages.

The result indicated that personal innovativeness affects individual's adoption behavior. This finding is important because it implies that innovation adoption in the organization needs to go beyond a traditional innovation adoption strategy. A research and implementation program must include individuals' habits and predispositions towards innovation that they bring to the job. Individual employees who are innovative will be more inclined to use the innovation. Organizations can utilize these people as important agents of change because they are likely to influence others and thereby create a positive attitude regarding the acceptance of innovation.

Prior experience was not supported in the regression analysis but has a positive and significant relationship in the Pearson correlation analysis. The qualitative results also revealed that prior experience strongly influences adoption behavior. Findings from quantitative (Pearson correlations) and qualitative results showed that image and enjoyment of innovation have a positive and significant relationship with usage. Both variables are important in explaining usage behavior. Being an expert with a certain innovation helps individual employees to see themselves as capable and knowledgeable among co-workers. There is a certain amount of status that goes with being an expert in the area. It creates a positive image for employees and gives them special pride. Organizations that intend to introduce an innovation or system should recognize individuals' expertise and knowledge. This will motivate others and facilitate greater adoption among employees.

Enjoyment of innovation plays a significant role in fostering a positive attitude toward adoption and usage of innovation. Organizations which aim for a greater use of innovation should emphasize not only the advantages of adopting the innovation, but also those features that make individual employees enjoy using the innovation. This is because individual employees are motivated not only by extrinsic benefits but also the intrinsic outcome using the innovation. Organizations should therefore strive to include "fun" elements in the system.

Davis (1989) did not include a subjective norms construct in TAM because it was insignificant and was one of the least understood aspects of TRA. The researcher believes that social factors influence individuals' attitudes toward adoption. Therefore, in the development of the advanced model the researcher introduced social factors and extended TAM to form a new theoretical model. From the regression analysis it was found that both variables – peers and social network – are non-significant or insignificant. However, the Pearson correlation showed that peers and social factors play a positive and significant part in reference to usage. The qualitative analysis also supports the notion that both variables are important in affecting individuals' likelihood of adopting innovation.

The study found that assistance from peers is extremely important in understanding and using a new system. An individual is more likely to have a positive attitude toward an innovation when he/she receives help from one's peers. An organization should create a supportive social environment among peers to encourage greater productivity in using innovation. Organizations should ensure that employees show greater support to those who have just started at the company or business. To increase the adoption rate of innovation in the organization, peers should provide continuous feedback, support and encouragement for such individuals so that they can master the innovation skills within a short period of time. Employees are influenced by their social network to adopt or at least consider an innovation, since many employees do not want to be left behind. Instead, they want to be knowledgeable about the innovation. With the help of the Internet and virtual communities, individuals are able to get much more information and consequently be influenced by innovation users around the world.

This study investigated the factors that affect the level of usage by individual employees within the organization. However, the researcher also undertook an additional analysis to assess the impact of those factors on people's attitudes. A correlation between usage and attitude shows that there is a strong, significant and positive relationship between attitude and usage (Chapter 6, section 6.5).

Incorporating and testing demographic characteristics in the advanced model in this study is another improvement on previous innovation acceptance models. Ajzen and Fishbein (1980) and Davis (1989) did not include demographics characteristics in their TRA and TAM models but Ajzen and Fishbein (1980) mentioned demographics characteristics are important in explaining usage behavior. The findings have discovered that demographic variables influence the attitude toward adoption. The hierarchical multiple regressions with demographic characteristics as controlled variable and other independent variables together accounted for 60.6% of variance in the individual acceptance of innovation. Table 6.54 showed that the coefficients and significance of each demographic variable in the model predicted usage behavior. ANOVA tests in section 6.8 also discussed the significant differences in the demographic characteristics regarding innovation usage.

The study found that female, administrative (professional) staff and full-time employees have greater influence on attitude toward the adoption and usage of innovation compared to male, academic staff and part-time employees. Employees in the science and technology disciplines have a greater influence on adoption compared to individuals who are in the business or social sciences disciplines. Demographic characteristics such as age and educational qualification had no significant impact on attitude toward adoption.

Data shows that an organization should not allocate resources on training and other efforts to educate or encourage adoption based on age or educational qualification. Findings indicate that age and educational qualification do not make any significant difference in the adoption of innovation. Employees of all ages and educational background understand the importance of innovation and use it in their daily activities. Thus, the findings encourage organizations to develop training programs for male, academic and part-time employees to so that they can use the innovation more effectively. Organizations also need to design training and other educational programs that will motivate employees who work in business and social sciences to adopt and use innovation.

Finally, an organization needs to know what strategies it needs to embrace during the adoption process and the comprehensive approach advocated here can provide much detail in this regard. To implement and manage innovations that enhance human capabilities and performance, management must recognize the organizational, individual and social factors as well as demographic factors that influence individual employees. The findings of this study will help organizations to identify factors and provide favourable workplace conditions prior to implementation of innovation. They also contribute to a better understanding of the factors that promote adoption of innovation and its usage.

Some of the most common obstacles to innovation adoption are inadequate training, lack of human capacity and expertise and inadequate managerial support. Any innovation is likely to encounter a substantial amount of resistance and many problems. However, the advanced model demonstrates that it may be particularly important to the organizations and employees wanting to adopt and implement innovation. In short, the theoretical framework developed and utilized in this study provides a rich and potentially fruitful area for further research, as well as contribution to knowledge. It has practical implications for organizations, managers, administrators and the employees concerned with taking up innovation in the organization.

## 8.4 Contribution to Knowledge

The research has contributed to knowledge in three ways: by developing a new model, by examining the little explored area of individual adoption and by using innovative research methods.

## DEVELOPED A THEORETICAL CONSTRUCT THAT COMBINES INDIVIDUAL ADOPTION OF INNOVATION ISSUES INTO A COHERENT MODEL

The study has contributed to theory by proposing and developing an advanced model of innovation adoption that involves the combination of multiple variables found in previous innovation acceptance models. Considering the general lack of research on individual adoption and the scattered research in the area using few variables, it was imperative to derive a simple combination of variables and a coherent model that examines individual adoption in the organizational context. This study concisely addresses an extensive list of factors and tested them for their relevance and significance. It addressed the differences between these factors and therefore the study contributes to knowledge and a wider theoretical understanding of the phenomenon. The model also serves as the framework for future research on innovation adoption. Further investigation can be undertaken using this theoretical model.

## EXAMINING AN IMPORTANT ASPECT OF INNOVATION ADOPTION

Despite the fact that innovation has been studied extensively, the drivers of adoption and research on individual adoption of innovation remain limited. The current literature revealed weaknesses in the area and indicates that we know relatively little about the ways in which individuals adopt innovation and the factors that influence individuals' adoption of innovation in the organization. It was deemed timely and important to conduct research to examine the adoption of innovation by individual employees within the organization. This study addressed those concerns and investigated the factors that influence adoption of innovation by individual employees in an organization.

## IMPLICATIONS FOR METHODOLOGIES

Apart from the theoretical implications, this study also has some implications for research methodologies. Firstly, the study has demonstrated a good understanding of the factors influencing and determining employees' adoption of innovation through quantitative and qualitative analysis. The quantitative method used in this research was an online survey questionnaire, followed by qualitative research through interviews that validated the findings and supported the quantitative analysis. While this approach is not new, most of the innovation acceptance-related studies seem to focus on quantitative work, not a combined approach. The latter is more likely to lead to a better understanding of the phenomenon and conceptual framework. Moreover, the respondents were actual users of the innovation. And, as professionals and management personnel, they have a range of characteristics and experiences that better suits research of this nature than college students only, as is frequently the case in studies of this nature.

## 8.5 Study Limitations

This study is not without its limitations. The following section presents limitations of the study, followed by suggestions for future research. This study encompasses a single Australian tertiary education institution. The same research carried out in another setting might generate a different result as organizational, interpersonal and social factors could vary according to cultural, geographical and socio-economic context, etc. Due to practical constraints this study was cross-sectional in that all measurement was done at a single point in time. Nevertheless, this research tested a model based on theories and literature and was supported by empirical research. It is believed that the approach undertaken in this research is a logical extension of previous studies and that the variables and relationships tested were appropriate.

## 8.6 Future Research

The study derived a set of ten variables, not all of which would be equally important in a specific organizational setting. The study may have also ignored some moderating effects related to the considered variables. Future research may incorporate more moderating effects such as organizational size, age and structure, because these can influence attitudes and usage. It might also be useful to examine the relationship between the adoption of innovation and organizational performance.

The study used two social factors – peers and social network. There was some inconsistency in the results obtained by quantitative and qualitative methods. In the qualitative method these factors were considered highly important in affecting attitude and usage of innovation. However, in the quantitative method these factors were insignificant. Further investigation testing these social factors might provide greater insights and their impact on attitude toward innovation adoption and usage.

The study used three organizational factors – training, managerial support and incentives. Future studies could replicate them and take into account the effect of negative incentives such as threats and disincentives that were not examined in this study.

The study was conducted at a single point in time. Future work could use longitudinal research design to explain similar issues. A longitudinal study would allow for the use of growth as a measure of performance. Longitudinal studies should be undertaken to fully investigate the causal effect of various factors and their relationships over time.

Further research studies may address the differences in innovation between developed and developing nations. A cross-cultural study on the adoption of innovation may help us understand attitudinal and perceptual differences between employees in multiple countries.

The sample was chosen to represent individuals who use a system in practice but more research is needed to investigate other employees who do not use a system regularly. Future research studies could focus on identifying more determinants of innovation adoption such as ethnicity, lifestyle and psychological factors.

This research provides a useful understanding of individual innovation adoption in an organizational context. While the results reported here would seem to be generalizable to other organizations that have similar characteristics, the scope and the context are somewhat limited. The interpretation and implications of the findings of this research depend on the nature of the organization. Therefore, further research is needed to broaden and confirm the results and implications of this study.

This research could be extended to other industry settings; for example, manufacturing or production industries. It may also be possible to conduct similar research in other countries either in the same or different organizational settings. This might provide more insight into different organizational or cultural contexts.

The model of this research can potentially be applied to a large number of innovation adoption and management problems in innovation adoption areas. Future studies may seek to identify research areas in innovation or management so that they may benefit from using the advanced model of innovation adoption developed in this study.

# References

Abrahamson, E., & Rosenkopf, L. (1997). Social network effects on the extent of innovation diffusion: A computer simulation. *Organization Science, 8*(3), 289–309.

Afuah, A. (2003). *Innovation management: Strategies, implementation, and profits*. New York: Oxford University Press.

Agarwal, R., & Prasad, J. (1998). The antecedents and consequents of user perceptions in information technology adoption. *Decision Support Systems, 22*(1), 15–29.

Ahuja, M., & Thatcher, J. (2005). Moving beyond intentions and toward the theory of trying: Effects of work environment and gender on post-adoption information technology use. *MIS Quarterly, 29*(3), 427–59.

Ajzen, I. (1991). The theory of planned behavior. *Organizational Behavior and Human Decision Processes, 50*(2), 179–211.

Ajzen, I., & Fishbein, M. (1980). *Understanding attitudes and predicting social behavior*. Englewood Cliffs, New Jersey: Prentice-Hall.

Al-Gahtani, S., & King, M. (1999). Attitudes, satisfaction and usage: Factors contributing to each in the acceptance of information technology. *Behaviour & Information Technology, 18*(4), 277–97.

Attewell, P. (1992). Technology diffusion and organizational learning: The case of business computing. *Organization Science, 3*(1), 1–19.

Babin, B., Darden, W., & Griffin, M. (1994). Work and/or fun: Measuring hedonic and utilitarian shopping value. *The Journal of Consumer Research, 20*(4), 644–56.

Bandura, A. (1986). *Social foundations of thought and action: A social cognitive theory*. Englewood Cliffs, New Jersey: Prentice-Hall.

Bhatnagar, A., & Ghose, S. (2004). A latent class segmentation analysis of e-shoppers. *Journal of Business Research, 57*(7), 758–67.

Bhattacherjee, A. (1998). Managerial influences on intra-organizational information technology use: A principal-agent model. *Decision Sciences, 29*(1), 139–62.

Bhattacherjee, A., & Sanford, C. (2006). Influence processes for information technology acceptance: An elaboration likelihood model. *MIS Quarterly, 30*(4), 805–25.

Brancheau, J., & Wetherbe, J. (1990). The adoption of spreadsheet software: Testing innovation diffusion theory in the context of end-user computing. *Information Systems Research, 1*(2), 115–43.

Brown, S., & Venkatesh, V. (2005). Model of adoption of technology in households: A baseline model test and extension incorporating household life cycle. *MIS Quarterly, 29*(3), 399–426.

Bruner, G., & Kumar, A. (2005). Explaining consumer acceptance of handheld Internet devices. *Journal of Business Research, 58*(5), 553–8.

Burgess, A., Jackson, T., & Edwards, J. (2005). Email training significantly reduces email defects. *International Journal of Information Management, 25*(1), 71–83.

Chang, M., & Cheung, W. (2001). Determinants of the intention to use Internet/ WWW at work: A confirmatory study. *Information & Management, 39*(1), 1–14.

Chen, J., & Ching, R. (2002). A proposed framework for transitioning to an e-business model. *Quarterly Journal of Electronic Commerce, 3*(4), 375–89.

Cheung, W., Chang, M., & Lai, V. (2000). Prediction of Internet and World Wide Web usage at work: A test of an extended Triandis model. *Decision Support Systems, 30*(1), 83–100.

Cho, V. (2006). Factors in the adoption of third-party B2B portals in the textile industry. *Journal of Computer Information Systems, 46*(3), 18–31.

Clegg, C., Carey, N., Dean, G., Hornby, P., & Bolden, R. (1997). User's reactions to information technology: Some multivariate models and their implications. *Journal of Information Technology, 12*(1), 15–32.

Cohen, J. (1988). *Statistical power analysis for the behavioral sciences*. Hillsdale, New Jersey: Lawrence Erlbaum Associates.

Creswell, J. (1994). *Research design: Qualitative and quantitative approaches*. Thousand Oaks, California: Sage Publications.

Currid, C. (1995). What to do when money does not motivate. *Network World, 12*(14), 52–4.

Damanpour, F., (1996). Organizational complexity and innovation: Developing and testing multiple contingency models. *Management Science, 42*(5), 693–716.

Damanpour, F. & Schneider, M. (2006). Phase of the adoption of innovation in organizations: Effects of environment, organization and top managers. *British Journal of Management, 17*, 215–36.

Davis, F. (1989). Perceived usefulness, perceived ease of use, and user acceptance of information technology. *MIS Quarterly, 13*(3), 319–40.

Davis, F., Bagozzi, R., & Warshaw, P. (1989). User acceptance of computer technology: A comparison of two theoretical models. *Management Science, 35*(8), 982–1003.

DeVellis, R. (2003). *Scale development: Theory and applications.* Thousand Oaks, California: Sage Publications.

Dewar, R., & Dutton, J. (1986). The adoption of radical and incremental innovations: An empirical analysis. *Management Science, 32*(11), 1422–33.

Dielman, T. (2005). *Applied regression analysis: A second course in business and economic statistics.* Pacific Grove, California: Thomson Learning.

Easingwood, C., & Beard, C. (1989). High technology launch strategies in the UK. *Industrial Marketing Management, 18*(2), 125–38.

Farr, J., & Ford, C. (1990). Individual innovation. In M. West & J. Farr (eds.), *Innovation and Creativity at Work* (pp. 63–80). New York: John Wiley and Sons.

Field, A. (2005). *Discovering statistics using SPSS for Windows.* London: Sage Publications.

Frambach, R., Barkema, H., Nooteboom, B., & Wedel, M. (1998). Adoption of a service innovation in the business market: An empirical test of supply-side variables. *Journal of Business Research, 41*(2), 161–74.

Frambach, R., & Schillewaert, N. (2002). Organizational innovation adoption: A multi-level framework of determinants and opportunities for future research. *Journal of Business Research, 55*(2), 163–76.

Fulk, J., & Boyd, B. (1991). Emerging theories of communication in organizations. *Journal of Management, 17*(2), 407–46.

Fuller, R., Vician, C., & Brown, S. (2006). E-learning and individual characteristics: The role of computer anxiety and communication apprehension. *Journal of Computer Information Systems, 46*(4), 103–15.

Gauvin, S., & Rajiv, K. (1993). Innovativeness in industrial organizations: A two-stage model of adoption. *International Journal of Research in Marketing, 10*(2), 165–83.

Gopalakrishnan, S., & Bierly, P. (2001). Analyzing innovation adoption using a knowledge-based approach. *Journal of Engineering and Technology Management, 18*(2), 107–30.

Gopalakrishnan, S., & Damanpour, F. (1997). A review of innovation research in economics, sociology and technology management. *Omega, 25*(1), 15–28.

Hair, J., Anderson, R., Tatham, R., & Black, W. (1998). *Multivariate data analysis.* Upper Saddle River, New Jersey: Prentice Hall.

Han, J., Kim, N., & Srivastava, R. (1998). Market orientation and organizational performance: Is innovation a missing link? *Journal of Marketing, 62*(4), 30–45.

Higgins, J. (1995). Innovate or evaporate. *The Futurist, 29*(5), 42–9.

Hill, T., Smith, N., & Mann, M. (1987). Role of efficacy expectations in predicting the decision to use advanced technologies: The case of computers. *Journal of Applied Psychology, 72*(2), 307–13.

Holt, K. (1983). *Product innovation management: A workbook for management in industry*. Boston: Butterworths.

Huang, E. (2005). The acceptance of women-centric websites. *The Journal of Computer Information Systems, 45*(4), 75–83.

Igbaria, M. (1993). User acceptance of microcomputer technology: An empirical test. *Omega (Oxford), 21*(1), 73–90.

Igbaria, M., Guimaraes, T., & Davis, G. (1995). Testing the determinants of microcomputer usage via a structural equation model. *Journal of Management Information Systems, 11*(4), 87–114.

Igbaria, M., Parasuraman, S., & Baroudi, J. (1996). A motivational model of microcomputer usage. *Journal of Management Information Systems, 13*(1), 127–43.

Igbaria, M., Zinatelli, N., Cragg, P., & Cavaye, A. (1997). Personal computing acceptance factors in small firms: A structural equation model. *MIS Quarterly, 21*(3), 279–305.

Jasperson, J., Carter, P., & Zmud, R. (2005). A comprehensive conceptualization of the post-adoptive behaviors associated with IT-enabled work systems. *MIS Quarterly, 29*(3), 525–57.

Karahanna, E., Agarwal, R., & Angst, C. (2006). Reconceptualizing compatibility beliefs in technology acceptance research. *MIS Quarterly, 30*(4), 781–804.

Katz, M., & Shapiro, C. (1994). Systems competition and network effects. *The Journal of Economic Perspectives, 8*(2), 93–115.

Kennedy, A. (1983). The adoption and diffusion of new industrial products: A literature review. *European Journal of Marketing, 17*(3), 31–88.

Khoumbati, K., Themistocleous, M., & Irani, Z. (2006). Evaluating the adoption of enterprise application integration in health-care organizations. *Journal of Management Information Systems, 22*(4), 69–108.

Kim, H., Chan, H., & Gupta, S. (2007). Value-based adoption of mobile Internet: An empirical investigation. *Decision Support Systems, 43*(1), 111–26.

King, W., & He, J. (2006). A meta-analysis of the technology acceptance model. *Information & Management, 43*(6), 740–55.

Konana, P., & Balasubramanian, S. (2005). The social-economic-psychological (SEP) model of technology adoption and usage: An application to online investing. *Decision Support Systems, 39*(3), 505–24.

Kraut, R., Rice, R., Cool, C., & Fish, R. (1998). Varieties of social influence: The role of utility and norms in the success of a new communication medium. *Organization Science, 9*(4), 437–53.

Kukafka, R., Johnson, S., Linfante, A., & Allegrante, J. (2003). Grounding a new information technology implementation framework in behavioral science: A systematic analysis of the literature on IT use. *Journal of Biomedical Informatics, 36*(3), 218–27.

Kwok, S., & Gao, S. (2006). Attitude towards knowledge sharing. *Journal of Computer Information Systems, 46*(2), 45–51.

Lam, T., Cho, V., & Qu, H. (2007). A study of hotel employee behavioral intentions towards adoption of information technology. *International Journal of Hospitality Management, 26*(1), 49–65.

Lee, H., Lee, Y., & Kwon, D. (2005). The intention to use computerized reservation systems: The moderating effects of organizational support and supplier incentive. *Journal of Business Research, 58*(11), 1552–61.

Lee, J. (2004). Discriminant analysis of technology adoption behavior: A case of Internet technologies in small business. *Journal of Computer Information Systems, 44*(4), 57–66.

Lee, S., Kim, I., Rhee, S., & Trimi, S. (2006). The role of exogenous factors in technology acceptance: The case of object-oriented technology. *Information & Management, 43*(4), 469–80.

Lefebvre, L.A., Lefebvre, E., Elia, E. & Boeck, H. (2005). Exploring B-to-B e-commerce adoption trajectories in manufacturing SMEs. *Technovation, 25*(12), 1443–56.

Lerouge, C., Newton, S., & Blanton, J. (2005). Exploring the systems analyst skill set: Perceptions, preferences, age, and gender. *Journal of Computer Information Systems, 45*(3), 12–23.

Lewis, W., Agarwal, R., & Sambamurthy, V. (2003). Sources of influence on beliefs about information technology use: An empirical study of knowledge workers. *MIS Quarterly, 27*(4), 657–78.

Liao, Z., & Landry Jr, R. (2000). An empirical study on organizational acceptance of new information systems in a commercial bank environment. *System Sciences, 2000. Proceedings of the 33rd Annual Hawaii International Conference, January 4–7, 2000*, 1–7.

Ligon, J., Abdullah, A., & Talukder, M. (2007). The effect of formal education, technical and management training on information systems (IS) managers' managerial effectiveness as perceived by their subordinates. *Performance Improvement Quarterly, 20*(1), 23–37.

Likert, R. (1932). *A technique for the measurement of attitudes.* New York: Columbia University.

Lu, J., Yu, C., & Liu, C. (2005). Facilitating conditions, wireless trust and adoption intention. *Journal of Computer Information Systems, 46*(1), 17–24.

Mansfield, E. (1993). The diffusion of flexible manufacturing systems in Japan, Europe and the United States. *Management Science, 39*(2), 149–59.

Miles, M., & Huberman, A. (1994). *Qualitative data analysis*. Thousand Oaks, California: Sage Publications.

Mirvis, P., Sales, A., & Hackett, E. (1991). The implementation and adoption of new technology in organizations: The impact on work, people and culture. *Human Resource Management, 30*(1), 113–39.

Moore, G., & Benbasat, I. (1996). Integrating diffusion of innovations and Theory of Reasoned Action models to predict utilization of information technology by end-users. In K. Kautz & J. Pries-Heje (eds.), *Diffusion and Adoption of Information Technology* (pp. 132–46). London: Chapman and Hall.

Nelson, D. (1990). Individual adjustment to information-driven technologies: A critical review. *MIS Quarterly, 14*(1), 79–98.

Neuman, W. (2000). *Social research methods: Qualitative and quantitative approaches*. Boston: Allyn and Bacon.

Nilakant, V., & Rao, H. (1994). Agency theory and uncertainty in organizations: An evaluation. *Organization Studies, 15*(5), 649–72.

Nooteboom, B. (1988). Diffusion, uncertainty and firm size. *International Journal of Research in Marketing, 6*(2), 109–28.

Pavlou, P., & Fygenson, M. (2005). Understanding and predicting electronic commerce adoption: An extension of the Theory of Planned Behavior. *MIS Quarterly, 30*(1), 115–43.

Peansupap, V., & Walker, D. (2005). Exploratory factors influencing information and communication technology diffusion and adoption within Australian construction organizations: A micro analysis. *Construction Innovation, 5*(3), 135–57.

Poremsky, D. (2003). *Sams teach yourself Microsoft Office Outlook 2003 in 24 hours*. Indianapolis, Indiana: Sams Publishing.

Porter, C., & Donthu, N. (2006). Using the technology acceptance model to explain how attitudes determine Internet usage: The role of perceived access barriers and demographics. *Journal of Business Research, 59*(9), 999–1007.

Ram, S., & Jung, H. (1994). Innovativeness in product usage: A comparison of early adopters and early majority. *Psychology and Marketing, 11*(1), 57–67.

Robertson, T., & Gatignon, H. (1986). Competitive effects on technology diffusion. *Journal of Marketing, 50*(3), 1–12.

Rogers, E. (2003). *Diffusion of innovations*. New York: The Free Press.

Sappington, D. (1991). Incentives in principal-agent relationships. *The Journal of Economic Perspectives, 5*(2), 45–66.

Scandura, T., & Williams, E. (2000). Research methodology in management: Current practices, trends, and implications for future research. *Academy of Management Journal, 43*(6), 1248–64.

Schepers, J., & Wetzels, M. (2007). A meta-analysis of the technology acceptance model: Investigating subjective norm and moderation effects. *Information & Management, 44*(1), 90–103.

Sherif, K., Zmud, R., & Browne, G. (2006). Managing peer-to-peer conflicts in disruptive information technology innovations: The case of software reuse. *MIS Quarterly, 30*(2), 339–56.

Standen, P. and Sinclair-Jones, J. (2004). *eWork in regional Australia.* A report for the rural industries research and development corporation, Rural Industries Research and Development Corporation Publication No 04/045, Australia.

Stevens, J. (2001). *Applied multivariate statistics for the social sciences.* Mahwah, New Jersey: Lawrence Erlbaum Associates.

Taylor, S., & Todd, P. (1995). Understanding information technology usage: A test of competing models. *Information System Research, 6*(2), 144–76.

Thatcher, J., Stepina, L., Srite, M., & Liu, Y. (2003). Culture, overload and personal innovativeness with information technology: Extending the nomological net. *Journal of Computer Information Systems, 44*(1), 74–81.

Thompson, R., Higgins, C., & Howell, J. (1991). Personal computing: Toward a conceptual model of utilization. *MIS Quarterly, 15*(1), 125–43.

Trevino, L., & Webster, J. (1992). Flow in computer-mediated communication: Electronic mail and voice mail evaluation and impacts. *Communication Research, 19*(5), 125–43.

Vallerand, R. (1997). Toward a hierarchical model of intrinsic and extrinsic motivation. *Advances in Experimental Social Psychology, 29*, 271–360.

Van der Heijden, H. (2004). User acceptance of hedonic information systems. *MIS Quarterly, 28*(4), 695–704.

Van Everdingen, Y., & Wierenga, B. (2002). Intra-firm adoption decisions: Role of inter-firm and intra-firm variables. *European Management Journal, 20*(6), 649–63.

Venkatesh, V., & Brown, S. (2001). A longitudinal investigation of personal computers in homes: Adoption determinants and emerging challenges. *MIS Quarterly, 25*(1), 71–102.

Venkatesh, V., & Davis, F. (2000). A theoretical extension of the technology acceptance model: Four longitudinal field studies. *Management Science, 46*(2), 186–204.

Venkatesh, V., Morris, M., & Ackerman, P. (2000). A longitudinal field investigation of gender differences in individual technology adoption decision-making processes. *Organizational Behavior and Human Decision Processes, 83*(1), 33–60.

Venkatesh, V., Morris, M., Davis, G., & Davis, F. (2003). User acceptance of information technology: Toward a unified view. *MIS Quarterly, 27*(3), 425–78.

Westaby, J. (2005). Behavioral reasoning theory: Identifying new linkages underlying intentions and behavior. *Organizational Behavior and Human Decision Processes, 98*(2), 97–120.

Westphal, J., Gulati, R., & Shortell, S. (1997). Customization or conformity? An institutional and network perspective on the content and consequences of TQM adoption. *Administrative Science Quarterly, 42*(2), 366–94.

Yi, M., Jackson, J., Park, J., & Probst, J. (2006). Understanding information technology acceptance by individual professionals: Toward an integrative view. *Information & Management, 43*(3), 350–63.

Yi, Y., Wu, Z., & Tung, L. (2006). How individual differences influence technology usage behaviour? Toward an integrated framework. *Journal of Computer Information Systems, 46*(2), 52–63.

Youngblood, M. (2005). The user is the key. *Policy and Practice of Public Human Services, 63*(1), 12–14.

Yuan, Y., Fulk, J., Shumate, M., Monge, P., Bryant, J., & Matsaganis, M. (2005). Individual participation in organizational information commons. *Human Communication Research, 31*(2), 212–40.

Zaltman, G., Duncan, R., & Holbek, J. (1973). *Innovations and organizations*. New York: Wiley.

# Index

abandon the innovation 2–3
abstract idea 9
academic
   disciplines 25, 48–9
   divisions 72, 79, 115, 141
   interest 5
   qualifications 48–9, 69, 78, 124–5
   staff 25, 78, 92–5, 121
acceptance context 45
acceptance of innovation 2, 26, 36,
     112–13, 126, 140, 177
acceptance process 3
achievement 18–19, 22, 152, 158, 168
Ackerman, P. 1–2
acquired skills 24–5
actual behavior 34, 41, 48, 175
actual measures of usage 34
actual usage 2, 49
adequate resources 7, 47, 59
administrative
   duties 25
   innovations 10
   processes 10
   staff 25, 48, 73, 80, 92, 124
   systems 10
   and technical innovation 9
adoption
   decision 1, 13–14, 18, 22–3, 48,
     162, 168
   by individual employees 5, 7
   of innovation 2–4, 16, 20, 22, 38

   of new technology 2, 149
   by organizations 13, 26
advanced features 11, 53–4, 58, 87, 147
advanced model 17, 27, 42, 52, 174, 176
advanced product quality
     planning 153
advanced research model 7, 26, 37, 39
affect employees' adoption 27
affecting individual adoption 3, 36
affective determinants 33–4
Agarwal, R. 19, 34, 46
age group 25, 78, 117
aggressive strategies 14
Ajzen, I. 22, 29, 31, 175
Al-Gahtani, S. 17, 19, 22, 34, 52
allocation 17, 42, 53, 59, 178
analysis of variance 55, 71, 77, 107, 128
Anderson, R. 55, 65, 69–71, 99,
     103–5, 109
anonymity 73
anxiety 17, 21, 24–5, 158, 168
anxiety-provoking situation 24
approaches 16, 51
appropriate modifications 57
arts and social sciences 55, 78–9,
     118–21, 128–30, 139
aspects of adoption 6
attitude
   construct scale 26
   toward adoption 40, 44–5, 47,
     169–71, 179–80

toward innovation 7, 12, 16, 20, 26, 41, 99, 156, 167, 183
toward targets 31, 140
authentic interpretations 72
authoritarianism 32
autonomous 53

background of the problem 1
Bagozzi, R. 17, 23, 30–34, 37, 45
Baroudi, J. 16–17, 19, 21, 23, 43–4
behavioral beliefs 26, 31, 40–42, 44, 63
behavioral intentions 21, 26, 34–5
behavioral phenomenon 32, 40, 46
behaviors of individuals 2
belief structure 31
benchmark strategies 4
benefit from the change 3
benefits 1–3, 10, 12–15, 18, 33, 47
Bhattacherjee, A. 1–3, 12, 16, 18–19, 31
bias 55, 65
bonuses 18–19
broader theoretical understanding 5
Brown, S. 21–2, 24, 45–6, 166
Bruner, G. 33
build confidence 18, 21
building competitiveness 9
business environment 15
business partners 12, 15

calendar 51–4, 56–64, 66, 68, 77
calendar applications 53, 58, 66, 83–4, 87
capital budget 2
career advancement 13, 18, 152, 167
Carter, P. 17, 34
causal flow 74
Cavaye, A. 17, 34, 46–7, 57–9, 64
centralized organizations 14
changing of titles 18
characteristics 14, 16, 19, 29, 31

Chen, J. 19
Cho, V. 26, 31, 41, 45, 48
choice of behavior 20, 154
clarity 52, 67, 77
clerical staff 25
clients 10
coaching 17
coefficient of determination 71, 106
cognitive 19, 25, 33–4, 37, 42
cognitive interpretations 19, 42
cognitive structures 25
coherent model 3, 5, 48, 77, 105, 142
collinearity 70, 98–9, 103–5, 109, 111–12
combination of multiple variables 5, 182
combination of variables 3, 5, 35, 182
combined TAM-TPB 37
commissions 18, 152, 167
communication 14–15, 23, 25, 170
compatibility 14
competitive advantage 8, 52
competitive disadvantage 15
competitive market environment 15
competitors 12, 15
complex organizations 10
complexity 10–11, 14, 49, 176
comprehension 67
comprehensive 9, 36, 38, 49, 175–6, 181
computer acceptance 33–4
computer software 53
concept of newness 8
conceptual development 39
conceptual framework 29–30, 34–5, 38, 139–40, 142–3
conceptual model 7, 36, 39–40
concern of scholars 2
confidence of employees 18
confirmation 12, 27, 145
confirmatory approach 71
conscious intended behavior 30, 175

consequence 18, 20, 26, 31–2, 59, 63
consultative feedback 18
consulting 17
consumption 22
contact management 53
continued use of innovation 4, 5, 13, 16, 174
continuous improvement 13, 52
contribution to knowledge 5, 6, 173, 181, 182
control over employees 18
control over the job 20, 154
correlation coefficient 71, 98, 106, 126
correlation matrix 69–70, 98–9, 110, 134–5, 174
correlation of organization size 14
Cragg, P. 17, 34, 46–7, 57–9, 64
create awareness 15
criteria 55, 58, 64, 72
criterion sampling 72
critical barrier 18, 167
critical mass users 46
Cronbach's alpha 65, 99, 103
cross-tabulations 69, 74, 84, 174
cross-validation 55
crucial for guiding 5
customers 10, 12, 15

daily activities 9, 11, 27, 54, 57
data analysis 51, 55, 69, 73–5, 79
data collection 51–3, 55, 68–9, 174
data display 73–4
data examination 65
data reduction 73
data triangulation 65
databases 25
Davis, F. 1, 3, 17, 19–23, 29–37
decentralized environment 53
decision of employee 18, 23
decision processes 2, 12

definitions of constructs and measures 57
definitions of innovation 7–8
DeLone and McLean IS Success Model 29, 37–8
demographic 7, 16, 24–5, 27, 29, 31, 36, 39, 41, 47–9, 71
    characteristics 41, 69, 71, 77, 79
    factors 7, 25, 27, 29, 41
dependent 55–7, 69–71, 77, 98–9, 101
descriptive tool 69
desired benefits 2
determinants 4, 19, 29–30, 33–5, 45
    of behavioral intention 34, 45, 138
develop
    advanced research model 3
    new model 4
    theoretical construct 5, 77, 105
devices 10
dichotomous variable 126
diffusion of innovation 20
diffusion process 20
digital recorder 73
disciplines 25, 48–9, 65, 71, 91
discussion 110, 130, 136, 143, 153
diverse use of applications 17
division of business 55, 79, 88, 90, 129–30
divisions 47, 53, 55, 63, 67–8
domains 30, 32
dominance 32
drivers of adoption 3, 22, 173, 182
Duncan, R. 8–9, 13–14, 53–4
Durbin-Watson statistics 107, 112

ease of use 29, 32–4, 40, 42, 175
economic factors 9, 14, 23
economy 1, 9
education 17, 25, 32, 47, 55, 59
effect on system use 21

effective adoption and usage 5
effectiveness 1, 12–13, 15, 20, 37
efficiency 1–3, 8–9, 11–12, 15, 20
    into daily activities 11
    in performing jobs 2
effort expectancy 37
empirical study 3, 41, 48–9, 142
empirically non-significant 45
employees 43, 45–7 53–4, 56, 58
    behavior changes 2
    skills 13
encounter difficulties 17
encouragement 17, 23, 45, 47, 59
end-user acceptance 3
end-user applications 5
engineering 55, 78–9, 88–91,
        118–21, 130
enhance efficiency 20
enhance the understanding 32, 40,
enhance work efficiency 8
enjoyment 4, 7, 16, 19, 22, 44, 62, 141
    with innovation 7, 16, 19, 22, 27
enrich the innovation acceptance
        literature 3
ensure risk reduction 15
entertainment potential 22
environment 1, 3, 6, 11, 13
environmental conditions 1
equation 69, 71, 107–8, 128, 177
evaluation of outcomes 26, 63
examine the adoption of innovations
        2, 173
examine the relationship 5
expectations 1, 45, 138
expected benefits 1–3, 13
experience 2, 4, 7, 16, 19
expertise in using innovation 46, 58
experts' opinions 51, 65–6
explanations 1, 72–4, 170
explanatory power 49, 176

external
    factors 29, 32, 40–41, 46, 140, 142
    influence 11, 24, 46, 166
    stimuli 31
    variables 31–2, 35, 140
extrinsic 22, 179

facilitate adoption 14
facilitate an understanding 3
facilitating conditions 16, 37
factors affecting individuals'
        adoption 3
factors influencing 1, 23, 30, 182
favourable or unfavorable attitude 8
favourable outcomes 19
favourable perceptions 17
female 24, 71, 73, 78, 85
financial 15, 18–19, 146, 148, 151,
        154, 167
    rewards 19
    risk 15
findings 4–5, 11, 48, 52, 64
firm specific 35
Fishbein, M. 3, 22, 26, 29–33, 37
five-point scale 26, 57, 63
follow-up discussion 67
formal and informal recognition 19,
        152, 167
formal schooling 24
foundation of the models 29
Frambach, R. 1–3, 7, 12–16, 20, 23–4
frequency of use 17, 57, 80, 85, 88,
        92, 95
friends and family influence 46
full-time employees 25, 96–7, 122,
        129, 138, 180
function of beliefs 31
functioning 16, 23, 36, 46
future intention 41, 49
future research 46, 49, 171, 173, 182

gain competitive advantage 8
gain in efficiency 1
gender 24, 37, 47–9, 69, 73
general casual explanation 52
general lack of research 182
generalizability 55, 105,
generalizable findings 52
global economy 1
goodness of fit Chi-square tests 79
Gopalakrishnan, S. 9–11
greater learning in innovation 3
greater understanding 17
groups of practitioners 5
guidance 17, 59, 162

Hair, J. 55, 64–5, 69–71, 99, 101
health science 55, 78–9, 88–91,
        118–21, 128
hedonic outcomes 22
help managers 4
heteroscedasticity 105, 112
Higgins, J. 8, 17, 34, 37, 48
high tech market 15
histogram 112–14, 130–32
Holbek, J. 8–9, 13–14, 53–4
holistic picture 72
homoscedasticity 105, 112, 130
Howell, J. 17, 34, 37, 48, 175
human behavior 30, 32
human resources 10

idea 8–9, 12–14, 24, 26, 33, 53
Igbaria, M. 16–17, 19–21, 23, 34
image 4, 7, 16, 19, 21
impact of organizational factors 4, 174
implementation 4, 6–7, 10–13, 15, 27
    of innovation 12, 141, 181
    process 11
    risk 15
improve 3, 5–6, 8–9, 11, 13

current operations 11
performance 9, 26
service 8
the work environment 6
incentives 14, 16, 18, 27, 46–47
increase individual productivity 1
increased autonomy 19, 152 , 167, 178
increased profits 12–13, 18
incremental innovations 10–11, 187
independent variable 37, 48–9, 55–6,
        69–71, 98–9
in-depth interviews 72, 115, 143, 166,
        169, 173
individual 1–9, 11–13, 16–27, 30–33,
        35–40
individual
    acceptance 35–6, 48, 71, 106, 111
    adoption 3–5, 13, 16–19, 22, 24, 48
    attitudes 5, 7, 16, 133, 142
        toward innovation adoption 7
    characteristics 19
    employees 5, 7–8, 13, 17–18, 22–3
    factors 4, 7, 19, 27, 39
    feelings 26, 63
    interpretation 32, 53
influence individuals' adoption 41, 182
informal networks 15, 23
information
    processing activity 15
    products 37
    quality 37
    sharing 24
    systems 1, 19, 26, 35, 37
        research 1
        success 19
    technology 33, 55, 60, 79, 118
initiation 13
innate tendency 20, 156, 167
innovation 1–23
    acceptance 3, 36, 38, 48, 173–6, 180

adoption decisions 1, 14
adoption process 27
backgrounds 53
capabilities 52
decision process 12
as an idea 8
investments 1
skills 24, 43, 65, 160, 180
success 20, 141
usage 5, 25, 37, 46, 110
innovative 4, 7, 13–16, 18–21, 27
innovative organizations 15
inputs 10
insight 9, 34, 67, 70, 72–3, 140
institution 26, 32, 46, 63, 183
instructions 17, 59, 163
insufficient knowledge 25
intended benefits 2, 18
intention to adopt innovation 15
interconnectedness 24
inter-correlations among study
     variables 98, 102, 137
internal influence 23
internal reliability test 69
internet 24, 153, 164, 180
interpersonal channels 20
interpersonal contacts 23
interrelated organization 24, 63, 166
interview data analysis technique 51,
     73, 75
interview findings 145
interviews 51–2, 65, 72–5, 110, 115
intra-firm adoption 23
intra-organizational adoption 12
intrinsic 22, 179
introducing innovation 5, 141
introduction price 15
introduction to innovation adoption 1
introversion-extraversion
investigating multiple factors 4, 71

investment in innovation 2
IT usage 1

Jasperson, J. 17, 34
job
     activities 53
     performance 19, 33, 42, 60
     security 19, 152, 167, 178
journal writing 53
judgment 30

King, M. 16–17, 19–20, 22, 30, 33–5
knowledge 4–6, 8, 10–13, 17–18, 25
     and expertise 17, 46, 58
     enhancement 13

Lam, T. 26, 31, 41, 45, 48
large variation 53
learn 25, 61–3, 68, 119, 139
Lee, S. 3, 17–21, 43, 46
Lewis, W. 19–20, 23, 34, 42–4, 46
lifelong learning 13
Likert type scale 56, 171
limitations 38, 171, 173–4, 183
location of the study 51
long-term abilities 18
long-term study issue 1
Lu, J. 16

mailboxes 53
maintain market position 15
maintain superior management
     systems 8
major definitions 8
major problem for organizations 2
male 24, 71, 73, 78, 85
management
     encouragement 17, 47, 59
     personnel 183
     policies 41

strategies 36
  support 4, 7, 16–18, 27, 46–7
managers 64, 138, 141, 178, 181
manufacturers 15
market 1, 15, 24, 151, 166
  acceptance 15
  environment 15, 24
mass media 20
material artifact 8, 54
mean 3, 11, 26, 51, 53
methodological triangulation 65
methodology 49, 51, 74
methods of implementation 12
Microsoft outlook software 52
mixing different methods 51
model of PC utilization 37
moderating factors 4, 16, 37
moderating variables 24, 49, 176
modifications 3, 38–9, 48, 57, 64
moral support 23, 164, 168
Morris, M. 1–2, 20, 36–7
motivate innovation 4
motivating users 2
motivation 22–3, 37, 45, 62, 138
motivational model 37
multicollinearity 70, 98, 103–5,
  111–12, 130
multi-method approach 52
multiple correlation coefficients
  106, 126
multiple influences 53
multiple methods 51
multiple regressions 55, 74, 109,
  126, 177
multiple sets of variables 34,
multiple units 53
multivariate statistical technique 69

natural settings 72
negative attitude 26

network externalities 36, 46
neuroticism 32
new
  idea 8, 12, 24, 54, 168
  knowledge 8
  product 1, 13–14
  to society 8, 54
  system 8, 17, 20, 26, 54
  technological system 8
  technology 2, 8–9, 20, 25, 29, 61
  world 22, 162
newness to the organization 8
non-monetary 18
non-statistical methods 72
normal probability plot of the
  residuals 112, 130
normality 105, 113, 130, 132,
normative beliefs 22, 31–2, 39–41, 45
normative considerations 32
note taking 53
number of features used 58, 94

object 8, 24, 26, 63
objective 55, 70, 73, 105
observability 14
observations 55, 105
occupation 32, 47–9, 69
occupation category 47–9
older groups 24
ongoing involvement 2
ongoing practice 12
online data 52, 68, 74
online survey questionnaire 52, 55,
  68, 74, 182
operational risk 15
opportunities 15, 52, 72, 141
organizational 1–5, 7, 9–14, 16–19, 24
organizational
  achievements 18
  adaptation 14

adoption 12–14
advancement 19
advantages 12
attitudes 13
characteristics 14, 78
context 56, 72, 78, 105, 142
decision 2, 13
effectiveness 13
facilitators 36, 41, 46
factors 4, 7, 16, 27, 39–40, 46–9,
    103, 133–4
innovations 2, 173
investments 1
policies 4, 16
productivity 1
size 14, 183
strategic posture 14
structure 10, 14
support 11, 36, 47, 137, 150
targets 32
organizations 1–5, 8–16, 20, 24, 26
organizations' personnel 26
outcome 26, 31, 63, 74, 106
outline 39–40, 48, 69, 170
outputs 10

Parasuraman, S. 16–17, 19, 21, 23, 43
parsimonious 33
part-time employees 25, 79, 95–8,
    122–3, 129
past decade 1
patterns 65, 72, 74, 99
Pearson correlation analysis 98,
    177, 179
peers 135–6, 138, 140, 145, 152
people 152–6, 158–69, 178, 180
perceived
    benefits 15
    enjoyment 44
    productivity 22

social pressure 22
    uncertainty 14
perception of professionals 145
perceptions of an innovation 14, 15
performance 165, 181, 183–4
performance expectancy 37
performance of organizations 1, 9
person 4, 7, 11, 13, 16–20
person's reference 46
personal
    benefits 13, 155, 167, 178
    characteristics 11, 36
    dispositional innovativeness 43
    information manager 43, 53–4
    innovativeness 43, 48, 56, 60, 98
    values 36,
personality characteristics 29, 31,
    140, 175
personality traits 32
persuasion 8, 23, 27, 36, 47
phenomenon 55, 66, 72, 139, 182
pilot study 51, 65, 67
pleasure 22, 162, 168
policies 4, 16, 36, 41
positive attitudes 21, 45
positive impression 21
possible configuration 74
potential adopter 1, 12, 14–15, 17, 23
potential barriers 17
potential trading partners 15
powerful motivator 18
practical implications 139, 181
practice 2, 5, 6, 8, 10, 12
practitioners 2, 4–5, 33
praise for the adoption 18
Prasad, J. 20, 43, 48
pre-defined criteria 72
predicted values of dependent
    variables 112, 130
predictive effort 70

predictor 35, 55, 69, 104, 106
primary indicator 57
prior experience 106, 108, 134,
    136–7, 140
probability of adoption 15, 23
problem of underutilized systems 3
process 2–4, 8–12, 15, 17, 20
process of adaptation 9
processes of an organization 2, 10, 173
product and process innovation 9–10
product experience 36, 43
productivity 21–2, 60, 137, 141, 146
productivity gains 1, 13, 18
productivity of employees 11
productivity of the organization 5
products 1, 9–11, 14, 37
professional staff 52, 64–5, 92–5,
    115, 119
profits 12–13, 18
promote the adoption 4, 5
promotion of management awareness
    5, 105
propensity to adopt 14–15
proposed advanced model 142–3,
    169, 173–4, 176
proposed advanced research model
    26, 39, 41
proposition 74
public folders 53
public recognition 18
purchase 13
purposive sampling 72

qualitative 51–2, 54, 65, 72
quality 9, 37, 60, 153
quantitative 72–5, 77, 136, 138–9, 142
quantitative research method 51
quantitative study 52, 143, 166, 169–71
questionnaire 52, 55–7, 64–9, 73–4,
    77–8, 173

radical and incremental innovation
    9–10, 173
rationale 4, 52, 74–5, 139
receptive to innovation 14–15
receptiveness toward innovation 14
recognition 18–19, 152, 167, 178
recommendations 52, 153, 162, 164
reduce anxiety 21, 158, 168
regression analysis 55, 69–71, 77,
    103, 105–6
regression equation 69, 71, 107,
    128, 177
regularities 74
reinforcement effort 18
reject information technology 33
reject innovation 19
relevant factors 5–7, 27
relevant formal training 17, 148
relevant unit of adoption 8, 26, 54
reliability 51–2, 64–5, 67, 69, 77
religion 32
reporting the reliability coefficient 65
research
    design 51, 74, 184
    instruments 51, 64, 67
    on individual innovation 3, 173
    model 3, 7, 26, 37–42, 48
    questions 6, 52, 56, 74
researcher 9, 33, 39–45, 48–9, 52–3
residual assumptions 130
residuals 55, 105, 112–14, 130–32
resist change 3
resources 137, 141, 148–50, 167, 178
respondents 55–8, 64, 67–9, 72–3,
    77–97
risk reduction 14–15
robust 52
Rogers, E. 8–9, 12, 14, 20, 24
    role of innovation 52
role of organizational 3

salary raises 18
Sambamurthy,V. 19–20, 23, 34,
    42–4, 46
sample 51, 105–6, 109, 111, 184
sample size 51, 55, 68–9
Sanford, C. 1, 31, 45
satisfaction 22, 37
scattered research 182
scatterplots 99, 105, 112, 130
Schillewaert, N. 2–3, 7, 12–16, 23–4, 29
science and technology 25, 180
self-training 43, 61
self-reported measures 57
self-worth 19
semantic success 37
semi-structured interview 72, 145
senior administration officials 53
senior management 17–18, 47, 59, 178
separate major category 41
services 9–11
shelf-ware syndrome 2
short-term success 18
significant contributor 52
significant value 8
simultaneous assessment 70
single organization 52–3
single-study context 5
skills 13, 17, 21, 24–5, 43
skills of using innovation 21
small and medium-sized enterprises
    14, 15
social 44–9, 51–3, 55–6, 63, 69
    cognitive theory 37
    environment 22, 36, 44–6, 179
    factors 22–3, 26–7, 36, 44–5, 56
    group 22, 138
    influence 22, 36–7, 39–40, 44–5, 48
    network 105–6, 108, 135–6, 138, 140
    outcomes 22
    persuasion 23, 36, 47

processes 3, 175
psychology 30
research 51
science 55, 69, 74, 78–9, 88–91, 113
status 22, 161
and technical system 9
socioeconomic status 32
software productivity 2
sophistication level of features
    used 58
South Australia 3, 52, 64, 67
speed for users 3
spread of information 15, 23
SPSS (Statistical Package for Social
    Sciences) package 69, 174
stand-alone application 53
standard deviation 99, 103, 106, 115,
    118, 121–2, 124
standardized predicted values 73
standards 9, 158
statistical analysis 55, 69, 109, 174
statistical power 55
statistical testing 77,
statistically 77, 108, 115, 133
stepwise regression 109
stimuli 31, 35
strategic domination 12
strategic importance 13, 15
strategies 4, 14, 36, 41, 141, 152
strategy and culture 14
strength and limitations 3, 174
structural change 2
structure 10–11, 14, 25, 31, 41, 65–6, 68
study limitations 183
subjective data 54
subjective norms 29–32, 34, 45, 140,
    170, 179
subjective probability 31, 33–4
successful in future 21
successful technology 2

sum of squires for the model 107
summary of interviews 145, 166
suppliers 12, 15
supports the development 77, 145, 169
survey 51–2, 55, 64–9, 73–4, 77, 79
system 1–3, 8–11, 13, 16–22, 26
    quality 37
    use 19, 21, 33, 48
systematic error 65
systematic use of information 30
systematic way 54

targeted innovation 9
targeting 14
task performance 1, 17–18
task tracking 53
Taylor, S. 26, 37, 63, 142
teaching and research 25
technical innovation 9–11
technical success 37
technological changes 9
technological knowledge 11
technology acceptance model 3, 7, 29,
    33, 37–8
tenure 36, 47–9
test of linearity 69
testing of a wide range of factors 3
theoretical
    construct 5, 77, 105, 142, 173
    foundations 6
    framework 3, 7, 41, 145, 174–6
    model 179, 182
    triangulation 65
    understanding 5, 139, 182
theories of innovation 27, 38
theories of innovation adoption 29
theory of planned behavior 37
theory of reasoned action 3, 7, 29–30,
    32–3, 37
Thompson, R. 17, 34, 48, 175

time allocation 23
Todd, P. 26, 37, 63, 142
training 4, 7, 16–17, 27, 36
    courses 43, 58, 61
transition experience 2
trialability 14
t-statistic 111
types of innovation 9

understanding 1–5, 16–17, 25, 30, 32
    factors 1
    IT acceptance 1
    and support of innovation 5
    usage behavior 34
unified theory of acceptance and use
    of technology 36
unit of adoption 8, 26
university employees 53
University of South Australia 52,
    64, 67
unstandardized coefficient B-values
    107–10, 128–9
unsymmetrical 113, 130
usage behavior 34, 37, 49, 179–80
usage level 57, 79, 105, 110, 122–6
usage of the system 37
use of computers 24
use of innovation 3, 13, 16–17, 21, 25
use the system 2, 124, 129–30, 138, 146
use-performance relationship 19
user
    acceptance of innovation 1–3, 33,
        35, 141, 178
    computer experience 21, 24, 43, 53
    confidence 17
    perceives 19
    satisfaction 37
    unwillingness 1
using computers 24, 146
utilization of innovation 17, 167

validity 33, 51–2, 64–5, 67, 74
    and reliability 51–2, 64–5, 77
valued by management 18
Van der Heijden, H. 22, 34, 44, 162
van Everdingen, Y. 3, 23, 44
variables 3, 5, 14, 16, 24
    of the study 56
    redundant 70
variance inflation factor 103, 111
Venkatesh, V. 1–3, 19–22, 24, 34–7, 44–6
viewpoints 51
virtual communities 165, 180
voluntariness 37

Warshaw, P. 23, 30, 33–4, 37, 45
web browsing 53
well-being of employees 5
well-recognized factor 42
Wierenga, B. 3, 23, 44
willingness of an individual 20, 43,
        60, 110

women 24, 129
work
    activities 11, 123
    activity of an organization 9–10
    design 2
    environment 3, 6, 21, 45
    processes 2, 173
worker productivity 2
working agenda 18
workplace 2, 24–5, 169, 181
worldwide 52, 165

Yi, Y. 3, 20, 23, 31, 35
younger people 24
Yuan, Y. 17, 23, 148, 164

Zaltman, G. 8–9, 13–14, 53–4
Zinatelli, N. 17, 34, 46–7, 57–9, 64
Zmud, R. 2, 17, 34